Making Sense of Parenth

Caring, Gender and Family Lives

Following on from *Making Sense of Motherhood* (2005) and *Making Sense of Fatherhood* (2010), Tina Miller's book focuses on parenthood and mothers' and fathers' unfolding experiences as they manage caring and paid work in modern family lives. Returning to her original participants, it collects later episodes of their experience of 'doing' family life and meticulously examines mothers' and fathers' accounts of negotiating intensified parenting responsibilities and workplace demands. It explores questions of why gender equality and equity are harder to manage within the home sphere when organising caring and associated responsibilities, re-addressing the concept of 'maternal gatekeeping' and offering insights into a new concept of 'paternal gatekeeping.' The findings presented will inform both scholarly work and policy on family lives, gender equality and work.

TINA MILLER is Professor of Sociology at Oxford Brookes University. She is recognised internationally for her research on gendered and cultural practices in families and family transitions. She is the author of *Making Sense of Motherhood* (2005) and *Making Sense of Fatherhood* (2010).

Making Sense of Parenthood

Caring, Gender and Family Lives

TINA MILLER
Oxford Brookes University

CAMBRIDGE
UNIVERSITY PRESS

CAMBRIDGE
UNIVERSITY PRESS

University Printing House, Cambridge CB2 8BS, United Kingdom

One Liberty Plaza, 20th Floor, New York, NY 10006, USA

477 Williamstown Road, Port Melbourne, VIC 3207, Australia

4843/24, 2nd Floor, Ansari Road, Daryaganj, Delhi – 110002, India

79 Anson Road, #06–04/06, Singapore 079906

Cambridge University Press is part of the University of Cambridge.

It furthers the University's mission by disseminating knowledge in the pursuit of education, learning and research at the highest international levels of excellence.

www.cambridge.org
Information on this title: www.cambridge.org/9781107104136
DOI: 10.1017/9781316219270

First published 2017

Printed in the United Kingdom by Clays, St Ives plc

A catalogue record for this publication is available from the British Library

ISBN 978-1-107-10413-6 Hardback
ISBN 978-1-107-50428-8 Paperback

Contents

Acknowledgements

As with my previous writing forays, there are many people to be thanked for their support during the writing of this book. Rooms and houses have been generously lent for days and weeks of thinking and writing (thank you to all at the farm, to Miriam and to Hannah and Stafford, for the hospitality and encouragement provided). A particularly helpful and consistent writing companion is my sister-in-law, Diana Miller, who has wielded paint brushes to wonderful effect, serendipitously providing the cover for this book (www.diana-miller.co.uk). Others have kindly read and commented on the book chapters as they have developed (Abbey Halcli and Sarah Spain) and listened and responded to my unfolding ideas in helpful and critical ways (Gary Browning and Rebecca Asher). Thanks also to all the members of the research network ONEFaR (www.brookes.ac.uk/onefar) who encouragingly shared with me an academic curiosity about family lives and political contexts, viewed from different disciplinary perspectives and countries. The British Academy is also thanked for its valuable support of UK researchers generally and their generosity in my award of a Mid-Career Fellowship, which enabled me to dedicate time to the project 'Managing modern family lives: public understandings and everyday practises of caring and paid work' (Reference: MD130067), from which this book has emerged. Thanks also to my colleagues at Oxford Brookes University, in particular in sociology, for their forbearance during my fellowship year. Joanna Cooksey, our subject librarian, is also due thanks for her rapid and helpful responses to my library queries and reference needs. The support of my own growing and changing family (Frank, Hannah, Freya, Lydia, Stafford and Henry) has also been appreciated, and love, as always, goes to each of you. Finally, the most important thanks go to the women and men who have shared their experiences of mothering, fathering and family lives with me over many years. This book is only possible because of you.

Introduction

The 'naughty step'[1] had not been invented when my own children were small. When my brother was brought home from hospital (being the firstborn, that is where birth usually took place in the 1950s), he slept in a drawer taken from a chest of drawers for the first few weeks of his life. When my mother was a child in London, she was sent out alone on all sorts of errands by my grandmother, including delivering tea in a milk bottle to the local Park caretaker. Happily everyone has survived and lived to tell the tales. But these glimpses of childcare from my own family provide a perspective from which to think about how ideas and practises – and the paraphernalia – of caring for children have changed in recent generations. Historically, of course, changes in how 'small adults' and 'little people' have been thought about, and so how phases of childhood – and more recently the advent of the teenager – have become construed and recognised, are well documented and debated (Acocella, 2003; Aries, 1962). How adults care for their children and develop relationships and attachments of love and protection has been configured in different ways at different historical moments. It is clear, then, that ideas about caregiving are historically, culturally and, in the 21st century, increasingly politically shaped. This has been brought home to me as I have had the good fortune to live in other cultures and witness how caring for children and working are managed. In the Solomon Islands (I lived on the island of New Georgia for two years in the 1980s), the small village shared caring for and chastising the babies, young children and young adults as a collective undertaking and village responsibility. This was in stark contrast to how caring was practised back in the United Kingdom, where I returned to give birth to my eldest daughter. The maternal business of caregiving here was assumed to be instinctive and undertaken as a mostly solitary and largely invisible (at home) endeavour.

[1] www.jofrost.com/naughty-step-technique.

Some things, but not all, have changed in significant ways since then. The changes have included a reorientation of how paid work features in women's lives, including those who are mothers, and changes in ideas and practices of what men can do as fathers. But the shifts across caring and paid work – and who does what – do not equate in exact ways between mothers and fathers and vary across cultures. In the United Kingdom, the contexts in which couple and single parents manage work and family lives have also become more politicised through ideas of 'good' parenting, which too often fail to acknowledge the material and gendered circumstances in which 'choices' and practises are made and lived. Expectations of parents have grown, workplace demands have increased and everything has become intensified. This intensification forms a neoliberal backdrop to the individual stories followed in this book. These stories are explored through a focus on how a group of mothers and fathers living in the United Kingdom manage the daily activities and responsibilities of caring for their children (in couples and alone) alongside other aspects of their lives. These activities, responsibilities and relationships are now often generically referred to as 'parenting', a term that has become increasingly used in the Western world since the 1970s.

The title of this book uses the term parenthood, and it is important to emphasise that this is not intended to imply a singular way of being a parent. Lives, circumstances, caring and love are experienced in numerous and changing ways and contexts, even though ideals of parenthood are narrowly constructed in political terms. It is necessary then to think about parenting relationships as reciprocal, inter-generational, challenging, loving and fluid and to think of parenthood in the plural, as parenthoods. But the term 'parent' also glosses over deeply embedded gendered differences and histories in the responsibilities, activities and 'mental labor' (Walzer, 1996) associated with women who are mothers and men who are fathers. Even though gender equality may be an aim of how caring in families is practised, reflecting other significant changes such as those in the workplace, there is still a long way to go, even in countries such as Sweden where gender equality has been championed through policies since the 1970s. For this reason, this book focuses particularly on how gender shapes the domains of caring and paid work and the contingency of maternal and paternal possibilities, viewed over time. This book is the third in what serendipitously has become a series, through the extension of an original qualitative study, Transition to First-time Motherhood (Miller, 2005), and a subsequent companion study, Transition to First-time Fatherhood (Miller, 2010).

This third book revisits the original participants and focuses on how lives have unfolded as the children born in the original studies, which set out to explore experiences of transition, reach 18 years of age and early adulthood in the Motherhood study and 5 years of age and the beginning of primary school in the Fatherhood study. The longitudinal aspect of the studies has enabled later experiences of caring and work to be collected and compared with earlier data, revealing how intentions, hopes and plans have unfolded in families initially interviewed just before the birth of their first baby. In the earlier books and here again, it is necessary to place caveats around what follows, or at least make clear what the book can do and what its particular focus and contribution will be. The samples in the two studies have been described in earlier work as more privileged because of their occupational status (employed) and associated social class.[2] These first births were happily anticipated (even if not planned, although most were) in heterosexual couple relationships. In these ways the participants conformed to normative ideals of the 'good' mother and the 'good' father, who are employed, have planned parenthood at a culturally appropriate age and stage of their working lives and intend to build stable and 'forever' families. Sadly, life doesn't always turn out as planned, as these later episodes of navigating caring and work experiences reveal. However, because the samples have had 'choices' and (some) avenues of opportunity open to them that not all families enjoy, the focus on gender taken in this book is in relation to middle-class experiences, which will be both similar to and different from the experiences of families with less opportunities and whose parenting might be – or feel – subjected to

---

[2] Social class is a complex issue because occupational class does not necessarily match or overlap with how social class is felt or claimed as an identity or position. For example, in the Transition to Motherhood Study, one participant who was a qualified and practising lawyer described herself as working class. Another described herself as upper middle class, making a further distinction within a class classification. In the 2015 British Social Attitudes survey, the majority of people surveyed considered themselves to be working class (60%) compared with 40% who identified as being middle class, despite the fact that it is estimated that only a quarter of the population in Britain are in working-class occupations (www.bsa.natcen.ac.uk/?_ga=1.43472613.1332573774 .1467244789).

greater professional scrutiny and (negative) labelling. Even so, the earlier findings from these studies revealed just how diverse and complex
early mothering and fathering experiences could be, even in apparently
homogeneous groups.

Set against the shifting landscapes of modern family lives, the chapters that follow explore how caring and work unfold as families grow,
jobs change, mothers work more and couple relationships (sometimes)
breakdown. The rich longitudinal data enable everyday experiences
and narratives of caring, working and surviving to be traced over
time. The analysis of the data (comprising more than 200 hours of
interviews) over the years leads to the central question that occupies this book: can a *primary* caring responsibility for children be
equally shared? Groundbreaking scholarly feminist work, initiated several decades ago, began to question taken-for-granted assumptions
about women's maternal selves, lives and destiny, challenging essentialist associations in contexts etched through with patriarchal privilege and power. But there was ambivalence too, with some arguing that
mothering was a form of female empowerment. There have been significant changes since then, and continued debate, about how 'choices'
and 'preferences' operate in relation to maternal and paternal orientations as caregivers and workers. Global labour demands and economic
necessity have also changed the debates as the majority of families in
the United Kingdom are now also working families. More precise and
nuanced understandings of how gender operates across the domains of
caregiving and working, have also helped to show that arrangements
in these interwoven spheres can be organised in different and more
gender symmetrical or equitable ways. Many fathers also want to be
more emotionally involved in their children's lives, rather than replicate the remote, breadwinning father figures they associate with their
own childhoods.

But the question of whether a *primary* caring responsibility for children can be *equally* shared remains, even though a burgeoning research
literature, including my own, has charted men's increased involvement
in hands-on caring for their children. What becomes clear through the
unfolding accounts charted in the following chapters is that no amount
of preparation can prepare you for the fact that a small baby occupies
every space (emotionally and perhaps physically too, with all the 'necessary' paraphernalia a 'good' mother must have) and that a sense of
a '24/7 thinking responsibility' descends as a baby is born. Someone

has to take on that responsibility. Regardless of intentions to change gendered practises of caring by mothers and fathers and to share caring in equal ways, typically mothers quickly become the parent who is most practised at caring and doing the mental work of thinking about the baby, then toddler, then young child and so on. Exhaustion for everyone in the early weeks and months of becoming a parent make it a difficult time to challenge and try to disrupt gendered arrangements in the workplace and corresponding possibilities in the home. Becoming practised at caregiving leads to perceived 'maternal' expertise, and fathers can 'get it wrong' if they are left 'in charge': everyone falls back into traditionally gendered positions. What emerges then are practises of parental caring that indicate fathers' increased emotional engagement and possibilities of change as well as maternal and paternal 'gatekeeping' of particular practises. Patriarchal habits and dividends and motherhood wage penalties continue to underscore the terrain. But it is the daily, micro-processes of caring, documented over many years, which in this book shows how gendered practises become accepted, reinforced and quite quickly 'invisible' and where inequalities *and* gatekeeping co-exist.

This book is written with the intention and hope of reaching a wide audience, both within various academic disciplines and beyond to a general, interested public. There will be something to attract anyone with a curiosity in the ebb and flow of family lives and practices, as well as for those with more specific interests such as theorisations of gender/gendered practices and agency or those interested in how intensive parenting ideals are engaged with by mothers and fathers as children grow and responsibilities change. Across the chapters, discursive and critical attention is given to contemporary debates and theorisations of how sharing and responsibilities are navigated within households. In Chapter 1, the context of modern parenthood (as institution and ideal) is introduced alongside the intensified and 'biologised' neoliberal landscape of parenting and caregiving in the United Kingdom. Details of the two qualitative longitudinal research studies are also outlined in this chapter. In Chapter 2, a closer examination of the literature on care, caregiving and gender is examined to frame the subsequent empirical chapters as consideration of gendered orientations and care/work unfolds across these. Chapter 3 returns to fathers from the original Transition to Fatherhood Study (Miller, 2010) and explores their experiences of caring involvement and paid work as their children begin primary school. In contrast (in many respects), the following chapter focuses on mothers from the original Transition to Motherhood Study (Miller, 2005) as their firstborn child reaches 18 years of age. The mothers reflect on how they have taken up and managed caring responsibilities and paid work across the years. In Chapter 5, the focus turns to consider the experiences of families in the two studies where parental relationships have broken down and co-parenting is now practiced between households. Aspects of caring orientations, maternal and paternal responsibilities and how these unfold and become managed are examined in Chapter 6. In this chapter, data from the two studies are explored and compared, together with earlier interview data from the participants, revealing how gendered patterns of caring and types of maternal and paternal gatekeeping become practised. Finally, in Chapter 7, conclusions and theorisations are drawn and reflections on narrating gendered selves and identities as individuals, parents and workers are considered, along with methodological reflections.

It is necessary to explain how, in the empirical chapters, the terms 'caring' and 'work' are used. The term 'caring' in this context is used to describe caring for a child or children in a family (alone or in a couple), which is further defined and illuminated through the data as activities, tasks, thinking and planning. The term 'work' refers to paid work (usually outside the home), which is distinct from the caring in the home, even though caring can be experienced as a form of labour. It is appreciated that this distinction implies a separation, which is not necessarily experienced, especially by mothers, but nonetheless is used in the book to distinguish between gendered ('moral') orientations and practices of caring and paid work and their navigation and orchestration in family lives.

The book can be read in different ways as each chapter is written as a standalone piece, which also means that some arguments are restated as the work unfolds. The book is also a single text on experiences of parenthood. But as a third book in a series based on longitudinal data, it is also possible for the reader to go back to the two earlier texts, for example to follow the featured participants before they became parents and then through their earlier parenting experiences. Of course, interpretation means that other versions of events are possible, even likely, as we make sense of our lives and those of others around us from different perspectives at different times. In the narrative tales of mothering, fathering, caring and paid work that have unfolded and unravelled across all three books, this will certainly be the case. Nevertheless, the narratives of individual experiences, which are re-narrated and edited as lives unfold, provide unusually rich accounts of mothering and fathering and the (unforeseen) twists and turns of family lives.

So, finally, even though it must be possible (mustn't it?) for a 24/7 thinking and caring parental responsibility to be *equally* shared, why does this still seem to be so hard to achieve? Rather than focus on the division of tasks, their type and hours spent on them, in trying to promote more gender equitable choices in home and work spheres, at the heart of these matters sits the assumed *singularity* of a primary responsibility. For all the sharing, it is this singularity – so obdurately adhered to the institution of motherhood and not (so far) to fatherhood – that demands our critical attention and sets the scene for the chapters that follow. But the exploration and further consideration of this tricky terrain has only been possible because of the generosity of spirit of the participants. They have shared their time and unfolding personal experiences of transition and later practices of family caring and work, love and loss, and to them I remain indebted and grateful.

1 | *Parenthoods*
Setting the Contemporary Context

I was the first person out of my friends to have a child and I remember saying to them it's brilliant, it's the best thing in the world, but it's harder than what people say.

(Joe, Fatherhood study)

It's the scariest job in the world, but it's the best job in the world.

(Felicity, Motherhood study)

Becoming a parent changes lives in all sorts of unexpected and predictable ways. Across the chapters in this book, everyday experiences of parenting are explored through a focus on the micro-processes of daily family living as parenting experiences unfold. The book explores later episodes of parenting experiences in the United Kingdom as children begin primary school (aged 5–6 years) and the later teenage years – aspects of parenting not included in transition and early parenting research. The question of what constitutes parenthood at these various points in parenting journeys, along with contemporary understandings of 'parenting responsibilities' and daily caring practises, will provide recurrent themes across the chapters. The scrutiny of parenthood, gender and caring as concept and practise is timely and coincides with significant shifts in women's and men's lives, for example labour market participation, increased family fluidity and new theorisations of gender (Bryson et al, 2012; Dermott and Miller, 2015; Grunow and Evertsson, 2016; Harden et al, 2014; Sparrman et al, 2016). In the United Kingdom, most parents are now working parents. However, these shifts have been accompanied by an intensification of expectations associated with 'good parenting', bolstered by recent political preoccupation with neuroscience and its application to parenting behaviours and child development (Allen, 2011; Craig et al, 2014; Edwards et al, 2015; Hays, 1996; Lee et al, 2014; Lowe et al, 2015; Wall, 2010).

In this climate, parental responsibilities can be seen to have increased, as 'risk management' and responsibility for 'maximizing' a child's potential are taken as measures of 'good' parenting (Wall, 2013). Further evidence of this can be seen in the proliferation of parenting advice, early-years interventions, educational demands and other forms of parental and child monitoring, which move the political focus to individual (and apparently 'poor parenting') endeavours. Clearly parenting experiences are varied, shaped by personal and household circumstances, age and number of children as well as material and structural factors. In contrast, neoliberal ideals of the 'good parent' are narrowly defined and practicably onerous or unachievable. Contemporary parenthood thus occupies a confounding position, with caring for our children being both the most important relationship parents can come to experience ('the best thing in the world'), yet something continually undervalued and increasingly regarded as a problematic sphere of social life.

At the outset, it is important to make clear which aspects of the terrain of parenthood are explored in this book and which are not. The subjects of parenthood and parenting are vast and have garnered critical attention from academics and others working from different disciplines and political perspectives. Popular media are also fascinated with these topics, with publications telling people how to parent, how not to parent, how to be a 'tiger mom', 'tiger parent' or 'conscious parent', about 'attachment', 'bonding', 'positive' parenting, raising a 'successful' child, 'training' and 'taming' children as well as evocations to display and share images of motherhood (and increasingly fatherhood, e.g. see Swedish Dads at www.johanbavman.se) via social media forums (e.g. Facebook-motherhood challenge). Parenting now requires routines such as scheduling of 'play dates' and other planning activities, which in previous generations did not require such explicit or detailed organisation (Mose, 2016). Activities of parenting may also persist over a longer and more intensive period in the form of so-called helicopter parenting, which, it has been argued, impedes the child's or young adult's development of independence (Willoughby et al, 2015). In contrast, and rather than problematizing individuals who are parents, this book looks at how a group of mothers and fathers manage the daily activity and responsibilities of caring for their children (in couples and alone) alongside other aspects of their lives. It focuses on aspects of gender, parenthood and family-care work practises and relationships through the individual narrations of women and men as daily experiences unfold. This focus includes caring for children over time, and the term 'parenting' is taken to convey the activity and thinking aspects of caring for children; the term 'parenthoods' (acknowledged as plural) conveys the 'institution' and societal expectations in which parenting occurs in the same way that Adrienne Rich distinguished between mothering and motherhood (Rich, 1976). This institution of parenthood perpetuates an 'intensive parenting culture' (Lee et al, 2014), which forms a powerful backdrop of political rhetoric and dominant, increasingly expert 'knowledge', against which parenting efforts are undertaken.

Clearly these terms are not neutral and in their examination of the language of contemporary parenting; Lee et al (2014) note the growing 'targeting of parental behaviour as deficient', increasingly requiring surveillance (both of oneself and other parents) and the 'watchful gaze of experts' (p. 8). But this gaze is also more likely to be focused on some parents and their 'wrong type' of parenting practices than others, as assumptions about parents according to class and material resources, age, race, sexual orientation and gender are made (Dermott and Pomati, 2016; Duncan and Edwards, 1999; Duncan et al, 2010; Featherstone et al, 2016; Gillies, 2007, 2008; Golombok, 2000, 2015; Jensen, 2010; Macvarish, 2016; Reynolds, 2005; Wastell and White, 2012; Utting, 2007). The term 'parenting' also implies gender-neutral engagement in caring activities (see Chapter 2) that, given the gendered and daily aspects of caring histories, both within families and beyond, is problematic (Daly, 2013; Miller, 2013b; Ranson, 2015). Of note too is the issue of parenting responsibilities linked to the perceived needs and 'cultivation' of a child, which are currently 'central to parenthood' but, at different periods, have historically been assumed and practised in very different and gender-unequal ways (Fox, 2009:288; see also Bailey, 2012; Sparrman et al, 2016). Just as conceptualisations of 'childhood' have fluctuated, so too have ideas of children's status and their care and educational needs (Davidoff et al, 1999; Hendrick, 2016; James and James, 2004; Kehily, 2013; King, 2007). The terrain is complex, contested, changing and increasingly seen to hinge politically on narrowly construed opportunities, for example the very early years, in which parents can get parenting 'right'.

The tendency for second-wave feminist researchers to focus 'more on childbirth than parenthood' has been noted by others (Fox, 2009:285), with a more general concentration of research on transition and the first year of mothering or fathering being apparent in any review of the literature (Arendell, 2000; Coltart and Henwood, 2012; Grunow and Evertsson, 2016; Habib, 2012; Ives, 2014; Nilsen et al, 2013; Oakley, 1979; Thomson et al, 2011). Having also focused on transition and early experiences of motherhood and fatherhood in earlier publications, the chapters in this book now follow later experiences, but of the same parents followed in these earlier books as their children have grown. Taking this approach, the focus is on individual narratives of daily caring, familial relationships and paid work and how these are made sense of and managed (Andrews et al, 2013; Frank, 1995; Miller, 2017a; Riessman, 2008). Individual narrations are theorized using the lens of gender and presentations of self (what can and cannot be narrated and by who), paying particular attention to shifts between historically narrow and binary concepts of gender, 'choice' and power, and recent, more nuanced theorisations of gender and notions of choice and responsibility.

This chapter provides the theoretical, conceptual and methodological framework for the remainder of the book. Across the following sections, the contemporary and historical contexts are examined to show how the category of parenthood and expectations of parenting have been configured and conceptualised and family life theorised. This backdrop illuminates the context against which to explore individual experiences and everyday practices of parenting and is illustrated through data collected in two qualitative longitudinal research studies. Earlier phases of data collected in these two studies have reported on transition to first-time motherhood experiences (Miller, 2005, 2007) and transition to first-time fatherhood experiences (Miller, 2010, 2011). Now, using later phases of the data, parenting experiences as children reach school age (in the Fatherhood study) and the teenage years (in the Motherhood study) are examined. These later episodes of data provide unusually rich, longitudinal sources through which to explore how parenting is understood, negotiated, practiced and reflected on over time (Henwood and Shirani, 2012; Miller, 2015; Neale, 2015). For example post-separation parenting arrangements are (unexpectedly) captured through this longitudinal lens as once-hopeful couple relationships have broken down (see Chapter 5; Phillip, 2014; Philip and O'Brien, 2012; Smart and Neale, 1999). Further information on the qualitative longitudinal research design and participant details are provided later in the chapter.

Setting the Broader Neoliberal Context: Family Change and Continuities

In the sections that follow, the changes and continuities that have patterned practises of parenting and constructions of parenthoods in recent years – including neoliberalism as political ideology, family change, understandings of gender and care – are discussed. This begins with a focus on 21st-century neoliberal restructuring and the 'transformation of the administrative state, one previously responsible for human well-being', to a state in which individuals are 'reconfigured as productive economic entrepreneurs of their own lives' (Davies and Bansel, 2007:248). In relation to family lives, political preoccupations have emerged, including an (over)emphasis on the cultivation and production of the competitive, individual worker-citizen, with a corresponding emphasis on more intensified parenting, parenting education and the imperative of success for children at school (Davies and Bansel, 2007; Holloway and Pimlott-Wilson, 2014; Jensen, 2010). This has included a discursive and conceptual move away from notions of 'child-rearing' to a preoccupation with parenting, which as noted earlier narrowly links 'certain parenting behaviours' to particular 'outcomes for children' (Daly, 2013:162). The cultural preoccupation with uncertainty and individual control apparent in neoliberalist ideologies increasingly regards families and family life as an acceptable focus for policy intervention (Daly, 2013). Through interventions such as parenting programmes, governments are increasingly extending their reach into areas previously regarded as primarily private and a family responsibility (Edwards and Gillies, 2011; Featherstone et al, 2016). But the focus on 'the family' in neoliberal restructuring and interventions does not pertain in equal ways to *all* families; rather, policies have been shaped by middle-class values and then rolled out as interventions for 'troubled', 'failing', 'feckless' and 'feral' families (Crossley, 2015; Gillies, 2008; Holloway and Pimlott-Wilson, 2014; Klett-Davies, 2010; Ribbens McCarthy et al, 2013). For, as Crossley (2015) notes, 'official categorisations and policies serve to discursively and symbolically privilege certain types of family as more *natural* and acceptable than others' (p. 12, emphasis in the original), while others observe the ways in which 'affluence protects' and deflects scrutiny (Ribbens McCarthy, 2006). In addition, the current preoccupation with parenting education and the professionalization of parenting takes no account of the social and material contexts in which parenting is lived and undertaken, but rather assumes child-rearing to be 'practised independently from the social context' while privileging idealised versions of middle-class[1] parenting (Fox, 2009; Gillies, 2008; Jensen, 2010; Tyler, 2008). However, even though not so centrally targeted on some mothers, or parents, the intensified gaze and discourses associated with modern parenthood can be pervasive, leading to a general sense of surveillance and practices of self-scrutiny.

The discursive and practical importance of education also runs through neoliberal ideologies as 'competition and an emphasis on individual success measured through endless work and ostentatious consumption' is both prioritised and prized (McGregor, 2001). Education of parents (to parent) and parents ensuring educational success of their children are associated with neoliberal concerns for 'the development of a skilled population' and notions of self-reliance and 'future social stability' (Holloway and Pimlott-Wilson, 2011, 2014). Family responsibilities to produce and nurture the competitive individual has a central focus for neoliberals as ideals of collectivism and any sense of the community are supplanted. These responsibilities are considered further in later chapters as experiences of school, work and family are explored in fathers' accounts of their primary school–age children (Chapter 3) and mothers accounts of their teenage children (Chapter 4). How are notions of parental responsibilities and 'success' configured, 'felt' and narrated in these accounts?

It becomes clear then that ideals of intensive parenting, especially in relation to time-intensive activities associated with measures of 'successful' parenting, for example 'concerted cultivation' of children and their success in the education system, are increasingly expected to be part of everyday family practises; but this is a time too when most parents are also employed outside the home and increasingly report

[1] The samples were all white, heterosexual women and men (some in ethnically mixed couples). In many ways this sample conforms to normative ideals of the 'good parent', as they were predominately middle class, white, and either married or in partnerships. Yet the longitudinal data have revealed diversity and complexity as caring and working relationships have unfolded even in this apparently homogeneous group.

feeling time-poor and 'stressed' (Harden et al, 2014; Henderson, 2012; Irwin and Elley, 2011; Lareau, 2003; Vincent and Ball, 2007). Significant research has accrued since American sociologist Sharon Hays coined the term 'intensive mothering' more than twenty years ago, drawing attention, among other things, to 'the tensions between the values of parenthood and the values of the market place' (Hays, 1996). In the intervening years feminist and other scholarship has continued to examine, problematize and critique the contours and practises of intensive mothering, and more recently fathering too: the focus on an 'intensive parenting culture' underscores the need for such continued endeavours (Craig et al, 2014; Jensen, 2010; Lee et al, 2014; Shirani et al, 2012). In political terms, 'good' parenting requires intensive amounts of time to be spent on child cultivation to ensure healthy emotional and psychological development and attachment, whilst inculcating competitiveness and producing a 'successful' individual worker-citizen (Dermott and Pomati, 2016; Irwin and Elley, 2011; Jensen, 2010; Lareau 2003). But parents are also expected to be productively engaged in paid work.

The framing of parenting in this way has been influenced by 'developments' in brain science, which have further concentrated political interest in intensive parenting 'to optimize child brain development' and reduce costs to government of 'failing' children and parents (Wall, 2010; Wastell and White, 2012). Increasingly, brain science is argued to play a role in reshaping the relationship between parents and the state, both in the United Kingdom and in other Western countries. Yet questions about the scientific credibility and 'truth' of findings have also been raised, as have concerns about how findings in neuroscience are being translated into professional parenting advice, especially in relation to early years interventions and 'poor' child-rearing practises (Bruer, 1999; Edwards and Gillies, 2011; Lowe et al, 2015; Wastell and White, 2012). Encapsulating the concern expressed by commentators and practitioners, Wastell and White (2012) note that while 'there is much to commend a "progressive" agenda of help for the most disadvantaged children', the rush to interventionist policies based on 'pseudo-scientific expertise' and misperceptions about brain development and 'the first three years' is clearly not the way to support such children or their families (p. 398; Featherstone et al, 2016). There are then myriad contradictions and inequalities embedded in the ideology of intensive parenting, which, together with social class bias, have more profoundly affected women who are mothers than men who are fathers. However, this is a more fluid situation than in previous times and, as Shirani et al (2012) note, if a 'maternal lens' is revoked, 'the ways in which parenting may become differently intensive for men' becomes more apparent (p. 37; see also Dermott and Miller, 2015; Doucet, 2016). But this remains a contested area, and a finer focus on individually perceived mothering and fathering 'responsibilities' in relation to care for their children, over time, is explored in greater detail in the subsequent chapters of this book. In particular attention will be given to the question of gendered and/or moral orientations to care and, in particular, how the 'mental work' of more intensified parenting becomes taken on, by whom and how practiced? (Walzer, 1996).

Gender, Work and Doing Family Life

Regardless of political invocations and increased development of models of 'good practice' and programmes to 'train' parents, at the everyday and household level mothers and fathers get on with the daily practises of 24/7 caring for their children in various ways and in increasingly varied family formations (Biblarz and Stacey, 2010; Dunne, 2000; Golombok, 2015; Herrera, 2013). Here too, various shifts, for example in reproductive technologies and legal arrangements (e.g. surrogacy, sperm donations, embryo donation, divorce, shared custody) have changed possible routes into and out of more traditional family arrangements and increased the diversity of family types (Golombok, 2000, 2015; Herrera, 2013; Murphy, 2016). Family formations now encompass same-sex, never-married, separated, adoptive, lone and co-parenting family relationships (Duncan and Edwards, 1999; Duncan et al, 2010; Jones and Hackett, 2011; Philip, 2014; Philip and O'Brien, 2012). Not surprisingly, one effect of these changes has been to challenge taken-for-granted assumptions around how caring for children is organised in families and how maternal/paternal/familial responsibilities are thought about (or not) and practised (see Chapter 2). Other changes contributing to shifts in family lives and practices have included labour market participation so that increasingly in the United Kingdom and more widely across Europe, it is clear that there is no longer one dominant model of employment arrangements in couple households as most children 'are being brought up by parents who are engaged in some form of paid work employment outside the home' (Connolly et al, 2016; Harden et al, 2014; Office for National Statistics, 2013). For example, recent research shows that almost one-third of working mothers (30%) across all age groups, income groups, and family types are 'earning as much as or more than their partners' (Ben-Galim and Thompson, 2013) and so are 'breadwinning' in ways previously exclusively associated with men and fathers. But even though the increase in maternal employment is a significant trend, a gender pay gap and 'motherhood wage penalty' continues to shape experiences, both in the workplace and caring arrangements in the home (Ben-Galim and Thompson, 2013; Budig and England, 2001; Costa Dias et al, 2016; Perrons, 2009, 2010). Recent research in the United Kingdom reports that following the birth of a child, there is 'a gradual but continual rise in the wage gap and, by the time the first child is aged 12, women's hourly wages are a third below men's' (Costa Dias et al, 2016:2). Research also indicates that some behaviours and practices may be more resistant to change than others, for example the division of domestic labour in the home (Ekberg et al, 2013; Miller, 2011; Norman and Elliot, 2015). I return to this in later chapters (see Chapters 3 and 4).

Alongside the intensification of parenthood ideals and workplace demands, expectations around men's involvement in their child's life provide another dimension of change. Even though mothers have been assumed as 'the main audience' for the policies and programmes increasingly being rolled out by successive governments, these are framed as gender-blind (Daly, 2013:172). However, developments in theorisations and practises of gender demonstrate that some shifts have occurred in relation to parenting and care work (see Chapter 2). Theorisations of gender that capture more fluid and contingent understandings of femininities and masculinities – and so gendered possibilities – have been associated with pockets of significant global change in countries where gender-equality policies are a central concern (e.g. Finland). Even though claims around biological predispositions and determinism continue – and may indeed be claimed by fathers ('*it's kind of instinctive*'), other research continues to challenge biological determinist arguments, especially in relation to capabilities to care (see Chapter 2). In earlier periods bringing together reproductive, caring realms, and facets of hegemonic masculinity would, in many Western societies, have felt contradictory, but more nuanced theorisations of pluralities of masculinity have challenged earlier hegemonic constructions and/or at least indicate new possibilities in relation to how masculinities are understood and lived (e.g. Anderson, 2011; Brandth and Kvande, 2016; Connell 1995; Connell and Messerschmidt, 2005; Elliott, 2015; Flood 2002; Johansson and Klinth, 2007; Kimmel et al, 2004; Messerschmidt, 2009; Murphy, 2016). For example, even though the normative worker may continue to be presumed as masculine, notions of 'caring masculinities' and examples of stay-at-home dads who may assume characteristics and activities once defined as feminine, also co-exist (Doucet, 2006, Elliot, 2015; Johansson and Klinth, 2008; Ranson, 2012, 2015). Similarly, research has shown the simultaneous ways in which both 'doing' and 'undoing' gender may be enacted in masculine practises of caring for children (Deutsch, 2007; Miller, 2011; West and Zimmerman, 1987). Change, then, may not be radical but piecemeal and co-exist in hegemonic displays and caring practises.

The concept of 'caring masculinities' has more recently been subject to further theorisations. For example, Elliott (2015) has drawn upon feminist care theory in claims to 'reveal new ways of thinking through masculinities' (p. 17). Through the development of a practice-based framework, Elliott recasts 'caring masculinities' as encompassing a 'rejection of domination' and the integration of 'positive emotion, interdependence and relationality' in place of traditional masculine values such as protection and provision (2015:2). Such theoretical developments – Elliott brings together critical studies of men and masculinities and feminist care theory – illuminate the ways in which practices and categorisations of gender require continual monitoring and reflection, both as everyday practises and broader, global processes. Even so, in the United Kingdom there is no national data collected on fathers, which means even basic demographic information is not available (Burgess et al, 2017). Similarly, fathers have been less likely as a group to be a focus in many publications except as figures bearing an economic responsibility if no longer living with their children, and/or positioned as figures of 'threat' and 'risk' (Featherstone, 2003, 2009).

But evidence of changing masculine practices in relation to behaviours once exclusively associated with femininity and nurturing capacities raises new questions in relation to the organisation of family lives. For example, questions about 'gatekeeping' and the taking on or giving up of responsibilities in relation to our children. To date theorisations of 'maternal gatekeeping' have been overly simplistic, failing to adequately take account of the historical legacy of gendered arrangements, how 'preferences' and 'choices' emerge and how power might operate (Allen and Hawkins, 1999; Hakim, 2000; Lewis et al, 2008; McBride et al, 2005; Puhlman and Pasley, 2013; Schoppe-Sullivan et al, 2008). But as theorisations of gender challenge previous arrangements, what are the implications? How far might 'paternal gatekeeping' come to feature as a strategy – or constraint – in caring too? These questions are returned to in subsequent chapters (see Chapters 6 and 7).

From a historical perspective, men's increased emotional involvement in child-rearing and care work is still relatively novel, as understood in contemporary (sharing) terms (Bailey, 2012). Ideas about who should be engaged in child-rearing and who in paid work have of course fluctuated through history (Davidoff et al, 1999). Aspects of these family arrangements have been underscored at different historical moments, emphasising particular attributes of motherhood and fatherhood and their differences (Hendrick, 2016). For example, the period following the Second World War in the United Kingdom (1950s and 1960s) usefully illuminates the ways in which the categories of 'motherhood' and 'fatherhood' are socially constructed and culturally inflected at different historical moments. During this period, the emphasis was on mothers to be 'homemakers' and nurturers, caring for their family at home (rather than in the outside jobs they'd undertaken during the war years), while men recommenced their work outside the home, providing economically as the family 'breadwinner'. Maternal and paternal responsibilities were further delineated (and separated) through the development of attachment theory and its emphasis on maternal bonding and associated maternal responsibilities (Bowlby, 1971). Here 'the notion that continuous and solicitous maternal attention in the early years of a child's life was crucial to the healthy emotional and psychological development of children' was emphasised by the 'experts' of the day (Wall, 2010:254). Practises of maternal and paternal agency and 'acceptable' behaviours have then been etched through with historical precedent and shaped in modern times in relation to patriarchy and political ideology (Davidoff et al, 1999; Ruddick, 1997). But in many contemporary Western societies, both parenthood *and* paid work have become intensified and so pose daily challenges for mothers and fathers (and increasingly grandparents too) in how these competing demands are undertaken and 'balanced'. Even so, in the United Kingdom women who are mothers are more likely to work flexibly, fitting their employment around the perceived needs of their husband/partner and children (Gatrell, 2005).

Working Parenthood

Working parenthood has become the norm in the United Kingdom[2] (and across other European countries), and the political rhetoric of the 'hardworking family' has also become a mantra of the Conservative government elected in 2015. Politically the 'hardworking family' exemplifies the neoliberalist ideals of the productive worker-citizen and competitive, autonomous individual. However, managing, negotiating and reconciling the competing demands of paid work and family life leaves many working parents feeling time-poor and 'squeezed' (Harden et al, 2014:124; see Chapters 3 and 4 of this book). For example, gaps in childcare provision mean that many families can find themselves involved in piecing together informal care arrangements using grandparents, other family members and friends and/or expensive, privately provided childcare services (Ben-Galim and Thompson, 2014; Lewis et al, 2008). Even though high-quality childcare provision should be a fundamental part of any state infrastructure, where families either economically have to, or want to, combine family life and paid work (e.g. as in Sweden), day-care provision in the United Kingdom is expensive and provision ad hoc. Recent research in the United Kingdom also shows that grandparents take on significant amounts of childcare and so play an important role in plugging childcare gaps for working families (O'Brien, 2009:209; see also Hoff, 2016; Lewis et al, 2008).

However, policies to 'support' hardworking families may in reality mean 'intervention' in the United Kingdom context, where standardised parenting programmes and models of compliance (for example in promoting appropriate parental interactions with schools) are used to '(re)skill or (re)train parents' (Daly, 2013:159). Less contentious forms of support to working families include policies regarding flexible

---

[2] In 2015 in the United Kingdom 79.8% of people aged 16 to 64 with dependent children were employed. Those with dependent children make up 37.0% of all workers who were employed in 2015. Employment rate for married or cohabiting men was 91.8% and for women 72.9%. www.ons.gov.uk/employmentandlabourmarket/peopleinwork/employmentandemployeetypes/bulletins/workingandworklesshouseholds/2015–10–06.

working and parental leave. In 2003 paternity leave was introduced in the United Kingdom that for the first time allowed fathers (who were eligible) to take 10 days leave at or around the time of the birth of their child or at the time of an adoption. Subsequent initiatives (e.g. a right for a parent to request flexible working, fathers to take additional paternity leave) have culminated in the most recent Shared Parental Leave (SPL) policy, which came into operation in April 2015. This policy was heralded in some political quarters as a challenge to 'the old-fashioned assumption that women will always be the parent that stays at home', and claims to recognise that 'many fathers want that option too' (Clegg, 2014). The new policy (in theory) enables parents to decide together how to share care during the first year following the birth of a baby and provides some flexibility in relation to this (www.gov.uk/government/news; Working Families Employer Briefing, 2014). Interestingly, a political intention to extend this leave to enable working grandparents to also share parental leave entitlement (from 2018) has also been mooted (www.gov.uk/government/news, October 5, 2015). However, in the first year following implementation of SPL policy, take up has been disappointingly low and reflects a political naivety about the complexity of aspects of family lives and the possibility of 'choices' within pervasive cultures of paid work and care (Moss et al, 2012). In reality this is not surprising because a policy can signal change but not ensure its take-up (unless significantly incentivized), as new 'choices' and negotiations within families are engaged from pre-existing unequal relationships and assumed responsibilities around work and family. The gender pay gap and 'motherhood wage penalties' add a further dimension to household considerations as well as deeply ingrained work practices (Budig and England, 2001; Costa Dias et al, 2016). But over time, and drawing on examples from Nordic countries, change can be achieved, but only by making expectations and intentions explicit in policy and incentivising individual leave policies and entitlement appropriately (Miller, 2013b; Moss et al, 2012).

It is now well recognised that a country's policy framework, particularly the level of financial incentive, is a key variable in shaping fathers' propensity to take family leave (Feldman and Gran, 2016; O'Brien, 2009; O'Brien et al, 2015). It is clear that working parents – mothers and fathers – populate home and work spheres in ways that are less segregated than in recent historical times. Even though historically some mothers have always had to work through economic necessity – and this remains the case in many households up and down the country – other aspects of being in the workplace can be experienced as personally satisfying and/or rewarding. The workplace can be a setting for identity work, career development, economic growth and visible success, all aspects of the social world that have been much more associated with men's lives and successful and valued forms of hegemonic masculinity. Men, on the other hand, as they become fathers, have more opportunities (e.g. through policies) to engage in what have been maternally etched areas of the social world, the home, caring for children and domestic chores, all largely invisible, undervalued and taken-for-granted aspects of the social world. But some areas are more impervious to change and the sharing of household chores remains a primary site of gender inequality (Norman and Elliot, 2015; see Chapter 2).

Researching Family Lives: Discourses, Narratives and Everyday Practices

In contemporary society, individuals and couples come to be parents in a landscape that is more demanding and subject to new forms of surveillance than in previous times. As Ramaekers and Suissa (2012: vii) observe, 'parents today have various claims made on them in the sense that they are expected to perform in certain ways and to achieve certain outcomes. Discourses around parenting, societal and personal expectations, the number of experts and amount and types of parenting advice has all burgeoned in significant and often perplexing ways. What sits at the core of broader macro and structural features are individuals and couples with children trying to manage family practises, relationships, caring and work in the best ways they can in different, and sometimes very difficult, circumstances. Even though managing these demands might seem daunting (or perhaps because they are), research continues to demonstrate that families 'remain of great importance to people, even as patterns of residence and family household arrangements are now more varied' (Charles et al, 2008:122; see also Edwards et al, 2012; Jamieson et al, 2014).

As a research focus too, families continue to provide a critical area of study for academics as family formations, relationships and their durability and complexity become more variable as well as increasingly subject to external surveillance. As a human activity, being a parent includes relational and intergenerational connections, obligations, responsibilities, love, frustration, disappointment and joy. But the claims of parenthood expressed in dominant discourses invoke morally, culturally and historically grounded expectations of parenting practises that are taken to constitute 'good' parenting. Yet ambiguity and contradictions run across these domains – the activity and discourses – reflecting the messy lived experiences that unfold in daily family practises (Ramaekers and Suissa, 2012; Jensen, 2010). Mothers also continue to be held more responsible in parenthood discourses – and their practises – because fathers are still more able to acceptably prioritise paid work over care (Bass, 2015; Miller, 2017b). Although scholars have continued to examine the contours of family lives, there has been debate on the relevance and retention of the concept of 'family' and its ability to encompass the complexity and diversity of contemporary relationships and experiences (Edwards and Gillies, 2012; Edwards et al, 2012; Morgan, 2014; Ribbens McCarthy, 2012). The increasing use of the language of 'personal life', 'intimacy' and 'kinship' are seen to potentially obscure 'other meanings and significances' that are denied or distorted through an individualist lens (Edwards and Gillies, 2012:67). Because the focus taken in this book is on experiences of parenting, family lives form a significant, variable and changing backdrop against which the mothers and fathers make sense of their unfolding parenting, working and everyday relationships. The participants are connected through families and wider/intergenerational familial networks (e.g. grandparents), their experiences are shaped by expectations – cultural and political – that permeate their lives through dominant and counter discourses. These discourses provide the discursive tools through which to narrate their selves as mothers and fathers in relational ways, which can reproduce and reinforce stereotypical modes of 'good parenting' and can (sometimes simultaneously) challenge and disrupt taken-for-granted assumptions about parenting, parenthood and family lives.

Different discourses – for example discourses of parental responsibility – then provide different discursive resources and possibilities through which to situate (or not) experiences. Discourses are also morally and politically imbued and so can shape expectations and ways of telling in particular 'moral' ways (Ribbens McCarthy et al, 2003). In the data used in the subsequent chapters of this book, the ways in which mothers and fathers provide accounts of their experiences as these have unfolded is a particular focus (Miller, 2005, 2017b).

Because the data used are longitudinal, attention is paid to time and the temporal ordering of events associated with unfolding experiences as parents of growing children provide accounts of these (Neale, 2012). This approach, and comparisons between the two studies, has importantly revealed the gendered aspects of behaviours and narrative possibilities: what can be said, when, and by whom as well as the obdurate assumptions that persist around paid work and caring. Philosophically this approach is located within traditions and debates about 'storied human lives' in which we 'are not only the actor, but also the author' (Frank, 1995; MacIntyre, 1981:198; Ricoeur, 1984). It is argued, then, that as human beings, we are storytelling animals. We act with intention and purpose and make sense of past experiences, present and future hopes and expectations, in relation to particular historical, cultural and social contexts. And it is this ability that provides us with an identity and a sense of existing through time and of acting with intention and purpose in the world. Taking a narrative approach in the study of subjective experience enables the researcher to access and explore individual identities: the ways in which social actors actively produce narrative accounts and present their selves to others.

In earlier episodes of the participants' experiences of becoming mothers and fathers, intentions, expectations and early practices were explored. These included expressions by the women of conventional expectations (especially in relation to mothers) of 'being there for others' (Adkins, 2002; Bailey, 2001). But the fathers also expressed intentions of 'being there' in physical and caring ways as first-time fatherhood was anticipated (Miller, 2010). However, daily practices did not necessarily map onto intentions and following the birth of a child, the new mothers and fathers typically assumed traditionally gendered behaviours despite their earlier intentions (Miller, 2011). The ways in which the birth of a first baby crystalizes gender differences in the home and paid work has also been well documented (Asher, 2012; Perrons, 2009; Sanchez and Thomson, 1997). Less so are the negotiations, or absence of these, that couples engage in as parenting practises and relationships with older children develop (Fox, 2009). How do parenting relationships and sharing of caring responsibilities and practices unfold as children grow and start school, become teenagers and anticipate their adult futures and as family contexts and parental relationships shift? The following section provides details of the study methods before the empirical data are examined across the subsequent chapters.

The Studies

The two UK-based qualitative longitudinal studies that are drawn upon in this book have focused on women's and men's transition experiences as they became parents for the first time and has followed later, unfolding experiences of family lives, caring and paid work. The initial Transition to First-time Motherhood Study followed 17 women through a year in their life as they became mothers for the first time (Miller, 2005, 2007). The participants were interviewed on three separate occasions; before the birth, in the early weeks following the birth and at a later interview when the baby was approximately 9 to 10 months old. Semi-structured interview schedules were designed for each of the three interviews. Recruitment commenced in 1995, and data collection was completed in 1998 and analysed/reanalysed in subsequent years (2005, 2007, 2012). More recently it was decided to go back to the women in the original sample because their firstborn child would be approximately 18 years old. Going back would enable the capture of much later episodes of the women's experiences as well as their reflections – a longer view – on their mothering and motherhood experiences. University research ethics approval, which had not been a requirement when the original study was carried out (Miller, 2012), was gained for this later data collection phase, and the 'Motherhood Revisited' study commenced in 2013. The hope was that these later interviews would facilitate data collection at another transitional stage in the women's lives as they care for their older, teenage children who will have reached early adulthood (18 years), where decisions about futures (e.g. education and work directions) and other more immediate concerns can occupy both young lives and mothering identities and experiences. The research would also gather participant's reflections on the ways in which their mothering 'careers' had unfolded and the ways in which these are/can be narrated (Ribbens, 1998).

The companion qualitative longitudinal Transition to First-time Fatherhood Study was commenced several years after the Motherhood study, with interview data initially being collected between 2005 and 2007. However, although this study followed the same research design as the earlier Motherhood study, once the study commenced it was decided to extend the time frame to include an additional (fourth) interview with the fathers, when their child reached their second birthday (Miller, 2010). The sample in this study also consisted of 17 men who were becoming fathers for the first time. During the interview carried out at 2 years with the fathers, the possibility of being contacted for a later interview when their children reached school age was discussed, and general agreement was expressed. In 2012 university research ethics committee approval was gained to re-contact the participants as their firstborn child reached school age (5–6 years of age). The rationale for keeping the study 'live' was both to add to a gradually growing literature on early years fathering experiences and to return to a sample seemingly comfortable ('socialised') with the qualitative open-ended and iterative interview format. It has been noted elsewhere that research on parents and parenthood has tended to focus on mothers because of their availability as main carers to provide details of family lives to researchers. It thus seemed important to try to add fathers' voices to these descriptions.

Sample Details

The sample in the Motherhood study consisted of 17 white, heterosexual women who had a mean age of 30 years at the time of the first antenatal interview. This was slightly older than the national average age for first births in the United Kingdom when the original data were collected (mid-to-late 1990s) but typical of the trend among professional women to delay decisions about reproduction. In many ways, this sample conformed to stereotypes that are held in wider society about those who are positioned as 'good' mothers. These women were predominately middle-class by occupation, white, and either married or in partnerships. Yet the data revealed how diverse and complex early mothering experiences can be, even amongst an apparently homogeneous group (Miller, 2005, 2007). The sample of 17 men recruited in the second study, which focused on Fatherhood, had a mean age of 33.7 years at the time of the first interview; ages ranged from 24 years to 39 years. The men were employed in a wide range of skilled jobs that would mostly position them as middle class; they were partnered (some married), white (several in ethnically mixed partnerships/marriages) and heterosexual. Their socio-economic location (by occupation) and corresponding choices could be argued to be greater than those that less advantaged groups might enjoy. Both samples were recruited from dual-earner households. The longitudinal data have been collected through repeat face-to-face interviews, initially on three separate occasions across the first year of transition to parenthood (late antenatal period, early and late postnatal interviews), followed by an end-of-transition-study postal questionnaire used to collect demographic data and feedback on experiences of participating in the transition studies. The data collected in these earlier interviews provide vital context and earlier episodes of intentions and unfolding experiences, against which the more recent data collection phase has been undertaken and the new data analysed. The subsequent interviews were conducted with the participants in the Motherhood study as their child reached their 18th birthday (see Chapter 4) and in the Fatherhood study as their firstborn child reached 2 years of age and again in the year their child started primary school (see Chapter 5). It is this later data that provide the major focus for the empirical chapters of this book (Chapters 3–6). In the Transition to Fatherhood Study, 13 of the original 17 fathers were re-contacted (using existing contact details) about participating in the later (school-age children) interviews. Of these 13, 10 fathers 'opted in' to the new phase of interviews. In the Motherhood study, 17 years after the last interviews 10 of the original participants were traced (using a variety of means see Miller, 2015; Oakley, 2016) and invited to participate in a further interview. Of these 10, 6 women agreed and participated in a subsequent interview (for further details, see Chapter 4). Across the two studies approximately 200 hours of interviewing has been carried out (in 125 interviews) and inform the analytical and theoretical work undertaken in this and the two earlier (companion) books (see Chapter 7).

The practise of undertaking qualitative longitudinal research has grown significantly in recent years, becoming recognised 'as a distinctive mode of social enquiry' (Neale, 2012). Through its focus on unfolding experiences over time, the approach in these two studies has specifically examined the ways in which intensions, expectations, experiences and reflections in relation to motherhood, fatherhood, parenting, family care and paid work can be narrated.[3] Going back to

---

[3] For further details of taking a narrative approach see Miller (2005), *Making Sense of Motherhood* (Chapter 1) and Miller (2017a), *Doing Narrative Research*.

participants can raise new issues for the researcher; for example the accumulation of new data may provide alternative and/or contradictory versions of earlier accounts and more broadly prompt questions of what constitutes 'the data' (Miller, 2015). Similarly, 'which versions of events carry authenticity' and what analytical insights and dividends may be gained through the analysis of cumulative (over a longer time period) and so more richly textured episodes of experience and narration (Neale, 2012:12)? Going back into lives and experiences that have unfolded in unexpected ways, and reminding the participant of an earlier version of their self, can enrich theorising of temporal subjectivity, but also unintentionally reinforce feelings of sadness or expressions of failure, for example when parents are no longer together (see Chapter 5). The accumulation and weaving together of episodes of experience gained through qualitative longitudinal research helps to illuminate – in these particular research projects – the 'tenuousness' of selves and selfhood, the ways in which powerful discourses associated with family lives and parenting shape what is felt to be permissible to say, when and what remains unspoken, such that earlier theorisations can be confirmed, re-evaluated and refined. The woven together accounts of everyday experiences, narrated in sometimes contradictory and edited ways, from different vantage points through parenthood journeys, illuminate subjectivity as fluid, recognisable and reflexive. Subjectivity is also narrated through particular discourses of parenting drawing upon available/acceptable storylines, aspects of which are gendered, classed and 'raced' and for some parents subjected to particular scrutiny (Gillies, 2008; Lash, 1994; Mac an Ghaill and Haywood, 2007). But the claims that are increasingly made about and on parents can be hard to escape and eventually come to shape ideas about parenting practises as the language of contemporary parenting is (imperceptibly) taken up.

Conclusions

It is clear that a dependent child has needs that must be met for survival, but the ways in which these are understood, regarded as individual and/or shared responsibilities and practically met, has varied historically, culturally and globally. In the Western world, the practices of meeting children's needs is generally and generically understood as parenting, but the rudimentary components of caring for a child,

providing sustenance, shelter and love have become overlaid in myriad ways with additional demands of intensive, child-centred care in
which children are positioned as *more* 'needy, vulnerable and dependent' than in previous times (Wall, 2013). Alongside this shift, parents in Western societies are now subject to an 'overwhelming array of
advice on how to bring up their children', which continues to be dis-
proportionately aimed at mothers and especially mothers living in circumstances where their choices may be more limited (Raemaekers and
Suissa, 2012, viii). Contemporary discourses of parental responsibility
invoke morally inflected, and at times, a gender-neutral language of
parenting, where parenting is intensive and child-focused, yet research
also shows that women are more likely to be primary caregivers as well
as increasingly contributing to household incomes through paid work.
At the same time, families have become a focus of political interest as
successive governments 'cost' the apparent consequences of 'poor parenting' and front campaigns about the importance of getting parenting
right in the first year, '1001' days, 3 years (Department of Health, 2016;
Edwards and Gillies, 2011; Lee et al, 2014). There are various claims
too that permeate the public sphere about parents and how parenting
should be undertaken. Against this backdrop, how do the mothers and
fathers followed in this book narrate their experiences of being parents
and doing parenting? How do mothers and fathers manage the daily
activities and the 'mental labor' of caring for their children (in couples and alone) as family lives unfold in unpredictable ways (Walzer,
1996)? What discourses are drawn upon to locate or challenge ideals of
'good parenting', and how are responsibilities divided? Is it possible to
escape the dominant, contemporary discourses of intensive parenting
and how/or are these experienced (differently) by mothers and fathers?
At its core, parenting involves the daily activity and thinking responsibility of caring, including providing and protecting a child. This is
often assumed to be and taken on as a primary responsibility, associated firmly with assumptions of maternal instincts and capabilities.
But men can care too. So in the following chapter, a finer focus is taken
on what care is, what it means and how caring comes to be practised.

2 | Caring Landscapes and Gendered Practices

I always felt that I was a primary carer – I would always do all the things for the children. That was my job.

(Gillian, Motherhood study)

We've been very busy at work, so there was like a three-day period when I didn't see him awake and that's horrible, you really start to miss him then.

(Gus, Fatherhood study)

This chapter focuses on caring and explores how everyday practices of parental caring become shaped and managed. It sets the scene for the following chapters in which caring activities and responsibilities are navigated and narrated. Caring is a fundamental human activity, which in this chapter is explored through thinking about daily practices in families that involve caring activities and the emotional, mental labour of care and care work.[1] These activities and responsibilities have historically been associated with women and their assumed natural capacities to care and still today women do more caregiving than men. But the picture is more complicated than these statements suggest and different biological, cultural, moral and ethical explanations for how caregiving in western societies evolves and is practised, have occupied philosophical thought, political theory and feminist debates and research agendas over many years. More recently, research has demonstrated that structural and demographic shifts are reconfiguring caring practices as caring trajectories also extend, with care work

---

[1] It is necessary to acknowledge the breadth of the concept and practice of care and caring. Care operates in different domains in paid and unpaid, assumed and dependent/unwelcome scenarios. It involves a range of moral and ethical orientations and motives. It may be vital for sustaining life and may produce broader benefits and values. In this chapter, a narrower focus on care and caring is taken as one way to explore family practices and how these are navigated and managed.

becoming more visible and increasingly politicised and public (Ben-Galim and Thompson, 2014; Crompton et al, 2007; Williams, 2010). These changes urge a more critical review of the concept and practise of parental caring in these neoliberal times, when parenthood and paid work expectations have become simultaneously 'intensified', as noted in the previous chapter.

Care is notoriously difficult to define because it involves 'an ethic defined in opposition to justice, a kind of labor, and a particular relationship' (Ruddick, 1998:4). In this book the focus on care is concerned with the 'labour' of parental care work and the relationship, both broadly as parental relationships of care for their children and specifically in terms of a *primary* care responsibility and how this is practised by mothers and fathers in contexts of family care. Thus the focus on care and caring taken in this chapter encompasses an examination of recent and more nuanced understandings of gendered moral orientations in relation to care and caring. This includes masculine capacities to care and women's increasingly significant participation in the workplace. These shifts have helped to change the parameters of debates and discourses as policy initiatives (e.g. flexible working and additional paternal leave) apparently signal new opportunities for how care and paid work could be organised in the United Kingdom and more broadly (Lyonette et al, 2011). It is also clear that 'how well a society rewards care work impacts gender equality' (P. England, 2005:381). How far, then, do expectations of modern fatherhoods and motherhoods – and evidence from northern Europe – affect the ways in which parental caring is imagined, shared and narrated in families in the United Kingdom? What happens to parental intentions and practices of caring as families grow? And how do increasingly active 'care markets' (Williams, 2010) fit with ideals of increasingly intensified 'good' parenting? These areas are examined across the later chapters in the book using qualitative longitudinal data as caring and working arrangements in families are explored. But first, a review of care debates and conceptual frames is discussed here.

It is not uncommon to hear parents-to-be express their intention that the impending birth of a first child will not change their lives to any great extent. Indeed it seems to be impossible to convey before the birth the 24/7 sense of caring responsibility that descends, as new parenthood is first experienced. But these unfolding responsibilities, which rapidly become evident, as new parents leave the care of the hospital[2] and commence caring for their new baby at home, pattern lives and household arrangements in all sorts of ways. As Paula England (2005) notes, the 'most time-intensive care work' is parenting (p. 384). Historically caring work has been assumed to be a 'natural', biological and so essentialist aspect of being a woman. Hence motherhood and the caring responsibilities and practises associated with mothering have been positioned as private, largely invisible and undervalued (Hochschild, 2003; Miller, 2005, 2007; Rich, 1976; Walzer, 1996). Not surprisingly such assumptions have been subject to many years of feminist critique and challenge, associated in particular with second-wave feminism. The social benefits (of having children) and opportunity for virtue that can arise as an aspect of caring and extends beyond its immediate practice, being foregrounded in debates (P. England, 2005; Noddings, 2003; Tronto, 1993, 2005). But the domain of parental caring has been a highly contested arena in which obligation, love, essentialism, gendered histories of unequal opportunities, 'preferences', 'choices' and power have played, and continue to play, out. As noted in the previous chapter, shifts in contemporary lives in relation to education, employment, practices of gendered individualisation and identity, reproductive choices and selfhood present new questions in relation to understandings of care and responsibilities and how these are arranged and managed in families. The increasing visibility of men as fathers also contributes to debates on how caring and work lives can be managed (Dermott and Miller, 2015; Doucet, 2006, 2016; Dribe and Stanfors, 2009; Gerstel and Gallagher, 2001; Inhorn et al, 2016; Marsiglio et al, 2005; Ranson, 2015; Rehel, 2014). Together these broadranging changes have led to what Sevenhuijsen calls 'a relocation of care' and an associated 'relocation of politics' (2003). Helpfully, the concept of relocation provides a useful device through which to explore changes in relation to care as a growing need, a moral, ethical and political concern and an everyday relational family responsibility and activity. These areas are explored further in the sections that follow and provide a broad overview of the contemporary landscape against which everyday practices of caring – and especially caring for children in families – is undertaken.

---

[2] Ninety-eight percent of births in England and Wales take place in hospitals. www.ons.gov.uk/peoplepopulationandcommunity/birthsdeathsandmarriages/ livebirths/bulletins/birthcharacteristicsinenglandandwales/2015–10–08.

Relocation of Care: Meeting Growing Care Needs

Changes in global labour-market demands, welfare state regimes and coinciding extended life expectancy[3] found in many countries have resulted in increased care needs and work. These shifts have resulted in a relocation of where care may take place, who provides it and how care is framed in political intentions and policies (Daly, 2013; Ehrenreich and Hochschild 2002; K. England, 2010; Williams, 2010). An ageing, and so increasingly dependent, population has also extended caring trajectories and family responsibilities (Skills for Care, 2015). For example a spouse and/or adult children can find themselves caught up in caring for a dependent partner or parent, which may overlap with care responsibilities for their children. At the same time, most families in the United Kingdom are working families with households dependent on two incomes. Although this has involved a model of (mostly) one full-time and one part-time wage earner, the 'dual full-time earner model' is, according to recent research, 'growing in significance' for parents of young children in Britain (Connolly et al, 2016:838; see also Perrons, 2009, 2010). These spheres of work life and caring are of course interwoven so that even where care provision is physically relocated – for example day care for a child – responsibilities for organising care and caring remain a factor in managing everyday family life. The question of how far relocating care provision to a 'care market', from unpaid to paid care, reduces a sense of caring responsibilities or changes gendered understandings in relation to responsibilities is explored later (Williams, 2010; see also Chapter 6 in this book). But whatever the response, 'the nature of caring practices' according to Sevenhuijsen (2003), is changing. This change includes increased political interest in an hitherto largely 'invisible' and undervalued activity of caring in families and raises the question of whether the relocation of aspects of care to political scrutiny and policy agendas changes the actors and meanings involved. Interestingly, in relation to this Fiona Williams has argued that 'the very surfacing of needs as matters for political concern has the effect, in and of itself, of denaturalizing them' making visible otherwise taken-for-granted or hidden aspects

[3] Life expectancy has increased in the United Kingdom, but with significant social class variations (Dorling, 2015).

carers become visible

of the social world. If this is so, then it has the potential to challenge and disrupt traditional and gendered caring arrangements and their 'natural' association with the 'duties attached to being a wife, mother or daughter' (Williams, 2010:3).

On

But others have noted the obduracy of deeply etched assumptions that continue to situate women as 'natural' carers and workplace expectations and cultures that shape and/or constrain choices and practices in care and paid work domains (Bass, 2015; Gerstel and Gallagher, 2001; Hochschild, 1989; Miller, 2011; Pedulla and Thébaud, 2015). Even though it is recognised that 'the most direct and far reaching policy to encourage fatherhood involvement' is through paternity leave and especially in policies 'that give exclusive rights to fathers' (Feldman and Gran, 2016:96; see also Brandth and Kvande, 2016:2), in the United Kingdom, policy intentions or interventions have not gone far enough. And so the gendered conflation of women and *their* responsibilities for caring (around paid work) continues (Connolly et al, 2016; Moss et al, 2012; Norman and Elliot, 2015). But effec-tive policy can have traction in reframing traditional gendered con-figurations of care and paid work as developments in Sweden and other Nordic countries have shown. Here policies couched in terms of individual rights and entitlements have been introduced over the past 40 years as a means to achieve gender equality and allow both parents to share child caring and paid work (Björnberg and Kollind, 2005; Ekberg et al, 2013; Klinth, 2008; O'Brien et al, 2007; Plantin et al, 2003). Fathers' participation in care has been encouraged in the Nordic countries by the introduction of leave policies 'that give exclu-sive rights to fathers' (Brandth and Kvande, 2016:2). However, in Swe-den amendments to the original 1974 legislation had to be introduced to engineer their original intention of *shared* parental leave. An amend-ment to the legislation was implemented in 1995, and the 'Daddy Month' (allocated to fathers and non-transferable) was introduced to try ensure fathers take up of the leave. By 2006 each parent in Sweden had two non-transferable leave months and nine additional months to be shared (Ekberg et al, 2013; Haas and Hwang, 2008). This has recently been increased to three non-transferable leave months for each parent. Interestingly, during the debate that accompanied the original policy amendment, the Swedish government spoke of a determination to change work cultures so that both men and women could 'dare to

Configuration of care + paid work

take parental leave without a feeling of jeopardizing their career or development opportunities at work' (Ekberg et al, 2013). I return to this theme in later chapters.

Any review of the history of caring in families across Western societies underscores the political framing and fluid dimensions of welfare regimes, care arrangements and assumed 'responsibilities' (Saxonberg, 2014). For example, before the collapse of communism in Eastern Europe, the responsibility for caring for young (preschool) children was undertaken in large part by the State, so that (all) parents could be productive workers. High rates of female employment were supported by the state, but women were also valued as unpaid care-takers and homemakers, whilst also economically active for the state. But post-communist reconstruction, for example in Poland, reframed the very same responsibilities as individual and private with the 'good' mother managing these competing demands with little or no state support (Awsiukiewicz-Tomczak, 2009; Sikorska, 2014). In other parts of (especially northern) Europe, fathers are increasingly framed in policies that promote or assume gender equality and situates them as equal carers too, with a particular emphasis on the first year of their child's life (Dermott and Miller, 2015; Eydal and Rostgaard, 2016; O'Brien, 2009; Westerling, 2015; Wissö and Plantin, 2015). But although policies can signal societal and cultural shifts, there can be resistance too, especially when caring is viewed at the individual and household level. How do conceptualisations of care as a universal human virtue and/or an essentialist and/or gendered responsibility influence ideas and practices at the family level?

Care as Moral and Ethical Concern

There is a growing interdisciplinary literature arising from questions about care and gender. This has arisen as a consequence of many years of theoretical exploration of agency and moral thinking in relation to caring, autonomy, gender and the opportunity to exercise virtue (Gilligan, 1982; Held, 1987, 2006; Hollway, 2006; Hochschild, 2003; Kittay, 1999; Noddings, 2003; Ruddick, 1989; Sevenhuijsen, 1991, 1998; Tronto, 1989, 1993, 2005). In particular 'patterns of moral thought' and 'moral orientations' and how these (may) differ between women and men (mothers and fathers) have provided a focus of debate among feminist philosophers, political theorists, sociologists, psychoanalysts and others over the past 40 years (Gilligan, 1982; Kittay, 1999; Sherwin, 1992; Tronto, 1993, 2005). While Gilligan's claim that 'women are more likely than men to understand moral- ity as consisting of caring for others' and that men perceive morality in terms of universal rules, have been challenged, it nevertheless crys- talizes gendered differences often assumed in care and other domains (Sherwin, 1992). However, the need to include context as a way to understand moral reasoning and thus practises of agency is more gen- erally accepted. One attempt to address context has involved calls to elevate caring both through disciplinary recognition and, more broadly, by making it 'visible' and positioning it as public and ethically relevant: an issue for moral and public consideration (Williams, 2010). But it is interesting to consider further how the context shifts perceptions of gender-specific caring as well as activities and levels of involvement.

A conceptual distinction between 'caring for' (activity) and 'caring about' (relationship) has been emphasised in care ethics (Fisher and Tronto, 1990; Skeggs, 1997). And the development of 'an ethic of care' has involved care-focused feminist theorising and debate in relation to core care values, public responsibilities and care domains (Fisher and Tronto, 1990; Hochschild, 2003; Hollway, 2006; Kittay, 1999; Sevenhuijsen 1998; Skeggs, 1997; Walzer, 1996). Notions of 'relation- ality' and 'interdependence' have been theorised, drawing attention to the broader moral capacities of actors and through Sevenhuijsen's (2003) work an understanding that 'everyone is in principle capable of giving care' (p. 20). But nevertheless, debate continues in relation to universal versus contextual forms of moral reasoning related to human and/or gendered capacities to care and have responsibility for others and in particular in relation to the privileging of the mother- child 'bond' (Held, 2006). But importantly, 'meanings of care are gen- dered' and so the 'acquisition of the capacities associated with caring is never a gender-neutral process' (Hollway, 2006:5). This helps to under- score the complexity of gendered caring but also offers the possibility of change.

As noted earlier, this chapter has a principal sociological concern with examining how 'caring about' and 'caring for' children becomes practised in families over time. More specifically, how caring becomes assumed as a sense of responsibility, an amalgam of the '24/7 think- ing responsibility' (Miller, 2010); 'maternal thinking' (Ruddick, 1989), 'emotion work' (Hochschild, 1983) and 'mental labor' (Walzer, 1996) identified in other research, and how this and practical activities of caring become managed. This focus implies a distinction between thinking and doing that is not as neat in practise as implied but nevertheless provides a useful frame through which to begin an analysis of caring undertaken in families (see later chapters). These actions of thought and activity are grounded in morally inflected, subjectivity, ideas of dispositions and practices of gendered agency. Similarly, care needs and responsibilities are fluid, changing and age related. But meeting different care needs according to Sevenhuijsen (2003) involves 'a social practice, a form of agency, the value and meaning of which can best be *learnt by practising it*' (p. 23, emphasis added). This particular version of care encompasses possibilities of caring that do not then assume feminised care as necessarily primary – or preferable. And in many ways this takes us to the crux of current sociological and policy debates in many Western societies about capacities to care, especially in relation to mothers and their assumed 'moral responsibility' in relation to caring for their children. In contemporary parental caring arrangements for children, who cares, how and why?

Care Work: Who's Caring?

Caring takes place in concrete daily experiences and 'in our patterns of moral thought' (Sevenhuijsen, 1998) even though in our practises of meeting daily care needs, particular moral orientations almost certainly will not be at the forefront of our minds or activities. Further, the relocations of care and politics noted earlier circumscribe fluid and increasingly globalised care contexts. These encompass dynamic and contextual care activities, undertaken across a life course and (potentially) by multiple and different, often migrant and female actors (Ehrenreich and Hochschild, 2002; Hochschild, 1989).[4] Significantly, caring contexts have been further relocated from unpaid to paid care as growing levels of 'women's employment means that more of the care for children and disabled elders is provided by paid workers rather than unpaid female family members' (England, 2005:381). Care work is still mostly provided by women, built upon the history of the 'globalization

---

[4] It is interesting to note that in England the social care workforce is predominantly white (80%), whereas more than 1 in 10 workers hold a non–European Economic Area nationality. Both ethnicity and nationality profiles also vary considerably by geographical region (Skills for Care, 2015).

of traditional female services' (Ehrenreich and Hochschild, 2002:25). But (some) men have also become more visible actors as caregivers, 'contributing more to the daily care of children, partners and family members' but this is 'occurring at a much slower rate than the relocation of women's activities to the public (work) sphere' (Doucet, 2016; Jacobs and Gerson, 2015; Pedulla and Thébaud, 2015; Sevenhuijsen, 2003:15). As noted in Chapter 1, these shifts have occurred as part of broader movements in global labour markets, changed educational opportunities (for women) as well as economic recession and adjustment, leading to the emergence and dominance of a 'two-earner household model', split in various ways between full-time and part-time work across Europe (Dribe and Stanfors, 2009:33; see also Connolly et al, 2016; Yarwood and Locke, 2016). A further shift in shaping how caring is/can be practised results from more nuanced theorisations of gender and in particular masculinities. But regardless of the theoretical developments and any associated structural shifts, it is the advent of first-time parenthood that provides the 'most time-intensive example' of unpaid care work. Becoming a parent crystalizes and can reinforce the gendered divisions of caring labour (Asher, 2012; England, 2005; Sanchez and Thomson, 1997).

It has been suggested that mothers' increased participation in the labour market across Europe has been 'one of the most significant social developments of the 20th Century' and that 'fathers active participation in family life' is set to be a significant development in this 21st century (Deven, 2014). Certainly the ways in which parental caring for young children is negotiated, supported and managed between mothers, fathers and others has become a more visible personal activity and a political interest and focus. Yet overcoming deeply entrenched ideas and changing normative assumptions about women as 'natural' (unpaid and paid) carers is a slow process and a key factor in the 'stalled revolution' of gender equality (P. England, 2010). In 1998 it was argued that only 'when care is re-evaluated and freed from its gender-load and its associations with sexual difference' would men be more likely to 'identify with care and to adopt a caring identity' (Sevenhuijsen, 1998:111). In the intervening period it is possible to see that policy interventions can help to reframe in more gender equal ways some early aspects of parental caring (e.g. as seen in Sweden and Iceland), but reshaping men's participation in care and overcoming the 'persistent gender essentialism' that patterns the workplace and home remain a challenge (P. England, 2010; Miller, 2011; Sweet, 2011). For example, even though research shows that fathers are more involved in their children's care than in previous generations, women still retain primary responsibility for childcare and the housework in most Western countries (Doucet, 2006; Lyonette et al, 2011; Rehel, 2014). Similarly, men's engagement in practices that involve 'caring masculinities' do not necessarily lead them to share all aspects of family care. Research has shown that they are less likely to undertake routine housework and may selectively undertake particular activities of care, for example those associated with 'fun things' (Crompton and Lyonette, 2008; Elliott, 2015; Johansson and Klinth, 2007; Norman and Elliot, 2015). The question then of *who* takes on the responsibility for thinking about, anticipating and planning care needs in families – the mental work of caring – and *why* provides a key focus across the subsequent chapters (Gerstel and Gallagher, 2001; Hochschild, 1983; Rehel, 2014; Walzer, 1996).

Changes in gendered household caring arrangements and paid work practices are then discernible, but the balance of activities varies significantly within households, between groups and between countries (Biblarz and Stacey, 2010; Dermott and Miller, 2015; Dribe and Stanfors, 2009; Klinth, 2008; Lyonette et al, 2011; Norman and Elliot, 2015; Sweet, 2011). In a review of the household division of labour in Sweden after the advent of parenthood, daily time use data from 1990–1 were compared with data from 2000–1. The authors found that the traditional gendered division of labour in the earlier data was much less evident in the later data. They conclude that 'parenthood might have increased the time devoted to childcare somewhat more for women than for men, but the difference was no longer statistically significant' (Dribe and Stanfors, 2009:43). These findings appear to indicate the ways in which political commitments to gender equality and policy initiatives can *slowly* change cultural norms and gendered, household level practises, but structural and cultural constraints should not to be underestimated (Eydal and Rostgaard, 2016; Haas and Hwang, 2015). Gradual cultural change also requires shifts in acceptable discourses and language associated with care, so that different discursive possibilities and claims become acceptable and accepted (Westerling, 2015; Wissö and Plantin, 2015). Care, as activity and thinking, needs to be understood in the workplace not as an optional activity (undertaken by mothers) but as a vital shared human activity and an aspect of being a parent, or having caring responsibilities for a dependent parent/relative. But while it is clear that the most significant changes in relation to caring responsibilities and practises occur in countries where policies actively promote gender equality, even here change is not wholesale or rapid (Eydal and Rostgaard, 2016; Haas and Hwang, 2015). In other countries assumptions about the normative (masculine) worker can persist, even where pockets of change may also be simultaneously apparent, for example men doing solo caring of a baby or children at the weekend or evenings when the mother works (Miller, 2011). Changes in family arrangements – such as a separation or divorce – can also change how responsibilities for children become practised, sometimes increasing men's involvement (see Chapter 5). It is interesting then, to think about what is visible in contemporary childcare arrangements and activities and what remains taken-for-granted and so is less-visible/invisible (Ranson, 2015). Freeing family caring and family working from its 'gender load' continues as a longer term, but vital, endeavour in this complex terrain. However, given that this is a fluid and changing scene, what does the 'relocation of care' and associated policy changes look like in concrete practises of caring? In the following section, the landscapes of daily caring in working, dual-earner households with children in Britain are considered.

Landscapes of Daily Family Caring in the United Kingdom

Caring takes place in different family formations in myriad household types and in taken-for-granted and often invisible ways throughout the United Kingdom (and globally). But significantly, families, in their variety of forms and types provide 'the crucible of subsequent caring relationships' (Hollway, 2006:6). Care needs and care relationships are fluid, may be context- and age-specific, unexpected, borne of love and/or guilt, purchased, given, received and experienced within a nexus of intergenerational familial relationships across a life course; and of course not everyone has children. In the United Kingdom, profound changes in family structures over past decades (including decisions to remain child-free) and changed workplace demands have 'implications for the realisation of family care in today's society' (Brannen et al, 2004; Hoff, 2009, 2015). They also raise the question of what (economic) factors drive policy change. The Office for National Statistics (ONS) confirms that female labour market participation has increased markedly over the past 40 years in the United Kingdom, while there has been a fall in the percentage of men's employment (ONS, 2013). Even though support for a traditional division of gender roles has declined, there continues to be a majority view that women should retain the *primary* care role for young children (ONS, 2013; Scott and Clery, 2013:115). Men with children are also more likely to work than those without, while the opposite is the case for women with children (ONS, 2013). Findings from a British Attitudes Survey shows that even though men are more involved in care for their children more generally than earlier generations of fathers (Hoff, 2015; Scott and Clery, 2013:115), involvement and time spent in caring for children and household chores remain less than for women. According to the survey, 'Women report spending an average of 13 hours on housework and 23 hours on caring for family members each week; the equivalent figures for men are 8 hours and 10 hours' (Scott and Clery, 2013:115). This is even though the 'dual full-time earner model is growing in significance for British parents of young children' (Connelly et al, 2016:838). Using British data collected between 2001 and 2013, researchers examined the work–family household arrangements adopted by parents in Britain and concluded that 'a new gender egalitarian equilibrium has not yet been reached' (Connolly et al, 2016:838). Mothers' employment outside the home has not yet been matched by changes in fathers' corresponding engagement in the home.

Further changes in who is providing care and how have resulted from the need for care provision for young children when both parents work as well as care needs resulting from the ageing population in the United Kingdom. Demographic trends have also resulted in a shortage in caregivers, so that the United Kingdom is 'increasingly reliant on migrant care workers imported from Eastern Europe, Africa and Asia' (Hoff, 2009:1, 2015). The growth in formal 'care markets' to address these care needs was noted earlier (Williams, 2010). However, it is still the informal care sector (families and friends) that comprises 5.8 million carers in England and Wales (White and the Office for National Statistics, 2013) and who undertake significantly more care work than the formal care sector provides (Hoff, 2015). Even so, the formal care sector has been an area of employment growth (often involving poorly paid female providers) since the early 2000s. Although some families may prefer or be able to provide family care, economic reasons can also pose a barrier to formal service use. For example, the costs of childcare in Britain are amongst the highest in Europe; they are not only unaffordable for many, but there are also significant gaps in provision (Ben-Galim et al, 2014). In particular state-provided or subsidised childcare for children under 3 years of age is a significant gap in childcare services the United Kingdom. 'It is in this period between paid parental leave ending at 9 months and the free hours kicking in at 3 years that many parents are locked out of work [and] cite the cost of childcare as their biggest barrier' to returning to work (Ben-Galim et al, 2014). This is a very different experience compared with parents in Sweden where the country's family policy is aimed at supporting the dual-earner family model including the provision of affordable, high-quality childcare (http://europa.eu/epic/countries/sweden/index_en.htm). Not surprisingly, recent research findings in the United Kingdom show that 'half of new mothers now depend on informal care provided by grandparents' (Ben-and Thompson, 2013) and that 'informal childcare use is common among families across all socio-demographic groups' as 'pragmatic solutions' are found (Bryson et al, 2012; Irwin and Winterton, 2014). Intergenerational care responsibilities have increased, including for some the coinciding of care responsibilities for young children and an ageing, dependent parent – the so-called sandwich generation (Bornat and Bytheway, 2014; Bryson et al, 2012; Grundy and Henretta, 2006). Significantly, grandparents, including grandfathers are increasingly helping to bridge the care gap in the United Kingdom for working parents (Lyonette et al, 2011). Not surprisingly, research has found that grandparents in Britain now 'spend more years with grandchildren than they spent with their own young children' (Hoff, 2015:5; see also Lewis et al, 2008).

While all families, regardless of their increasingly fluid formations, will have some caring responsibilities, not all will be combining paid work outside the home with these. But decisions about whether to combine paid work with being a mother (or father) are often not a matter of choice, but for most families are an economic necessity (Connolly et al, 2016; Lewis et al, 2008; Lyonette et al, 2011).[5] This is borne out

---

[5] Any review of history of the family will show that some mothers through economic necessity have always had to combine work outside the home with other caring responsibilities, but this was not particularly visible and so not part of mainstream concern as is increasingly the case now in relation to how families 'balance' paid work and care demands.

by recent figures on the reduction in the number of 'inactive' women not engaged in paid work at all but undertaking full-time childcare for their children (Scott and Clery, 2013). As noted earlier, the care gap left through inadequate childcare policies creates significant problems for many families in the United Kingdom. As maternity leave or shared parental leave ends, parents face a childcare gap until statutory childcare provision commences for children aged 3 years. Childcare is also costly in the United Kingdom with part-time nursery care provision for one child under 2 years costing more than £6,000 for a year (Rutter, 2015). It is little surprise that the birth of a second child can mean families find it too costly for both parents to work; when this happens, it is still much more likely that the mother will be the parent to stay home. These arrangements then reinforce the gender pay gap and 'motherhood penalty' and disrupt career opportunities, presenting a cumulative penalty on women who spend time out of the labour market (Budig and England, 2001; Costa Dias et al, 2016). In contrast, the working culture in the United Kingdom has been based on a model of (men) working long hours (among the longest in Europe) and women working part time and flexibly and so 'balancing' or 'reconciling' their paid work and family childcare needs (Lewis et al, 2008; Lyonette et al, 2011).

Caring for Children in Families: *Primary* Responsibilities of Care?

More nuanced understandings of care work and its practise by more individuals, who are not only women although still predominately so, offers glimpses of how paid work and family lives could be organised. But how do daily practices in couple (and separated) households come to be navigated and managed? If we understand so much more about how gender operates and that biological determinism is not only reductionist but fallible and that structures of power can be challenged and dismantled and productive policies introduced, why are women still (mostly) taking on a primary care role even though fathers are now more involved in care than previously? This question sits at the core of this book and is examined by exploring how a primary caring responsibility becomes assumed and then practised from the early days and weeks after the birth of a baby, up to early adulthood. This involves exploring the ways in which apparent parental 'choices', 'preferences' and 'constraints' configure experiences and narrations of parenthood and the possibility of a primary responsibility being shared (equally?), rather than assumed to be a singular (feminine) endeavour. Why in contemporary times when so many aspects of women's and men's working lives have shifted, have mothers continued to take on the mental work and '24/7 thinking responsibility' for children in ways that can exonerate fathers – and/or potentially 'gatekeep' activities and exclude fathers? And conversely why aren't fathers taking this primary role? How does contingency operate in relation to mothering and fathering caring responsibilities and how these are taken up (Gerstel and Gallagher, 2001)? And how do caring responsibilities change over time as children grow? Clearly this is tricky terrain, with competing interests, shaped according to long practised, unequal historical precedents, but the longitudinal data collected over the years of the Transition to Motherhood Study (Miller, 2005, 2007) and Transition to Fatherhood Study (Miller, 2010, 2011) facilitate this endeavour.

Returning to the findings from the British Social Attitudes Survey (Scott and Clery, 2013:124), it is interesting to note that only minimal support was found 'for splitting the breadwinner and carer roles equally (with both parents working part-time)' among those surveyed. The authors concluded that 'the public retains a view that there should be a gender divide in terms of caring responsibilities' but also acknowledge that 'the idea that a mother works part-time, rather than not at all' was now an accepted attitude in Britain (Scott and Clery, 2013:124). Other research has reported the ways in which women manage a 'work-life balance' and take responsibility for 'who will do what', by 'carrying the mental and emotional work of ensuring that everyone's needs are met' (Irwin and Winterton, 2014:145). This links to ideals of the 'good mother' (which has also become intensified) and relates back to an earlier point about the increased outsourcing of childcare. Here the responsibility for organising childcare is still (mostly) being undertaken by mothers, but they 'reframe good mothering as being "in charge"' (Christopher, 2012:73). Clearly there are elements and evidence here of continued expectations of women (especially mothers) being there for everyone (Adkins, 2002).

In the past, caring responsibilities, especially for children, have been unquestioningly assumed to be instinctive and deterministic, a

natural *and* moral capacity that a mother possesses in ways that are
different to (or sometimes assumed to be absent from) a father. But as
moral engagement leads to a position where care has been relocated
and theorised more broadly as a human activity and so 'part of the
practices of active citizenship', how does this position fathers? When
Sevenhuijsen (2003) notes the moral responsibility of the mother as
'a form of morality that is literally unthinkable without affection
and emotion' (pp. 25–6), couldn't this equally be applied to fathers?
Wouldn't they share this description of their own moral connection
to their children and meeting (even intermittently) their care needs?
But it seems the moral weight and repercussions of (more intensified) parenting expectations continue to be felt more extremely by
mothers – and they are much more likely than fathers to be judged in
various domains on their efforts. Men continue to be able to escape
this particular gaze. Even so research, increasingly shows that they
are able to develop competence in practises of parenting, but not
necessarily in ways that exactly match or mirror mothering practises
(Brandth and Kvande, 2016; Ranson, 2015; Rehel, 2014).

It is useful to think then about how the same caring needs met
in different ways are 'seen' and how they are regarded in the context of heterosexual couple households (living together or apart), a
focus examined in later chapters of this book. It has been argued
that 'entrenched ideas about fathers and masculinity' are responsible for having 'diverted attention from men as caregivers' (Ranson,
2015:171). As noted earlier, others too have suggested that 'revoking
a maternal lens' enables aspects of paternal behaviour to be seen and
understood in different ways (Shirani et al, 2012:34; see also Crespi
and Ruspini, 2016). Even as intentions to be involved and sometimes
equally share caring for a new baby are increasingly expressed or
assumed by men as they become fathers, analysis of their practices can
privilege maternal ways of doing caring. For example, the following
extract is taken from an interview with a father in the earlier phase
of the Fatherhood study as his firstborn child approached his second
birthday (see Miller, 2010:141–2). In the interview I ask the father,
Ian,[6] if there is any aspect of caring for his son that he does not do.
He calls out to his wife who has been sitting in the next room. She

---

[6] All names of participants and any family members are pseudonyms.

replies '*packing his bags for Brenda*' (the childminder). The following exchange between Ian and Polly then unfolds:

POLLY: Yeah I tried to get Ian to do that [pack the bag], I decided, when I was ill at the beginning of the year I said right 'you do a Monday' and I had a list. But my list was all scribbled on and then Monday maybe he'd be out and so we haven't kept that up. But we ought to do that again. But I suppose the only thing I can think of [that he doesn't do] is choosing what [their son] wears. It's partly again because I have a system and he has, if he wears disposable nappies, he wears smaller trousers than if he's in bigger bulky washable ones. So I know which trousers to put on and I'm saving that for this occasion and Ian doesn't know. So he might get his head bitten off if he chose the wrong thing!

IAN: Yes so I think that looks interesting to put on and then it's invariably the wrong thing.

POLLY: Or I say 'why have you changed to that'.

IAN: 'So...'

POLLY: You don't have confidence in doing that, do you?

IAN: No.

POLLY: I also I tend to be responsible for the washing as well so I'm aware of what [son] needs and what he's wearing and what fits him and again because I'm responsible, I tend to be responsible for the change bag as well, I pack that [pause]. Yes and I buy them as well.

IAN: Yes and if I get involved it does sometimes make it more difficult because Polly then has to throw what I've done ... [laughing].

POLLY: Poor Ian!

IAN: Disputes about how many washable nappy outers have been used.

POLLY: Were there any clean ones?

IAN: They can be reused on a short-term basis and whether they get reused or whether new ones get got out.

POLLY: You see I have systems.

This exchange (which will be instantly recognisable to many parents) illustrates how practices and behaviours are taken on and become part of the gendered, accepted and daily-ness of routines of caring. But even if Ian doesn't always pack the bag with the 'right' things, couldn't he develop confidence and competence by packing it differently to Polly (who has 'systems')? But Polly also asserts her responsibility for several aspects of care (washing the baby clothes, choosing what their son wears and knowing what is being saved for another, future occasion) and has taken on a primary overview of their son's care needs.

The primary responsibility assumed in Polly's account of caring for their son positions Ian as secondary and supportive. Which returns us to a question posed earlier – can a primary caring responsibility be shared equally – and how might 'maternal gatekeeping', or indeed paternal gatekeeping, operate in family caring contexts? Again, this, like so much in debates about how modern family lives are lived and our children cared for alongside paid work, stomps over all sorts of tricky, emotional and emotive ground. I am reminded of a friend who, in the fall out from a divorce, wanted to claim and privilege the primacy of a maternal–child bond and her superior attachment to her two young sons even as she had been the 'breadwinner' in a shared caring household. After years of scholarly work to wrest moral ideas of care work from 'symbols and norms of femininity' and a 'logic of unselfish nurturing', masculine forms of care necessarily become part of the debate (Hays, 1996; Sevenhuijsen, 2003:21). But when in many countries and contexts responsibility for children continues to be 'one of the most fundamental elements of good mothering', which has also become subject to further scrutiny, a lot can be felt to be at risk if/as change occurs (Rehel, 2014:113). In earlier work conceptualisations of 'maternal-keeping' have been used to explain how women's 'beliefs and behaviours' may limit fathers' opportunities for involvement in family care practices (Allen and Hawkins, 1999). More recent research has also reported on 'maternal encouragement' and 'relative father involvement' (Schoppe-Sullivan et al, 2008:389) and has examined 'determinants of maternal gatekeeping' during transition to parenthood (Schoppe-Sullivan et al, 2015) and in dual-earner households (Radcliffe and Cassell, 2015). Other research has considered maternal gatekeeping after divorce (Pruett et al, 2007) and made attempts to reconceptualise and produce a new 'model of maternal gatekeeping' (Puhlman and Pasley, 2013). To date, conceptualisations of maternal gatekeeping have tended to rely on quantitative, survey data and resulted in conclusions that hold women responsible for restricting men's involvement in care, rather than examining other constraints that shape attitudes and practises and complicate this sphere. Across the following chapters a more finely focused and contextualised view of how maternal and indeed paternal gatekeeping may operate are explored. Importantly, this will take account of how we produce narratives of intent and experience in contexts that are already historically highly gendered.

Conclusions

Gender and gendered arrangements continue to pattern and constrain caring 'choices' and practises in various ways, both individually and within families and structurally through government policies and provision. Even so, change in how caring for children is organised and practised is increasingly evident in parts of northern Europe where a combination of policy commitments, well-funded childcare provision and associated cultural shifts in workplaces and households have led to more egalitarian family practises (Feldman and Gran, 2016; O'Brien et al, 2007, 2009). These shifts in northern Europe indicate men's capacities to care and women's capacities to be successful in the workplace. In the United Kingdom change has not been so dramatic or so supported by political will, which has been identified as a constraining factor, but change is still discernible. This includes the growing significance of 'the dual full-time earner model' among parents with young children, but unlike the Nordic countries, 'a new gender egalitarian equilibrium has not yet been reached' (Connolly et al, 2016:838). Societal attitudes have changed, but with respect to how working families combine caring for their children the view is retained 'that there should be a gender divide in terms of caring responsibilities' (Scott and Clery, 2013:124). The shift, then, has 'been in accepting the idea that a mother works part-time, rather than not at all' (Scott and Clery, 2013:124). But women's increased participation in the labour force has been part of future economic growth projections (Eurostat, 2016) and clearly, the question of how working parents manage economic activity and caring responsibilities will remain a persistent concern. How can work and family lives be made more compatible?

In this chapter some of the constraints and confounding aspects of caring for and about children in working families have been introduced as a backdrop for the empirical data that follow. Attempts to disentangle philosophical aspects of care orientations and practises alongside structural constraints (policies and political will), and unequal gendered histories, serve to underscore the complex landscape in which modern parenthood and caring and work is situated. The chapters that follow explore the ways in which fathering and mothering and combinations of paid work and caring are organised and narrated. Significantly, the data include recent accounts of fathering (as children begin primary school) and mothering (as firstborn children reach

adulthood at 18 years) and re-assessment of their parenting relationships and practices when families separate (Chapter 5). But these current accounts are grounded in several years of interviews, which has
enabled a longer and more richly informed view to emerge of how
caring practices unfold, become managed and change. The following chapters privilege individual, relational accounts of family care
and paid work as the micro-processes of unfolding family experiences
have been documented in the two qualitative longitudinal studies (see
Chapter 1). The search here is not for determinants, correlations or
causations but rather engages with the complexity, tenuousness and
enduring aspects of narrations of family living and everyday and longer
term hopes, fears and practises.

3 | *Fathering*

Caring, Work and School-Age Children

I mean there are dads in the playground at the end of the day and start of the day, but there are very clearly more mums than dads.

(Nick)

I guess that work requirements have maybe framed what we do as a family and how we work it all out.

(William)

But there's things that we kind of make him do and his tennis lessons, music classes, he's taken up the guitar, which he sort of likes and sort of doesn't, that's through school. So do we push him to carry on with these things.

(Ian)

In this third chapter the interrelated themes of caring, gender and managing paid work and family life as a parent, outlined in the previous chapters, are explored. Uniquely this chapter uses later episodes of data collected in qualitative longitudinal research on fatherhood and explores men's unfolding experiences of fatherhood and being a parent, family caring and paid work as their firstborn child reaches primary school age (Miller, 2010). The data drawn upon were generated from interviews carried out with the men as their firstborn child (born during an earlier phase of the study) was aged between 5 and 6 years. In a climate of heightened interest in parenting practises and their (successful) execution, this chapter focuses on everyday practices of family life and paid work as narrated by the fathers. For example, do 'ideals' of intensified parenting associated with 'maximising' a child's potential' appear in the men's accounts, especially as their children begin school? Similarly, how far have the shifts documented in research literature on societal attitudes led to parenting behaviours becoming less gender-defined or segregated and more gender-neutral (Brandth and

Kvande, 2016; Deutsch, 2007; Elliot, 2015; Miller, 2011)? In a context where most parents in the United Kingdom are now also working, have practises among this group of fathers changed in the home to reflect the changes in mothers' lives outside the home and how are family and work lives 'balanced'? What emerges from the data are accounts in which parenting a growing and more responsive child (along with subsequent children born since the earlier interviews) leads some fathers to more active involvement in particular parenting activities, and reinforces and makes more visible a gendered gap between others. This includes thinking about and organising (sometimes outsourced) care arrangements and working 'flexibly' alongside continued commitments to work colleagues and careers. The rich qualitative data capture men's experiences of paternal agency and activities through their descriptions of caring involvement and typical workdays.

Setting the Scene

To go back, the landscape of contemporary fatherhood was explored through the men's accounts of becoming fathers for the first time in an earlier text, *Making Sense of Fatherhood*, published in 2010. In that volume, the men's experiences of transition were documented up to the time their child reached 2 years of age; in this chapter their later experiences are explored. At the time of the last interview, any sense of going through a period of transition had past: '*I guess there is . . . a kind of the shift from dealing with transition to becoming a new father to being now an established one*' (Richard); but recurring themes related to family involvement and responsibilities, time and paid work continued. By the time of the 2-year interview, the men had been interviewed on three earlier occasions (before and after the birth and at approximately 1 year). In the first (antenatal) interview, first-time fathering was narrated in terms of 'being there' and 'sharing caring' (initially envisaged as equally) and in later interviews, there was a sense of life having (just about) returned to 'a new normal' after the birth of a first child. This new normal revolved around paid work outside the home and 'fitting in' fathering into early mornings, evenings and weekends and in spaces that were created by, for some, changing their working *patterns* rather than number of hours worked. The emotional highs and lows experienced as men juggled and managed family, work and relationships was apparent, but there was also a sense of the men developing a new expertise in relation to fathering/parenting and an associated confidence that would have been unthinkable before the advent of fatherhood.

Over time the men have become more practised and thus more confident in their fathering, and importantly there was the beginning of a greater sense of having a more interactive relationship with a child (aged 2 years at the time of the last interviews) who was now in turn much more responsive and expressive. At this time fathers described daily 'routines' as they narrated their caring involvement and made visible their fathering practises. The routine enabled things to be managed and a sense that life was in control and being coped with ('*a good routine and we have a manageable system*'). Similarly, changing feeding patterns, '*weaning*' and '*introducing solids*' had also provided an opportunity for some of the fathers to talk of becoming *more* involved in caring for their baby/child than in the earlier months when some saw their wife or partner as more accomplished at caring ('*because of time*', '*she's a natural*') for a new baby. The men often cited their inability to breastfeed as limiting aspects of their involvement. Focusing on these routines in the earlier data analysis illuminated how maternal and paternal 'responsibilities' were assumed and where and how differences, similarities and overlap in relation to caring practises occurred. Discourses of nature and instincts *and* time were also linked together in the men's earlier narrations as they explained why their lives as fathers had become organised in the ways they had, which was not how they may have intended in antenatal narrations (see Miller, 2010, 2011). But the participants demonstrated levels of involvement and a capacity to 'be there' as fathers in emotionally caring and invested ways that they felt were different from their own fathers and earlier generations.

In the data collected in the later interviews and used in this book, the children have reached 5 to 6 years of age, and their fathers[1] now reflect back across the intervening years. There is no longer any uncertainty about their identity as a father ('*that is now who I am, I am now a father, whereas before I was a new one. I don't feel like a new one anymore*'), and several years of being a dad have led to increased

---

[1] For the interviews in this phase of the Fatherhood study (not originally planned when the first transition phase of the research was undertaken), 13 of the original sample of 17 fathers were contacted (using existing contact details) and invited to participate in these later (school-age children) interviews. Of these 13, 10 fathers 'opted in' to the new phase of interviews.

confidence. The fathers now narrate from a position of experience, for example appreciating that children are much more 'resilient' than they had first thought (*'you know I think through that, the biggest thing I learned was how durable and resilient kids are actually'*). They talk of *'being more grounded'*, having *'maturity'* and *'being better at reading stories'*, *'being a role model'* and *'setting an example'*. The routines that shaped family lives in the earlier interviews are just as evident (as described later), but there is much less sense that the fathers need 'debriefing' in relation to practical aspects of caring, which had felt essential when they were less practised as new fathers. The now older children, whose agency is also a relational factor, are able to articulate needs for themselves in relationships that are much more interactive (*'but I think with certain comments and points that daughter has made and with wife kind of backing her up, I'm like "oh really, am I really a grumpy old git?" Okay, it turns out I actually am!'*). But there are also feelings of guilt, failure, frustration and unfulfilled intentions as well as imminent (*'get him to learn to ride a bike'*) and longer term (*'she has a university fund'*) hopes for their children. Some of the fathers talk about their experiences of fathering as being 'hard' (*'I never thought it was going to be a breeze, but it's hard'*, *'I didn't really worry about anything before and now I just worry'*), and for all it is almost impossible to remember life before children and how they had filled their time (*'what did we do, because every minute of the day is taken up with, once they are in bed then it's doing stuff in the house, what did we do before?'*). But across the narrations there is a deep sense of the fathers having established loving (*'I love them with all my heart'*) and enduring relationships with their children (*'but kind of there is the lingering sense of kind of fear, what would happen if something happened to one of your children'*), brought into sharp relief by Sean, who's second child, Jack, died at just 4½ months of age (see Chapter 6). Reflecting on his loss, Sean says, *'I mean he's not here, but he's very, still very ... a key part of the family'*.

Research in the United Kingdom has demonstrated the continued popularity of the family in all its forms (Edwards, 2008; Holland and Edwards, 2014). In this study too, continuity and the importance of familial relationships are emphasised even if relationships break down or become reconfigured. Deaths of parents or grandparents are described in the data as new generations of family lives unfold. Death of their own parents prompts questions for these fathers of their own mortality, especially when this coincided with their own children still being young and regarded as dependent (*'I'm thinking I don't want to die when my children are like 5 and 2, so there was something kind of overwhelming about that. My mum dying kind of yeah . . . did the mortality bit'*). There have been subsequent births in the intervening years as well as miscarriages (*'I guess it was quite strained then for the next few months, until she got pregnant again'*) as well as reported *'failed attempts at pregnancy'*. As fathers the second time around, the men were much less likely to attend any preparation classes during the antenatal period (*'I think because obviously we're so experienced with having a child before and . . . no I think there is an element that with your firstborn you don't know what to expect'*). Some spoke more openly of feeling *'helpless'* and a *'spare part'* at the second birth, while others described *'much better'* births this time around and knowing what to expect. All took the 2-week statutory paternity leave available to most fathers in the United Kingdom or annual leave (or both) as subsequent children were born, and managing two children had become a matter of family *'logistics'*. In the intervening years there had been changes in the men's employment, redundancies and place of work, sometimes as a result of attempts to achieve more flexible working conditions. Paid work has remained a key factor in practises of father involvement in caring activities, responsibilities and family life (discussed subsequently).

In the data collected in the earlier phase of the study and reported as a generic finding in numerous other studies on fatherhood, 'being there' as an emotionally attuned and involved dad was a major theme, and it remains so across the more recent interviews (Harden et al, 2014; Henwood et al, 2014; Ives, 2014). But 'being there' is now sometimes understood and practised in different ways, for example 'not being there' (as a separated dad noted, *'I've always wanted to be the best dad I could possibly be and then sometimes I think well how can you say that by not being there now?'*). Relationship changes and separation[2] feature in these later interviews and are explored in more detail in Chapter 5. A recurrent theme pursued across this and the remaining

---

[2] Of the 17 fathers followed in the original Transition to Fatherhood Study, at least three couples have since separated or divorced. Thirteen of the original 17 fathers were contacted (using existing contact details) about participating in the later (school-age children) interviews. Of these 13, 10 fathers 'opted in' to the new phase of interviews.

chapters of the book teases apart aspects of caring practices (activity) and caring thinking (the mental work of caring) and how these are shared and managed in working households as the demands of work and care are navigated and combined.

Managing the Logistics of Family Lives and Caring Involvement: Fathers' Perspectives

Fathers' involvement in caring for their new baby was explored in earlier phases of this research, and now most have additional children.[3] This changes the 'logistics' of their involvement as Nick explains:

I think possibly I've done less with the second baby, but I think part of that may be, actually when you've got two parents doting on one that's different from two doting on two and there have been times when it's become I'll look after [older child] and you take [baby] to the health visitor or whatever. Whereas the first time 'round I went to all of those things. So there is a logistical part of it. (Nick)

The '*hard work*' of having two children, of '*engaging*' with two children and having '*quality time*' or '*individual time*' with them is commented on by the fathers, even though attempts are made to treat children '*equally*'. As Joe says, '*we're always trying to do things exactly the same as what we did with our first child*'. The birth of a subsequent child poses new concerns for the fathers, both practically, for example how they will manage two children, when one has consumed so much time, and emotionally in terms of another loving relationship ('*will I be able to love another child as much as I love her [first child]?*'). There was a sense for some of still coming to terms with the 'surreal' feeling of being a dad to growing and competent children, as Mike explains in the following extract:

It was still that whole kind of surreal moment of hang on a minute I've got a two and a half year old and now a new born, is this, am I babysitting, are they actually mine and even now I still sometimes get into this kind of surreal world of [daughter] being able to write beautiful sentences and [younger son] coming out with spellings and words. (Mike)

---

[3] Three fathers have not had more children, one of these already had twins and another commented that 'I think we've kind of missed the boat'. Of the others, all had had a second child, but none a third (ONS, 2016).

The birth of a subsequent child has implications for how family lives are managed, which is also significantly determined in the data by parental working patterns.[4] The fathers are all employed in (mostly) full-time work and the wives/partners also work, although they are more likely to be employed part time, a pattern that has been common in the United Kingdom (Connolly et al, 2016; Fagnani, 2007; Lewis et al, 2008; Lyonette et al, 2011; O'Brien et al, 2015). All the fathers have been involved in aspects of caring for their child or children in ways that are more intensive and emotionally invested than their own fathers, but time is felt to be 'squeezed' further as subsequent children are born (*'the other obvious difference is you've got two and they are at different stages'*). Even though original intentions of shared caring and *'splitting things down the middle'* were expressed in the men's very first antenatal interviews (see chapters 3 and 6 in Miller, 2010), these intentions were mostly not realised when the realities of combining the demands of caring and paid work were experienced (*'I'm just not going to be able to do this'*). Even though the men are now much more experienced at hands-on caring and have developed a significant relationship with their firstborn child and subsequent children, (*'how different they are is just really surprising'*), no one has changed places to become a 'stay-at-home dad' (Doucet, 2006, 2016). But their experience and, importantly, the relationship they have developed with their children means that they talk in confident ways about their practices ('doing caring') and selves as fathers. How far this extends to taking on the 'mental work' or '24/7 thinking responsibility' is considered later.

The importance of 'routines' was noted earlier and becomes clear in the men's accounts of everyday family practises as multiple demands on parents are managed and/or 'balanced'. The fathers talk of *'routine and structure'* (*'I like structure'*), *'programmed activity'*, *'sequences of events'* (related here to bedtimes) and being able to sustain *'everything routine based'*. A father of twin boys, Frank, says, *'We've kept them in that routine, it's always about a routine because it's worked well'*. In their accounts, the routines provide a sense of having control, or at least trying to bring control and order to multiple and competing demands. Busy family lives now include getting (at least one) child to

---

[4] At the time of recruitment in the original phase of the research, all but one of the participants were living in dual-earner (mostly one full-time and one part-time earner) households, the temporarily single-earner household was due to a partner having a periodically debilitating chronic health condition.

school ('*my daughter's at school now ... it's stressful, harder, getting them ready and so forth and making sure they've had breakfast*'). A child reaching primary school age[5] also brings with it a sense of him or her being less dependent on the parents as other socialising agents and influences come into play ('*you've got the influence of the school*'), and the realisation '*that you can't live their lives for them*' (Ian). Having a child at school brings about other changes as well, as demands on parents shift as Richard explains:

the interesting thing I suppose is that [daughter] being at school certainly means that quite a lot of the caring time with her is of course actually tied into school it's to do with homework and stuff like that as well. (Richard)

It is interesting to note here how activities once almost entirely undertaken during school time now become activities for the home. These nudge the boundaries between home and school and what gets measured and associated with (new) parental responsibilities.[6] It is also interesting to note that homework becomes a new dimension of caring and another activity that requires the investment of time. As noted earlier, all the fathers are also in (mostly) full-time work, and although they may be involved in morning and evening routines and dropping off and (less often) collecting their children from school, hours and location of employment continue to pattern fathers' involvement in significant ways. So even though the men are accomplished at caring for their children ('*the two of them seem equally comfortable with either of us*'), the ways in which caring for the children becomes practised hinges in part on time available around paid work during the week and the flexibility within their jobs ('*I would feel sorry for anybody who hasn't got that sort of flexibility*'). This in turn has an impact on how caring practises and tasks are shared or divided and more critically on how the 'mental work' or '24/7 thinking responsibility' – and so primary carer role – is understood and becomes practised.

Time, lack of time and feeling the pressure of time were dominant themes in how the fathers described typical working days, especially where there were now two children ('*it can be tricky to give them both*

---

[5] In the United Kingdom, 'primary school age' is generally 5 years of age.
[6] It is interesting to note (in Chapter 4) that feeling unable to help their two (now older) teenage children with their schoolwork leads Lillian to worry, '*because I'm not really highly academic and I worry that has ... you can only give so much knowledge if you haven't got it*'.

kind of individual time they need') (Harden et al, 2014). This had a knock-on effect for weekends when family or domestic tasks had to be caught up with (*'trying to catch up a bit and sort of trying to make up time when I was back'*). In the men's accounts of fathering and caring, the ways in which tasks and responsibilities became shared or divided and practised was very clearly related to time. As Frank says, *'It's all back to time, being there, having the time, making the time'*. Changes in employment, for example becoming self-employed (Frank), reducing the pattern of hours worked into longer days and shorter weeks (Graham), being able to sometimes work from home (Richard, Sean), moving house and/or working geographically very close to home or school (Joe, Nick, Graham, Richard) and working in a job that included having school holidays (Nick) all shaped the fathers involvement in caring activities. So too did changes in wives' and partners' working patterns (especially once there were two children) and their proximity to work and school or childcare. As Richard explains, after a house move to be closer to his wife's full-time job, which reduced her daily commute and *'makes life easier'*,

Our routine is probably much more sort of divided than it was and it's divided because we are both there, rather than one of us being there and one of us not being there. (Richard)

What becomes clear from a comparison of the earlier and later interview data is that in couple households family patterns of caring – what mothers and fathers 'do' – becomes established very early once a baby is born. This has also recently been reported by Fagan and Norman (2016) in their research results. As seen earlier, practices are configured in relation to structural features and especially paid work. Changes in patterns of employment experienced by two of the fathers since being interviewed in the earlier phase of the research, illustrate this further. Ian, who is now a father of two children (a son and younger daughter), no longer works from home but goes out to work in a new job following a period of redundancy. William, whose job had always taken him abroad for periods of time (*'I think I calculated during the first year I was away for 7½ months'*), describes himself now as having been a *'weekend dad'* and has recently changed jobs and is now able to 'commute daily'. In the following extract, Ian reflects on his caring responsibilities for his second child, which has not been *'quite to the same extent'* as with his first child:

I mean obviously I'm not there now since July last year in the house all day. I get her up every morning and I'm not there every evening to do bed times every evening, so I do quite a lot of bed times, both of them. . . . I was still at home most of the time until July when [second child] was 8 months or whatever, then during that time I think I was as involved as I was with [first child]. (Ian)

But he is at home at the weekends:

Saturday yes, we both . . . I think we are equally involved on Saturdays. I perhaps have slightly more things that I do out of the house than Polly does, so the balance might not be quite as I think it is, because when I'm not there, I don't take that into account. (Ian)

These extracts demonstrate how (now experienced) fathers caring can be practised in activities (getting the baby up) in pockets of time around paid work (mornings and some evenings), tasks that can be more 'equally' shared at weekends. But crucially they also illuminate how 'sharing' and 'balancing' is perceived and understood when not observed *'because when I'm not there, I don't take that into account'*. Interestingly, this apparent throwaway line draws attention to how involvement is dependent on presence and the visibility of the act for Ian (and others). It hints at the ways in which the invisible mental work of thinking, planning and holding lots of past, present and future-oriented responsibilities together may elude fathers when they engage only in supportive, helper care activities: especially (and only possible) if someone else is orchestrating and taking on a primary responsibility. Is a thinking care-orientation for the fathers tied in to physical presence and the moment, but all-encompassing (24/7) for mothers? These questions are considered further in subsequent chapters.

In contrast to Ian, William talks about the weekend as an opportunity to try to '*to maximise time*' with his daughter and wife. In the following extract he reflects on how his work has framed their family life:

But then from September last year I started work [closer to home]. . . . I'm able to do a daily commute, which is fantastic. So that means with [daughter] she's now obviously staying up a bit later in the evening, I get home and see her each evening. I'm gone before she wakes up in the morning, but then we have weekends together and I try and do all the work activity I need to so I don't bring any work home. . . . I guess that work requirement has maybe framed what we do as a family and how we work it all out I guess. (William)

William then describes his involvement when he was away in the week and so what he calls '*a weekend dad*':

So for that time it would have been, my wife took the strain big time in terms of looking after our daughter and you know that, it was trying to catch up a bit, and sort of trying to make up time when I was back home. I think we all felt that I was always on the, you know, it wasn't desperation, but there was a sort of feeling to sort of compact everything into the time I had with her and that can, it can get wearing if you're not careful, because you're trying to do too much and you've got to just relax into it. So actually now the balance has shifted back to normal. (William)

This extract conveys the pressures all family members can experience when trying to combine and manage work and family life, and there is 'too much to do'. Fathering here involved trying to '*compact everything into the time I had*', which also implies someone else has responsibility for the rest of the time that William does not have. But William's sense that '*now the balance has shifted back to normal*' assumes a 'normal' that is not shared across his other accounts. He goes on to differentiate between '*fun stuff*' and '*the caring bits that aren't the fun bits*' (and homework looms again) in the next extract:

When I was squashing stuff in I think I was trying to squash in the fun stuff, you know and I was trying to squash in good memories for her in a way, so she'd have a great time with dad and then, and I think there was a degree of friction because of that because [wife] quite rightly would say well that's great for you to do the fun stuff, but actually there are all the other jobs that need to be done and the caring bits that aren't the fun bits that need to be done. Silly things like homework needs to be done, you know and if you aren't covering it now then that leaves me more to do during the week. So there's, it wasn't a big thing but every now and then you'd recognise that yeah we've got to do the boring stuff as well. (William)

These extracts from Ian and William help to convey how practises of caring can be individually conceptualised, practised (or not) and 'seen'. Ian hints at the caring activities which he doesn't see and so doesn't 'count' or include in his perceptions of how caring is shared in their family, there is a significant sense that sharing is linked to physically 'being there'. William classically conforms to the dad who is there for '*fun times*', not '*boring stuff*', when in practical terms a lot of caring activity is associated with repetitive and (invisible) boring stuff. But these extracts lead us to consider further the parameters and detail of caring, sharing and balancing family lives and paid work. What is the (new) 'normal' in managing caring including demands from school ('*homework needs to be done*') and employment and how are any differences between mothers and fathers and caring practises and responsibilities understood and narrated?

There is no question that the fathers are practised and skilled (just like the mothers) in meeting the needs of their child/children ('*you know I worked at home today, I can do the caring part*') having engaged in multiple practises that they see as constituting caring. These include transportation to school, bath time, bedtime, shopping with kids, cooking, ironing, cleaning, ferrying children to extra activities and homework. These activities are described as '*shared*', '*balanced*', '*trying to get a bit of a balance*' and two fathers use the term 'interchangeable' ('*It's mostly interchangeable I think*', Graham). As Nick (who is now a father of two boys) explains in the following extract,

I think sort of 90% of the family, the home and stuff is interchangeable. I think there are sort of aspects which we've never spoken about but they are very clearly role orientated. I'm not sure that I've ever bought a pair of shoes for the children and I've never said I'm not going to buy shoes . . . that is sort of how it's fallen. Then there will be other bits that I will sort of do, but I think most of it is very interchangeable; bedtime, bath time, story time, homework time, taking the kids to school, collecting them. (Nick)

But having different working patterns also shapes how much of any one activity is taken up:

I mean I think [wife] does more because she's at home, she works 2½ days a week, but whoever is at home that day makes the meal, and at the weekend it could be either of us. So I think the children see that we both cook. I think they probably experience that I make breakfast more and that mum makes tea more, partly because I'm always here for breakfast and I'm not always here for tea . . . and in the school holidays yeah they would experience that I do lots of washing and stripping the beds and making the food and hoovering . . . 'dad is going to do the hoovering', then we play. (Nick)

Here again time, rather than ability to undertake these practises, defines the ways in which the fathers narrate their involvement. But this can also of course influence perceived proficiency, amount of time taken over tasks and so forth, and thus how these are shared and taken up. Other fathers quantify their involvement ('*80% of the cooking and*

the shopping', *'ironing 50:50'*), yet for some involvement is still practised in a 'helping out' and supportive way rather than being 'interchangeable' or 'shared' or wholly directed by the fathers themselves.

For Mike who is now a father of two, paid work structures his
involvement:

> I think pretty much everything has been fairly similar [with second baby]
> so if he woke up in the night and I was in a position to be able to feed,
> as in if he's on a bottle, then yes... it's only fair in my mind, that I should
> be involved in helping just as I would expect a partner to do I guess. But
> also yeah sometimes in the early months and years, it is, I guess important
> to try and form that bond, because yeah sometimes work/life does get a
> bit hectic and does, rightly or wrongly does take over your life and I think
> any opportunity to kind of, to help out or to be involved in that process or
> whatever it is, I think that's been quite important.... I'm generally home in
> time for them, for me to be able to bath them and dress them and we used
> to read [them] a story.... So it's been key for me to kind of stay involved in
> that side of things as much as possible really.... I think it's expected and I'd
> want to get involved and see them develop and those kind of things.... So
> I was involved when I could be. (Mike)

Interestingly Mike, who referred to himself as having a 'feminine gene'
in one of the earlier interviews, has changed jobs and house and clearly
feels the pressure of 'hectic' work demands. But he also talks (again)
about bonding and staying involved in certain activities (bedtime routines), yet there is an optional note too in his descriptions (*'I was
involved when I could be'*) and the intensity of his involvement is partial, even though he talks about equity (*'it's only fair in my mind'*). Set
against the narratives of some of the other fathers (for example Nick,
Graham, Richard, Frank, Sean), Mike's description of his involvement
(in a 'helper' sense) is closer to William's experiences of being given
'duties', as in the following extract:

> So my, when home, all of my kind of duties if you like are the same, so I
> do the bathing, I do the reading and often if I'm home early enough I make
> her sort of evening meal and then the bathing and then the bedtime story.
> (William)

What emerges from the men's narrations of family practises is both that
societal expectations of father involvement (*'I think it's expected'*) and
actual daily/weekend practises have shifted when compared to previous generations. This reflects broader changes in understandings and

practices of paternal agency, relationships (e.g. 'bonding') and broader structural/workplace change. However, even though all the fathers are more involved in their children's lives (and sometimes domestic chores too) than their own fathers were, and even some contemporaries they see (*'Some of the dads do lots of DIY, lots of building and wouldn't be seen anywhere near the kitchen'*), they are still positioned as the secondary, rather than primary, carer. When asked who they would say was the main carer in the family, all but one (*'I think we probably split it fairly evenly, so I wouldn't say that we have a main carer'*) name their wife or partner as having that responsibility. What becomes clear is that while caring activities may be shared and even (sometimes) be interchangeable, the 'mental work' and '24/7 thinking responsibility' and future-oriented care planning is not. The person who has this primary responsibility is seen to be the mother of the children.[7]

Fathering Primary School–Age Children: New Demands

The ways in which political ideas and interventions have infiltrated ideals of parenting responsibilities and associated discourses was noted in Chapter 1. It is interesting to note the ways in which homework soon filters into the fathers' accounts of family life as their child reaches primary school age (5–6 years) and begin schools.[8] The fathers have mixed opinions on whether caring for older primary school–age children, rather than babies or toddlers, is easier (*'definitely easier because they can look after themselves much more'*) of harder (*'I think it's harder, at least when they are babies you put them down and they*

---

[7] Although divorce can change this perception; see Chapter 5.

[8] A focus group with mothers of school-age children was conducted by the author in 2015 after the fatherhood interviews used here. The data collected included areas of overlap with the fatherhood data in relation to their children beginning school and parental experiences of this period. For example, reflecting on the advent of a new form of socialisation in their child's life, loss of control, not knowing what happens at school and homework concerns. However, the mothers' accounts were shared in a different tenor from those of the fathers; they were saturated with the minutiae of their child's lives, of disappointment *'that was the innocent bit over'*, of tiredness and desperation for school to start (*'I actually can't do anymore hours with her'*) and worries (*'there will always be the other children who bully'*). The mothers narrate from central and primary positions in their child's life (even those who work), while the fathers in this chapter narrate from a less central, peripheral position, even though they are involved (see Chapter 6).

don't go anywhere') or just different. The interactive aspects of the relationship can be enjoyable and frustrating as the children become less solely dependent on the family (*'she started school and I'm really proud of her and you sort of see her developing to be her own little individual*). School introduces a new socialising agent into a child's life and another new structure into the family day (just as play groups, childminders and nursery schools will have done) and family 'routines' must shift to accommodate this change (*'going to school has been one of the biggest kind of logistical disruptions . . . it's actually very difficult because of the time you pick them up*'). There are new demands of homework, timetables and getting to school on time as well as interactions with teachers to be navigated (*'you don't want to be pushy at school'*, *'it's hard handing over your child to somebody you don't really know'*). While the fathers are involved in some aspects of their child's school life, for example in choosing a school, the 'school transporting' is still more likely to regularly involve the mothers. As Nick explains,

I mean I think out of most of our peers, possibly all of our peers, all the dads work full time and a couple of the mums work full time. I think most of the mums work part time, so do more of the school pick-ups and stuff. I mean yeah there are dads in the playground at the end of the day and start of the day, but there are very clearly more mums than dads . . . but the playground is still predominantly a female environment. (Nick)

The increasing political and professional focus in recent years on parenting and neoliberal ideals of maximizing a child's potential can be keenly felt through interactions with the school. Regardless of how parents might intend to care for their children, it can be hard to escape these increasingly prevalent strands of intensive parenting discourse, which emphasise and prize competition and individual (school and exam) success. As the fathers describe their child beginning school, it is clear that this had not been an arbitrary process as 'research' is undertaken (*'we went round and had a look both of us together and it was absolutely fine'*) and 'weighed up' (*'spoken to friend and colleagues and done some research'*), and there is a very clear sense that for most it is important to get your child into a 'good' school' (*'But yeah a very good school'*, *'we were fortunate I guess to get our first choice school, it sounded reasonable from an OFSTED [Office for Standards in Education] point of view'*). As Mike explains,

We soon discovered that from a schooling, primary school perspective there were three or four schools, one of which was really, came across head and shoulders as a recommendation from people and by coincidence our house was fairly close to that school as well. Because you've always got in the back of your mind, well it's okay aspiring to go to a certain school, but unless you are in the right catchment area, as the crow flies, then it's very difficult, or could be very difficult to guarantee getting that place. So yes we moved in ... [and] managed to get our first-choice primary school, which was a kind of a great relief to us. So yeah schooling was a major thing. (Mike)

Geographical proximity to home and work are other factors that were sometimes considered (*'He's at a school that is five minute walk away from us', 'We both liked the idea of a local school'*). Once at school the extra tasks now expected of primary school aged children – *'spellings'*, *'reading'* and *'homework'* has added to activities particularly undertaken by the fathers in evenings and weekends. Richard and Graham reflect on these in the following extracts:

School has been quite straightforward. I think we worry a bit about the sorts of things you tend to, is she kind of reading the right sort of stuff.... Yeah they started getting homework this term and I think, well even she knows that after Christmas school gets proper. So really the first year is really just a continuation of nursery and she has had sort of homework you know.... So yeah that is a bit scary.... I can't remember getting homework until I was about 15! Yeah and just sort of coping with school communications and that sort of thing. You know so that becomes part of the task. (Richard)

We have got quite a lot of, one thing I think we do now is quite a lot of homework with the children, particularly reading where, so that will often be a key part of the weekend, Sunday evenings as well. We make sure the boys have had some reading practice and [older child] has spellings to do and this sort of thing. (Graham)

While homework to Richard appears to be have been introduced at a much younger age than he recalls (his daughter is 5 and he was 'about 15'), homework has become one of the many activities that takes up family time. The importance of spending time together as a family is highlighted by several of the dads (*'and generally Sunday is a sort of family day and we try and do something altogether'*), but this is not always achieved and time-pressured households can have other consequences (*'I'm trying to find a way of not saying that it's put a strain on our relationship, but I don't think it has fundamentally, but it has on the surface sometimes'*). As Ian observes,

You know it feels like there must have been more time in the past, but literally finding time to do things as a family is difficult to get hold of. (Ian)

Even though working weeks are busy across all the households, time for many of the children (and so parents) is also now taken up with numerous other activities (apart from homework) outside the home (Henderson, 2012). As one father observes,

Yeah, we're looking for swimming classes, for example, we want to get them to do. But we have got friends who have got children who seem to spend every other day doing something and ours are not like that.

The intensification of parenting and ways that practices of 'concerted cultivation' can influence parenting 'strategies' and engagement in extracurricular activities was noted in Chapter 1 (Henderson, 2012; Lareau, 2003; Lee et al, 2014; Vincent and Ball, 2007; Wall, 2013). Across the families, the study activities outside school included swimming classes, ballet, ballet exams, karate, tennis (*'and she's learning to play tennis as well'*), guitar, music lessons, football, dancing, horse riding and more. So what emerges from the data is that a particular type of 'good' parenting becomes much more than just meeting a child's needs for sustenance, shelter and love, but developmental and time-intensive activities now occupy and intrude on (family) time. These activities require economic and 'organisational investment, which may differ by class, family structure and income' (Henderson, 2012:545). But such strategies can also be hard to ignore as other children are seen to engage in them (*'and they're like playing the violin at 8'*), and such activities become erroneously read as shorthand for 'good parenting'.

Although expectations of idealised 'good parenting' continue to be more associated with mothers, the men have their own ideas about how aspects of (good) parenting should be conducted. These emerge in the ways the fathers narrate their ideas and practices of parenting their now older children. For example, even though Frank talks about having to *'pretty much have to make it up as I go along'* as a parent, he still draws upon recognisable elements of 'good' parenting, which include regulating his twins, now aged 5 years, television viewing:

When you are on your own with them it's '*daddy, daddy, daddy*', and you think 'oh god be quiet' and the temptation to plonk them here and switch that [the TV] on, but you know it's not the right thing. But every so often you think 20 minutes/half an hour won't do them any harm just to get lunch ready or get something done, or just have a respite. (Frank)

Many parents will recognise the strategies that are used as trade-offs (TV for getting lunch ready) that Frank describes here. Other parenting strategies, such as '*reward points*' that their children can earn '*for doing things when asked the first time or you know eating a good meal*' (Graham), are also described. Others talk of the importance of '*having meal times together*' and allude to 'poor' parenting practises in others:

I see our friends with their children and they are a little bit disruptive and then they don't sit and they don't communicate to their children and I think it's all part of their development, talking and reading, you know it is one of those things you have to do.

Another father talks of following the same model of caring and parenting with a second child as the first, involving his wife staying at home until a free government-funded nursery place was available. He explains,

And using [first child] as a bit of a benchmark for want of a better phrase, it worked out really well and she is you know very confident now and has got some really good social skills and that kind of thing. (Mike)

Helping a child to have confidence and to develop '*good social skills*' is clearly seen as a successful outcome here, but this isn't always how things work out ('*I'm not saying she needs to be competitive, but she needs to try and she just gives up so easily*'). Drawing on examples from the fathers it could be concluded that good parenting/fathering includes helping their children to develop communication skills, table manners, self-control (e.g. in relation to TV and computer games) and lots of activities outside the home, as well as providing 'discipline'. But for all that, at some point most parents also just want a quiet life, and the best of intentions can be thwarted as Nick, who works with children in a professional capacity, describes:

You know I can spend all day understanding behaviour and helping other professionals understand behaviour and I can be home within ten minutes and feel fully frustrated. I don't want to understand the behaviour, I want it to stop! (Nick, laughing)

Other fathers also note the frustrations that can be experienced as a parent, regardless of the amount of advice they feel is now aimed at parents – or perhaps because of it. Here Graham, a father of two sons, responds to a question on what the hardest thing about fathering has been:

There were lots of really hard things so I find it hard to weigh it up.... But yes to feel that you are trying to work hard with these kids, it's taking a lot of your time and yet you still seem to be basically telling them what to do, telling them not to do things and leaving them to get on with things, rather than having, you know, rather than giving them a more sort of better experience of having a parent there, is a shame. (Graham)

The interactional and relational aspects of a caring relationship are evident in Graham's account and those of other fathers. Children can be expressive, articulate and demanding too (*'you start to understand how they work as individuals, they are their own people'*). The child's agentic development now makes possible a very different form of inter-action (compared with the interviews when the focus was on birth and the first 2 years) in which men's practises of fathering can now be assessed by those their efforts are focused upon – their children (*'and they were sort of oh you know we don't want you to get cross with us Dad'*). For example, some of the dads spoke of being disappointed with aspects of their fathering and were frustrated by not seeming able to be the sort of dad they'd originally envisaged they'd be, or initially had been.

In the following extract, Mike conveys the ways competing demands and self-expectations have worked out in unexpected ways:

I think I've seen in myself fairly recently as well, I think that I've become a lot more serious I think. So I think, I'd like to think that before... before children I was a lot more light-hearted and focused on fun and having a laugh and doing whatever it is I was doing, but I think I've almost taken on this 'I'm a Dad' therefore I have to be serious in front of the children and set an example or this perception of I'm a dad therefore whatever I say is correct and therefore you need to do it type of approach, which yeah, which has been an interesting one.... So... I've tried to make a, tried to have an approach where I'm a bit more relaxed and flexible and that kind of thing and it's really hard. It's very, very difficult to do that. I think you know it turns out that I'm perhaps not as patient as I could or should be at home as well and it's a strange scenario, because when you are at work I'm one of the most patient people ... but you come home and you're tired and you're hungry and you've had a rubbish day, but at the same time as [wife] reminds me, it's not the children's fault and they haven't seen you. (Mike)

Interestingly, in this extract Mike invokes a stereotype of a more traditionally masculine and authoritarian, father figure as '*serious*', '*setting an example*' and always being right. But contrast this to how he described his fathering involvement when his oldest child was 2 years old:

I still bath her ... it's now a case of trying to catch her as she legs it 'round the house because you know it's turned into a bit of a game. She's like hiding in wardrobes – and it's like where is she or under the bed covers or something like that which adds to a huge great amount of fun into it and if I've had a particularly rubbish day at work and just to have a little cheeky girl running around and hiding and stuff. (Mike)

Of course lives change and the birth of additional children add to parenting demands and parenting older children ('*my son is quite a grumpy person at the moment*') has new challenges as children now socialise much more regularly outside the home at school and in out-of-school activities. For some, parenting older children works out in ways that were not imagined as individual agency shapes paternal and child interactions and new sibling relationships too and there can be expressions of frustration and guilt. Stress too can arise in situations that are experienced as pressurised and time squeezed ('*you don't have any me time*') as attempts are made to meet in some way the demands of family care and work.

Explaining Family Practices of Caring and Paid Work: Theorising 'Fluffiness'

The data collected in these later interviews with fathers provide an innovative opportunity to explore how the men understand and explain the differences and overlap between paternal caring and maternal caring/mothering after several years of fathering involvement. How far is parenting less segregated according to gender or more 'gender-neutral' and the naming of their wife or partner as the primary or main carer (as noted earlier) a consequence of only (a lack of) time, as some fathers imply? Consider the following extract:

I would say [wife] is still the main child carer because she is about more often, but I would say yeah Monday to Friday it is probably 70:30 and weekends it's probably 50:50. (Frank)

Indeed, is it possible to disaggregate primary carer responsibilities as practises *and* thinking (the 'mental work') into pockets of time (e.g. weekends when Frank describes their caring as 'probably 50:50')? In the following section these questions are explored further, first through the language that the fathers use to describe their relationships and practices. In the interviews carried out in the earlier phase of the study, as the men became new fathers, they used the terms 'bond' and 'bonding' to express a connection they anticipated, said they felt 'immediately' at the birth of their baby or said was something they would develop over time. The language of bonding (*'a very strong bond'*), connection (*'the more time you spend with them, the more the connection comes'*) and love (*'I love them with all my heart'*) is volunteered and present again in these later interviews, but interestingly, with the passage of time, further distinctions are now drawn between mothers and fathers. In the following extract, Sean reflects on a bond being a two-way, reciprocal relationship:

with a maternal bond . . . well I don't share, but with a father who's there a lot, a bond . . . develops and although that might be a kind of instant thing for a dad, for the baby it may take a little bit more time. (Sean)

Sean acknowledges that his is not a maternal bond (which is something distinct) but alludes to time (*'there a lot'*) and the potential for 'a bond' to be instantly felt or developed, but that this being reciprocal (felt by the baby) is a longer term endeavour (see Chapter 6 for further discussion of Sean's experiences of fatherhood and loss). Talking of his firstborn and now 5-year-old daughter, Sean describes having established a strong bond with her:

But that is not to say that I haven't got a very strong bond with [daughter] and although she doesn't realise it, I hope that in years to come she will be grateful for the fact that I was around as much, and I did get to know her as well as I did. (Sean)

Interestingly, this extract raises a much broader question about generational change and the impact the increased involvement these fathers are having with their children will have on future paternal/familial arrangements. For example, what might his daughter's expectations of family caring practises and parental responsibilities look like? It also implies an individual investment in what is hoped will be an enduring familial relationship. James, who is now divorced and sees much less of his only daughter, is more focused than the other fathers on the enduring dimensions of relationships and is involved in the '*long game*':

That's what everyone says you play the long game on these things. So eventually she's going to grow up and discover what's right and wrong in life and make decisions I think. So I'm, you know the way I'm looking at it, you know I've got 40 years with her from the age of 18 onwards. (James)

The ways in which separation and divorce change caring arrangements and parental possibilities are explored further in Chapter 5.

Even though the fathers continue to engage discursive practices that have been seen as exclusively maternal in the past and imply elements of gender-neutral practises of care, they nevertheless draw distinctions between mothers and fathers in their actual caring practises (Doucet, 2006; Ranson, 2015). It is of course too simplistic to assume changes in language claims correlate straightforwardly to changes in everyday caring behaviours, even though there is evidence of both in the study. For example, Frank (father of twin boys) talks about seeing himself as 'more the disciplinarian' in the following extract:

I'm hands on. Definitely hands on. I'm probably more the disciplinarian. But I think that's always a, generally a man's thing, to be, you know when they're out of hand, bring them back into line sort of thing. (Frank)

But even though he links discipline and men ('*a man's thing*') in a very traditional way, he then goes on to describe his own mother as having been the 'disciplinarian' in his childhood family and that his '*dad was the softer touch*'. Even though Frank also describes his involvement in his sons care as 50:50 at the weekends, he also alludes in the following extract to a particular maternal connection to children and time (implicitly, 'being there'):

I think it's [parenting] as instinctive as how you've been brought up. If you've been brought up with values then I think it's a little bit more instinctive but I think it's more mothers having that connection more than the father. But

I think the more time you spend with them, the more connection there is. I think with children it's all about time, it's spending time with them . . . and you'll start to understand how they work as individuals and they are individuals. (Frank)

The implication across the data is that the fathers assume an instant and instinctive 'maternal' bond will be forged between mother and baby but that they may have to wait longer to establish 'closeness' and a bond. However, with time and practical involvement, the father can become, as one father put it, '*a perfectly good substitute*' for a mother. It is increasingly clear that men are capable of competently caring (in sometimes different ways compared with maternal practices) for their children (Brandth and Kvande, 2016; Doucet, 2006, 2016; Ranson, 2015). But how far do these shifts in caring correspond more broadly to practices of masculinities and do they disrupt more traditional gendered assumptions about the masculine subject?

In response to an interview question on what advice the men would give to friends becoming fathers for the first time, Joe challenged the idea and replied, '*As I said we're just blokes, we don't really speak about it*'. There are other examples across the data of the men experiencing ambivalent feelings as emotionally involved, caring fathers, 'successful' workers and 'real' men. The sense of navigating through changing times where multiple masculine identities are possible rather than solely hegemonic-oriented, traditional masculinity is conveyed in the following extract as Nick recounts being in the pub on a Saturday night:

So I was in the pub the other night with some dads and it was very male and they were talking about golf handicaps and you know downing quite a few pints whereas earlier that day I had been with one of the dads and we'd been talking about washing blackberry stains off the kids because they had been blackberry picking. But there was no way that was going to come up in the pub on Saturday night. (Nick)

But for William the 'roles' of mothers and fathers continue to be distinct and differentiated by his sense of gendered differences and orientations:

But I think still the roles are relatively distinct . . . so you know let me give you an example, what she [daughter] wears for me isn't too much of a hassle, as long as it's kind of you know appropriate in terms of the weather and what she looks like isn't completely atrocious then I'm happy with it, whereas [wife] is more particular about it and how it looks and the presentation.... Likewise all the house stuff largely is, and looking after [daughter] in that sense, you know buying in stuff for the house, getting the right shampoos for her, whatever else you know, I don't get involved in that. I think it's still the provider, me provider, wife nurturer sort of role I guess, still. But you know I'm allowed to sort of dabble in it on occasion. (William)

The continued arrangements/expectations of 'provider' and 'nurturer' roles along traditional lines of gender may be a consequence of William's absence due to his job, which involved him spending long periods of time abroad in the first years after the birth of his only child.[9] But this extract also illustrates how aspects of care can become taken on, assumed or even protected (*'I'm allowed to sort of dabble... on occasion'*) as aspects of 'maternal gatekeeping' are alluded to here (Allen and Hawkins, 1999; Puhlman and Pasley, 2013; Radcliffe and Cassell, 2015; Stevenson et al, 2014). (The concept and practice of maternal gatekeeping is explored further in subsequent chapters; see Chapters 6 and 7.) But in the following exchange, William also acknowledges aspects of change, compared with when he was a child:

TINA: Would your father have dashed back to do bedtime with you?
WILLIAM: No, no. Yes and no, I do recall him in that sort of fashion, but not constantly doing it, it wasn't like his job as such, his role. I think we're fluffier to use that term, now more than we would have been I think. There is this kind of metrosexual approach to it all, with all things to all people. I think no my parents' generation would have been much more – father, that sort of provider... than we have at the moment. I think it was a more formidable environment when I grew up.... I think now it's a lot more caring, sharing, checking how the child is, a lot more reflection and so on and so on, and I think that's changed.

In fact some of William's fathering practices quite closely resemble the description he gives of his own father as a 'provider', but he recognises that the broader social context has changed and is *'fluffier'* and more *'caring and sharing'* and less *'formidable'*. This fluffier contemporary context has implications of course for the ways in which gender more broadly and masculinities are understood and practised as seen across

---

[9] In other research the gender of the child has also been considered as a factor in how practices of contingent care become enacted, for example see Gerstel and Gallagher (2001).

the accounts in this chapter and other work[10] (Doucet, 2006, 2009; Miller, 2010, 2011; Ranson, 2015). These changes are noted too in the following extract, where Nick is curious about how his two sons will come to understand 'masculinity',

But I wonder what sort of masculinity my children see and you know say for example lots of the dads where we live meet up on a regular basis and go for beers and play tennis…you know they build extensions and stuff and we got somebody in to build our extension and you know my children see that I have a bottle of beer and that's it. So I think their view of masculinity of a father will be different from some of their peers. (Nick)

Nick is one of the fathers who said that he and his wife were 'interchangeable' in terms of their capacities to care for their children, clean the house and work. But he notes that even so, his sons love to play what he sees as traditionally 'masculine' games,

So they love fighting, you know sword fighting, they can turn anything into a sword…. and that is not what I play with them you know and I don't, play 'shoot them' games. I don't particularly sit and watch violent films with them but they pick that up and they have a very strong sense of we are knights, we are soldiers, we are battling and I think it's sort of quite a traditional masculine role, which I don't think they get from me. You know maybe they do. (Nick)

The complexities and nuances of (developing) gendered identities and gender fluidity and possibilities of change run across these two extracts as influences beyond the home and in the home are pondered by Nick. While he describes his own practises of caring as 'interchangeable' with his wife's these are lived in complex structures and contexts shaped in relation to significant gender differentiation and histories. The fathers' practises simultaneously challenge stereotypes of caring orientations and at times confirm and reinforce them.

Conclusions

As their children begin school, it is hard for the fathers to remember a pre-baby phase of their life. Their focus is now on 'what is good for the children' and helping them to be happy and successful

[10] See for example Chapter 2 in *Making Sense of Fatherhood: Gender, Care and Work* (Miller, 2010).

individuals. They have now developed greater confidence and skills as fathers. But the demands of school, work and family weigh heavily, and everyone feels that there is not enough time to squeeze everything into the day, evening, week or weekend. The quality of the time they have with their children can be felt to be compromised as routines structure the working family day. But it is not just about a lack of time but how the time they have is used and who orchestrates this. The fathers are aware of and respond to the demands of more intensified parenting expectations, but in reactive ways rather than taking the primary lead or overarching responsibility. The fathers are 'insulated against the demands of intensive parenting' to a greater extent than the mothers as they undertake responsibilities in different ways and sometimes ways that are seen as 'wrong' (Shirani et al, 2012:25).

Patterns of responsibilities have followed those established in the early months of their children's lives, with particular and changing tasks being taken on. But their involvement in practises is also responsive to the fathers' job, as well as the birth of subsequent children and more recently the demands of school. The fathers caring practises do not mirror those of women in exact ways, nor do they carry the same burden of caring in terms of time. In these households with school-age children, it becomes clear that the fathers' involvement is often orchestrated by the person who knows the daily routine best, who is most attuned to the vagaries of the school timetable, to the cleaning and shopping that has been done and who has spent more time doing the mental work of caring: the mother.

4 | *Mothering*
Caring, Work and Teenage Children

I mean I'm not saying the teenage years have been easy, we have had rows and hormonal outbursts from all of us you know. But on the whole we've reasoned with it in the end.

(Lillian)

And I kind of think, I've probably done a good enough job, not brilliant, but good enough.

(Rebecca)

But I just totally and utterly believe, it's part of being a parent you don't know, there is no book that tells you how to do it and it was just instinct, gut, I don't know...I just did it.

(Sheila)

In the previous chapter fathering experiences were narrated as firstborn children reached primary school age, and in this chapter mothering experiences are narrated as firstborn children reach 18 years of age and approach the end of their school days. Once again the overarching themes of caring, gender and paid work explored in the previous chapters will be returned to, and illuminated through empirical data, but from the perspective of a group of mothers. The background for this chapter is set with an overview of the findings from the earlier book, '*Making Sense of Motherhood*' (Miller, 2005) in which the same participants feature, before exploring their much more recent experiences as they reflect on 18 years of mothering/parenting. This longer, experience-rich view – from transition to motherhood to their child now reaching adulthood – provides an unusual opportunity to trace how 'mothering careers' have unfolded as adult children plan individual futures including leaving school and (potentially) leaving home[1] (Oakley, 2016; Ribbens, 1998). Over the years, how have the mothers gotten through the daily practises of caring, and have aspects of these practises been adopted or ring-fenced as specifically maternal or paternal? Is there evidence of any intensification of their parenting practises in response to political and cultural expectations of contemporary family life?

To go back, the original study involved interviewing a group of women across a year in which they became mothers for the first time. Three interviews (and completion of an end-of-study postal questionnaire) were conducted with 17 participants. Some 17 years later, 10 of these women were traced and invited to participate in another interview, and 6 agreed.[2] This process of going back was complicated by the fact that the original study had been conducted before the everyday use of e-mail or the advent of mobile phones as research tools (see Miller, 2015, for further details on this process). It is data from these new interviews that are explored in this chapter. But to set the scene, the following extract is taken from the original study that was published in *Making Sense of Motherhood* (Miller, 2005). This abridged extract is taken from a chapter in the book (chapter 6, 'A return to normal: Becoming the expert') and provides an account of the mothers' experiences when last interviewed as their firstborn babies were approximately 9 months old.

The passage of time enables the women to (re)construct and present challenging narratives of mothering. Over time, they reflect on and make sense of their experiences and now feel able to disclose unhappy and difficult experiences, which had previously been withheld. Shifts occur around perceptions of expert, authoritative knowledge as control in a life is felt to be regained. Women become the experts, through practice, in recognising and meeting their children's needs. Similarly, professional constructions of normal transition to motherhood and child development are also challenged. Perceptions of risk are re-evaluated from this more accomplished stage in the women's mothering careers (Ribbens, 1998). This is in relation to their children, and how they manage their own selves and are judged by others as mothers.

---

[1] Research shows that young people in the United Kingdom are continuing to stay in the family home beyond the age of 18 years (Office for National Statistics, 2016).

[2] Of the 10 women contacted, 6 agreed and 1 declined by e-mail. Of the other 3 contacted, 2 were to be contacted by the original gatekeeper (a member of their family) but did not get in touch, and 1 was sent a letter and a phone message was left on an answerphone, but she did not respond (see Miller, 2015).

Over time, and with practice, a social self as a mother is gradually developed and eventually incorporated 'into an overall schema of self-understanding' (Lawler, 2000:57–8). Movements in and out of the practised worlds of paid work, less anxiety about meeting a child's needs, and coping both within and outside the home, together with interaction with an increasingly responsive child, all contribute to the development of a sense of self – a social rather than essentialist self – as a mother. Yet for some women concerns remain about their abilities to mother and their responses to their children. The trajectory of a return to normal is differently experienced, and professional practices, including monitoring and measurement, often do not fit with experiential time. This leads some to challenge once sought and accepted authoritative, expert knowledge and to reassess perceptions of risk. For most, a schema of self-understanding is eventually enriched through becoming mothers and managing 'good enough' mothering, but not for all.

In this earlier book, the frames of selfhood, (embodied) performance, practises of surveillance and discursive possibilities were used to explore the women's experiences of *transition* to first-time motherhood. In retrospect one of the hardest things for the women to come to terms with was the enormity of the felt '24/7 responsibility' and 'mental work' of caring for a dependent baby, for which they felt ill-prepared despite lots of antenatal preparation (Walzer, 1996). Their sense of their self (as an individual) became subsumed into the identity of 'mother', which conveys expertise and yet is weighed down with assumptions about instincts, which most of the mothers did not initially or instantly experience. It seems that it is (almost) impossible to convey the 'mental work' of caring responsibilities to parents-to-be. Preparation for parenthood tends to focus on task-based caring practises (feeding, nappy changing and routines), and it is easy to make a miscalculation between a physically small baby and the amount of care and thinking time it will occupy: the emotion work is incalculable at this point.

Caring for a baby when the original study was conducted in the United Kingdom (mid-late 1990s) was still much more assumed of, and associated with, mothers rather than fathers (for example paternity leave legislation was not introduced in the United Kingdom until 2003). Reeling forward to the present day, a focus on experiences of mothering their now young adult (and any subsequent) children provides a powerful focus through which to examine change and continuities that have occurred during the intervening years. Although all the mothers in the original study lived in dual-earner households and most returned to part- or full-time work after maternity leave, rates of mothers' employment have risen significantly since the original study (Ben-Galim and Thompson, 2013; Connolly et al, 2016; Lyonette et al, 2011). The majority of families in the United Kingdom are now working families, which has led to expectations of fathers' increased involvement in family care and household chores (Harden et al, 2014; Scott and Clery, 2013). As noted earlier in this book, parenting practices have become more generally subject to increased political scrutiny and prescriptive notions of what constitutes 'good parenting' (see Chapter 1). The women have of course cared for their growing children against this shifting backdrop, and it will be interesting to see how they have navigated the competing demands of paid work, family and school life as their children become young adults. In the sections that follow, a short summary provides an update on key developments in the lives of the six mothers who are featured in this chapter (Gillian, Kathryn, Rebecca, Sheila, Lillian and Felicity[3]).

In the data collected in these much later interviews, the mothers reflect back across the intervening 17 years, which have gone by '*In a flash. I can't believe it is 18 years*'. Any worries about coping and being seen to be competent at caring for a first baby are long gone. Subsequent births ('*I wanted a bit more pain relief this time because it was horrendous last time*', '*and it was second time 'round and everything was easier and I didn't have any stitches*') have resulted in siblings being born. Just as in the previous chapter, the mothers, like the fathers, share a sense that children should be treated equally ('*you think you need to be treating your children the same*', '*I felt I should do it because I'd done it with the first one*') as families grow ('*being a mother of four is a huge part of me*', '*having one you realise is easy, once you have two it's like running a zoo*'). Between the six mothers there are now 16 children who at the time of the interviews were all aged 12 years and older, with the eldest being 18 years (the child born in the original study). The enthusiastic preparation undertaken as the first birth was anticipated 18 years earlier is not repeated ('*No I don't think I did any preparation classes, I'd done it all by then so I thought I knew it all*')

---

[3] Each of the mothers' experiences of the antenatal, early postnatal and later postnatal period as their first child was born can be followed through the chapters in *Making Sense of Motherhood* (Miller, 2005).

and there is a sense that having come to terms with the '*shock*' of the first birth, they were more prepared to cope with subsequent births ('*it was just easier because you know you've done it all once before, so it was much easier*').

All the women are working mothers, employed in either full-time or part-time jobs, which have mostly continued from their return to work in the original study with subsequent periods of maternity leave as necessary. Of the six women, two have been divorced for approximately 10 years (Sheila and Felicity) and have not re-partnered, two have separated/divorced more recently in the 2 years before the interview (Gillian and Kathryn; Kathryn is engaged), and two remain married to their original partners (Lillian and Rebecca) (see Chapter 5). Looking back, the dependency of younger babies and children and the 24/7 thinking and planning required to anticipate and meet their needs ('*learning to put someone else before everything else continually, was difficult*') is now viewed from the perspective of having a more independent 18-year-old young adult ('*they can get their own meals*', '*It's not as hard as it was, the responsibility is, well first it's shared and secondly they have to take some responsibility for themselves*'). So feelings of responsibility shift and are not felt so acutely but continue in other ways. Young adult children are not felt to have the same dependency ('*they were so dependent and I had no freedom and that was really hard*', '*because they were 17, they needed to make their own decisions*') and do not require the same amount of 'selflessness' on the part of their mother (or father). But time is still pressured as other aspects of parenting are felt ('*all that performance anxiety, every single day there is a test, there's a SAT or there's modular this or whatever*', '*Obsessed with it, Kumon Maths and doing this and doing that, learning this skill and being Grade 8*') as their now young adult children contemplate (or are encouraged to) their own, adult futures.

Like the fathers in the previous chapter, '*the logistics*' of doing things with more than one child are similarly commented on by the mothers. But parenting an adult child also involves the mixed emotions of *being there* in now different ways and preparing for them leaving and letting go ('*I'm about to send one off in the world with all the pressures that that involves and it is scary, it's really scary*'). Leaving home – for travel, a job or university – now features prominently in future hopes and orientations of the mothers and the young adults themselves ('*I hope he can fulfil his dream in the gaming industry*'). But helping their children to reach perceived desirable outcomes has involved practises of long-term parenting investment, examples of which run through the mothers' accounts (*'yeah, she had 18 years of intensive mothering which hopefully is enough to give her the confidence and the skills to do it herself'*), and these are explored further in what follows.

Mothering a Young Adult

The interviews with the mothers provided an unusual opportunity for them to reflect back across their mothering experiences (*'I just found sitting watching them on climbing frames mind numbingly boring'*) while imagining futures without the close, everyday proximity of their firstborn child. There are hopes, worries and regrets as well as a sense of personal accomplishment (*'she's had a good enough start in life and that's what I want for all of them'*). What is clear is that once school life begins, the intensity of some aspects of mothering (*'the toddler bit ... I found that incredibly hard because they are constantly there and they don't understand'*) is reduced, while other aspects have become intensified, especially in relation to managing a child's emotional and personal growth (*'well my daughter, now she has been quite down, she's better now but she went through a really bad time', 'he wasn't happy and I didn't know why'*). This occurs in an environment seen as more pressured and 'risky' and is sometimes felt to be beyond the control of the family (*'one of the hardest things about parenting is that you've taught them so much and you can't control their behaviour ... when they drink it all goes by the board doesn't it?'*) (Wall, 2013). Across the six families, extracurricular 'enrichment activities' outside the home were also taken up in busy days already filled with homework (*'but sometimes you feel like you know there is a lot of pressure from school to do a lot at home'*) (Vincent and Ball, 2007). Producing a 'successful' – that is, happy and healthy – young adult (*'making sure she gets to adulthood the best that she can and the best that I can provide for her as far as you know being emotionally stable'*) who would be able to make their own way in the world was a shared aspiration. But routes and types of outcomes varied (*'it's about developing them as human beings that I didn't anticipate'*). Of course parental aspirations will be 'shaped by many complex factors', including their own experiences of paid work, different ideas of 'a good job' and 'estimations of realistic possibilities for their children' (Irwin and Elley, 2012:127; Lewis et al,

2015). One thing the mothers recognise from having subsequent children is how different and individual they could be, requiring different types of support and care. As mothering and parenting has been argued to have become intensified and parental responsibilities shifting from sustaining, loving and caring for a child to also investing in and maximizing their potential, it is interesting to see how aspects of these expectations featured in the mothers' accounts (Jones, 2014; Wall, 2013). It is also important to note how, compared with the previous chapter on fathers and caring, the identity and use of the noun 'mother' is so culturally conflated with assumptions about caring that the combination of 'mother' and 'care' does not need to be stated in the same ways necessary when describing fathers and caring.

In contrast to the stage of parenting explored in the previous chapter, where fathers described their firstborn child beginning school, here schooldays are ending. Interactions with school and the activities that emanate from and around it have significantly shaped family lives and daily, time-pressured, practises and parental relationships (*'I think the pressure on them in terms of exams is enormous. The pressure on them in terms of jobs... there just wasn't that pressure that there is now'*). The school day is no longer just about the hours spent at school but seeps into home life, family time and parental responsibilities as the imperative for children to demonstrably succeed is recognised by the mothers (Wall, 2010, 2013). It is also publically measured, for example in regular testing and the publication of school league tables. It seems it is difficult ('risky'?) for parents[4] to resist this expectation and so already busy, working lives for the mothers also include helping with homework, interactions with schools and teachers and ferrying children between school and extracurricular and other activities. The word 'pressure' related to time is used in all the interviews. In the following extracts Lillian, a mother of two teenagers, talks about the pressure she has felt from her children's school and her worries about her ability to *'give so much knowledge'*:

But sometimes you feel like you know there is a lot of pressure from school to do a lot at home, you know and if we can't decipher what that means,

---

[4] The ways in which middle-class parents are particularly caught up in practices of 'concerted cultivation' and feel pressure to 'supervise, guide and direct children's activities and learning rather than letting children take responsibility for themselves' has been noted (Wall, 2013:166).

you know then how can we pass that on. So I think that is difficult I think. I mean some parents don't find that difficult, they might find other things more difficult ... you know academically wise, because I'm not really highly academic and I worry that has ... you can only give so much knowledge if you haven't got it. You know so how do they progress further than both me and their dad you know academically ... so I worry about that. (Lillian)

Lillian's concerns are recognisable in the context of increasingly intensive parenting expectations and perceived risks associated with not being seen to have managed this (Wall, 2013). In the following extract, Sheila, a mother of three sons, alludes to these risks of failure and her sense of her 'blame' as she feels she took her '*eye off the ball*' while fighting a Local Education Authority to get her youngest child a place at a specialist school,

But anyway so that tribunal was during a year which was also a very important year for the older two [twins] ... and I do blame myself that I wasn't there for them ... so I feel that I took my eye off the ball with them and didn't push them as much as I should have with doing their homework and doing everything to do with their GCSEs. You can't do everything. (Sheila)

Sheila goes on to respond to a question about what she has found hardest about mothering:

School, homework, I hate it, absolutely hate it! I wish somebody could find a solution. I don't know whether it's me, whether it's my problem or what, but I don't know how other parents manage, maybe they just don't worry. But I don't think my children would have got any exams if I didn't push them. (Sheila)

As noted earlier, research shows that the majority of parents are also engaged in paid work in the United Kingdom. But rather than diminish the intensiveness of societal expectations in relation to parenting, the opposite seems to be the case. All the mothers, just like the fathers in the previous chapter, described time-pressured lives and households, but where numerous and varied extracurricular activities were still taken up. Among these families these activities included music, drama, extra maths, trumpet lessons, violin lessons, football, keyboard and piano lessons, youth theatre, youth orchestra, gliding, rugby, Brownies, Beavers, Cubs, Scouts, swimming lessons, lifeguard training and air cadets.

The onus on a 'good' mother is still to 'be there' (a key finding in both earlier studies on motherhood and fatherhood) but in ways that the mothers feel are different from the demands associated with babies and young children. For example this now involves having the knowledge to help with homework, ensuring it is done and being available to listen, talk and advise (*'even on the end of a phone . . . still available'*). The practical aspects of caring may be reduced, or can be negotiated with a young adult, but the 'mental work' can be felt even more intensively as Shelia notes in the following extract:

Definitely with boys . . . it's much, it's physical when they are younger. I was constantly out because they would wreck the house. You have to be constantly one step ahead of them, taking them out on the bikes, rugby, swimming anything, out whereas now it's very much more mental. It's so hard. (Sheila)

There is a shared sense that even if their children are more independent, they are still needed in different ways as *'backup'* and *'support'* as children are going *'off in the world'*. Gillian (whose daughter is travelling abroad), Kathryn and Felicity explain aspects of this in the following extracts.

But yeah she had 18 years of intensive mothering which hopefully is enough to give her the confidence and the skills to do it herself. But with the backup, there is always the back up there isn't there, you are always there behind supporting, encouraging, sending messages, replying to her messages, Skyping. You know you are still there for them but just not in that, you don't have to be there on a 24/7 basis because you can't be. (Gillian)

So the focus on life has changed and I talk to people who have older children about when they need you and I don't think children need you any less, they just need you very differently and at different times. (Kathryn)

So it's a very different pattern of parenting I think than parenting young children. And exhausting equally, emotionally, mentally and physically but in a very different way. Somebody said to me your children get bigger and so do their problems and the consequences of those problems and that's very true. I can reflect back and think I can't, I can remember thinking that they didn't sleep through the night and it was the end of the world and now I'm about to send one off in the world [with] all the pressures that that involves and it is scary, it's really scary. (Felicity)

There is a sense too that their teenage children have to negotiate a more complicated and 'riskier' world (*'I think the pressures on teenagers now are huge and very diverse and different and very nasty, they have all sorts of things, everything is on Facebook'*). Forms of social media (*'the whole Facebook, Twitter, phone thing'*) are seen to play an influential role, both positive (facilitating contact and new forms of being there: *'they do Skype and they do chat on snap chat, so there is still that contact between the two'*) and negative (*'they spend far too much time on it and so they are very inward looking about appearances and what other people think'*). But the ways in which constructions and perceptions of 'risk' also change, over time and generation, are apparent too, as Lillian describes:

I mean we've been ... like I smoked very young at 13 years and my children, I would go mad if they were smoking and they haven't, you know. So there is, they are more aware of themselves I think younger now. I probably had more freedom you know, I could go out at a younger age. (Lillian)

Mothering teenagers who are *'more aware of themselves'* at a younger age, or are 'pressured' to grow up (too) quickly or are *'needing to find themselves'* was experienced as demanding (*'I hate my life at the moment with them, but you have to be there'*). When Kathryn observes that *'it's tougher to negotiate with a teenager'*, she alludes to the practises of agency and individualisation that teenagers might engage (*'It's really hard when they're smarter than you'*) and that are different from a baby or younger child. Aspects of caring become more explicitly reciprocal too (*'but she leaves the outside light on for me. I think that's just so lovely isn't it you know the tables are sort of turned'*) as well as interactions sometimes being more combative (*'I'm there and I'm nagging and I'm horrible and I won't give in and then they are so horrible to me'*).

Across the years, concerns over sleeping, weaning and early childhood milestones have been replaced by concerns for the mothers about their teenage children, which include *'sleeping around'*, *'sex, drugs, drinking, smoking and everything'* and helping them to be able to cope in the world. As they reach their 18th year, which culturally signals adulthood in many societies, the data indicate anticipated change in mothering responsibilities and relationships (Jones, 2014). This involves the mothers not only gradually supporting their children to become independent, including dealing with risks, but eventually *'standing back'* too, as Gillian explains:

Well as far as motherhood is concerned, [second daughter] is 16, so 2 more years really I feel of making sure that she gets to adulthood the best that she can and the best that I can provide for her as far as you know being emotionally stable and being here for her and teaching her everything I know … and I'm looking forward to sort of standing back a bit with oldest daughter [who is 18], letting her do what it is that she wants to do and letting that develop. So the picture is bright. (Gillian)

Gillian, like the other mothers, can see (or at least glimpse) a future in which she is able to stand back (a bit) as intensively felt responsibilities associated with mothering are less immediate (*'I'm always here for you, you know and I kind of think … oh, it makes me tearful'*). The ability for this to happen emerges from the solid foundation having been established through their caring (*'still being there, you know like there sort of rock for them'*). The changing but enduring aspects of mothering, being there and generational, parental relationships are summed up by Lillian in the following extract:

I think it always stays doesn't it, because I still you know, I don't say I rely on my mum and dad, but I do go to them, not for domestic things and things like that, but just you know they're there. So I think you've always got to be there haven't you. (Lillian)

But across the years leading to this point, how have maternal and paternal practices of caring unfolded across the participant's households? Are aspects of caring responsibilities regarded or practised as 'interchangeable' (see Chapter 3) and if so is parenting regarded as generic and/or increasingly gender neutral? (Brandth and Kvande, 2016; Elliott, 2015; Miller, 2011). In the following section, questions about how 'thinking about a baby', and so taking on the mental work of caring, corresponds with 'thinking about a young adult' and associated responsibilities are considered. This is followed by a focus on mothers, maternal selves and how 'choices' are made in relation to paid work, caring practices and individual selfhood, as well as how these are narrated and presented.

Unfolding Practises of Caring Responsibility: Doing Mothering

The daily practices of parenting narrated across the data were patterned in different ways by various factors. These include whether both parents were resident, lived nearby or were 'estranged', how paid work was organised as well as the number and age of the children and individual ideas on how parenting should be done (*'I think some fathers stand back and let it just happen don't they. . . . But I think sometimes he's in too much, he just needs to back off'*). The picture that emerges is mixed: fathers are depicted both in more traditionally gendered ways as disciplinarian (*'they don't answer their dad back. They walk all over me but they do not say a word to him'*, *'I mean he is the ultimate, "I'll tell your father"'*) and also as significantly involved in providing the majority of daily caring (*'You asked for this baby and you are going to jolly well look after her'*). Aspects of caring are also described as being shared (*'So there is no regular division, except he mows the lawn and I iron, that's the only jobs that are gendered'*). Some fathers are perceived to have been better at different stages of parenting (the mothers too, as discussed later); for example, in the following extract Sheila talks about her ex-husband who still has daily contact with their three children:

He loved them, but he just with little, he didn't quite, when they were tiny, tiny it was fine, when they did as they were told and he played with them, it was fine. But as they got a bit older and he had to sort of do what they wanted, he found that hard. (Sheila)

Others too talk of changing relationships and involvement between fathers and their children (*'He was fantastic when the babies were little . . . Not so good now they are teenagers, he is very prudish and totally out of touch with a lot of things'*), but the fathers (whether resident or not) are mostly described as continuing to be involved in supportive, task-based interactions rather than taking primary responsibility or having an interchangeable role with the mother.

All but one of the mothers (Lillian) describe themselves as the primary carer, including where one mother has worked full time (Rebecca) and her husband part time so that he can provide the daily childcare. Lillian also describes changing her part-time work to involve fewer hours *'because we just felt that the childcare was too much on him [husband]'*. But from the data it becomes clear that even though aspects of parenting *could be* interchangeable, very early practises of mothering and fathering set a pattern for how caring responsibilities are felt, even if they are practised in different ways as children grow and family circumstances change. The opportunity to reflect back across the years of being a mother and mothering led some of the women to question why they had held on to particular responsibilities when, with hindsight, family life could have been organised in different, less maternally intensive ways (see Chapter 6). Their reflections provide useful insights into how the mental work of caring merges into particular practises (or at least assumptions about responsibilities) based on how caring is initially practised and then continues to structure subsequent ideas and practices.

In the following lengthy extract, Rebecca (full-time worker and mother of three) provides a sense of how the daily practises of caring in her family are organised. At the time of the interview her husband had been employed in part-time work for a number of years. In the extracts Rebecca emphasises the planning and organisational, rather than purely practical, aspects of caring responsibilities.

Actually [husband] has done his bit because he was physically there for the younger two when they were little, but even so as soon as I came home, he would abdicate all responsibility and it would be me! But I've always and I've always arranged all the childcare and I've always been the one there, but he has been a house husband and a father more so than lots of other people.

So I'm more compassionate and loving and he's more, he's not strict but he can't be bothered to stand for any nonsense, he gets irritated with them, whereas I you know, as a last resort, I get cross. So discipline we kind of muddle through together really. But he is definitely very good at motivating them. And then childcare I always sort out, doing the washing, the feeding and stuff, we, well I always do all the washing, I tend to organise the buying of the food, sometimes he does the shop, but I tend to. But he does a bit of cooking when he's at home, you know we share that.

So I was always in charge of the transport and I'm always in charge of the arrangements which are always incredibly involved, you know somebody has got trumpet lessons, somebody has got drama club, somebody is going to somebody's house for tea, or somebody is coming to our house for tea **and I have to hold it all in my head**. Then I communicate it to them religiously every night and every morning and most of the time it goes over their heads, but most of the time they do actually remember where they've got to be, but I organise all that, [husband] wouldn't have a clue, not a clue. (Rebecca, emphasis added)

In time-pressured, working households many people will recognise Rebecca's description of family life, and her husband of course may have a different sense of how their family life is managed. But of interest here is how Rebecca positions herself as a mother and what she continues to hold on to and emphasise in her account, even though she is also the primary breadwinner and full-time worker and has been for a number of years. Could her ability to '*hold it all in my head*' be a reason her husband '*wouldn't have a clue*': because he doesn't have to? These questions are posed not to in any way blame Rebecca or align with her husband, but rather to try to disentangle how caring practises and planning and their orchestration become taken on as responsibilities in relation to our children, and how these are understood retrospectively. Does Rebecca narrate her experiences in this way to demonstrate that even though she works full time (and successfully), she is still a 'good' mother and sees her primary role as being that, which is evidenced not through physical daytime presence but by her continual connection to her children through thinking about and organising their daily lives? Are her narrations indicative of maternal discourses and assumptions that can individually (still) be felt hard to escape or reject? Would it be too risky for Rebecca to 'abdicate all responsibility' or be seen to do so?

Others too have noted the 'ways in which women take on themselves the task of synchronising conflicting timetables and the work of managing work–life balance . . . carrying the mental and emotional work of ensuring that everyone's needs are met' (Irwin and Winterton, 2014:145). In contrast to Rebecca, Gillian, a mother of two, has worked part time up until her eldest child was 16 years old, when, after the breakup of her marriage, she took on full-time work (see Chapter 5). In the following extract, she reflects back on her mothering:

. . . it's just you always, you know with hindsight, you think oh did I do that right. Like with the responsibility thing that is the first thing I said to you I think maybe I've taken too much responsibility, maybe I could have shared the responsibility more and I don't know if that was me. . . . I think that is probably my nature and with hindsight I think there probably were people around. I'm sure [husband] would probably have taken more responsibility if I made him. . . . And when they actually spend time on their own with other people, even from a young age, I think they do get a special relationship that you can't replace. So I think if I was doing it again, I would certainly watch that and might have handled that a bit more, a bit differently. I would have given away some of that responsibility I think because I think that weighed me down in a way that I felt was essential at the time, but with hindsight I'm thinking why did I feel quite so weighed down by it, why did I not share that. You know I have extended family, why didn't I use that more, yes I think so yes, for the benefit of the children I think, not just for my own benefit, but for them. I don't know why I did not just share it, but maybe that was just me, maybe I just needed to take 24-hour responsibility. (Gillian)

Given this opportunity to reflect back on the ways in which mothering journeys have (to this point) unfolded and with '*hindsight*', Gillian now questions her actions and motives and whose needs (retrospectively viewed) were being met. She thinks that she may have taken '*too much responsibility*' and recognises that children can benefit from time spent with other people (extended family in this case) and that in taking so much responsibility, she felt at times '*weighed down*'. Gillian now feels that she could have shared the responsibilities that she took on, with her husband and others, but her ideas about mothering and motherhood instead had involved her taking on '24-hour responsibility'. In retrospect she is (almost) bemused by this, perhaps in part because her ex-husband now does both the mental and practical work of caring for his teenage daughters ('*he's done an awful lot more parenting since we've been apart . . . because suddenly he had to take responsibility*') in a shared, post-separation arrangement (see Chapter 5).

In the earlier transition to motherhood interviews, the women endeavoured to present themselves mostly as coping and competent new mothers drawing on 'a limited repertoire of possible storylines' (Miller, 2005, 2007). But 17 years later, longer term practises and responsibilities can now be narrated in more revelatory ways. There is less perceived risk in how the mothers feel they may be judged as they have 'successfully' raised a child to young adulthood. Reflecting back from this position, the mothers talk more candidly: '*I'm not so good at the toddler bit. I found that incredibly hard because they are constantly there and they don't understand*'; '*you think you're coping and you're just, you know you're not*'; '*I probably did it all wrong*'; '*I think the most difficult thing about being a mother when they were little was having to put someone else first and not being able to do what you wanted to do*'; '*you know this whole façade of being a great mum*'. But although there is now less ambiguity in how the women narrate their selves as (experienced) mothers, self-sanctioning in relation to 'choices' made over the years are still also apparent and explored further in the next section.

Selves, Motherhood and Paid Work 'Choices': Reflections and Some Regrets

The women's earlier worries about (not) coping with the care of their new baby were connected to their sense of self as an individual who was also now a mother, but who (mostly) did not instinctively or instantly feel like a mother. There is now a shared sense that mothering eventually *becomes* instinctive and *'intuitive'* based on *'common sense'* and *'learning as you go through things'*, but also a sense that you are either 'naturally maternal or not' (Miller, 2007). In ways that reproduce and reinforce ideals of the 'good' mother, being maternal is associated with being 'selfless' (*'on the whole you have to become selfless really don't you'*) and not being maternal is equated with being 'selfish' (*'She left her husband and left the three children, she didn't have the maternal want and need, do you know what I mean? She is very selfish'*). But how are maternal and non-maternal 'selves' now understood as lives have unfolded and included 18 years of continual ('intensive') mothering and paid work? How, or have, schemas of 'self-understanding' shifted (Lawler, 2000:57–8)? Such schemas are of course fluid and changing but will have elements that are recognisable and more enduring; the women's desire in the original study to 'get back to normal' was a wish to recapture elements of their pre-baby (recognisable and rehearsed) selves (see chapter 6 in Miller, 2005). The combining of paid work (in some form a financial necessity for all the women) and family caring is narrated by the women through a mixture of necessity (*'It was only the imperative of having to earn some money'*), regret (*'the fact that I was a mother and that I had failed my children because I hadn't been a stay-at-home mother'*), setting an example (*'I hoped they would take something from it'*, *'a role model'*) and self-fulfilment (*'I'm probably a better mother as a consequence of going back to work'*). But there are regrets too.

'Being there' continues to feature in how the women narrate their mothering and work-life experiences, especially in relation to how they manage 'not being there'. For example, Rebecca talks of a less intensive mothering relationship with her two younger children due to lack of time (*'I didn't do anything with either of them because I hadn't got the time*') even though she earlier described their full and active lives. In the following extract she reflects further on this:

Now I look back and as I said the days with [first baby] and being part time were the happiest days because I was still working [part-time] and really enjoying it and feeling fulfilled and really enjoying her even though she was quite demanding. But then I went back full time and then I had [two more babies] and I carried on working full time . . . we needed the money and isn't that stupid? Yeah your life revolves around money. So I just carried on working full time and I wished I'd have gone part time and spent time with them I think. (Rebecca)

But it is interesting that she concludes with a note of uncertainty – '*I think*'. Kathryn has always worked full time (with housing supplied as part of her job) except for two periods of maternity leave. Both Rebecca and Kathryn describe aspects of their mothering in strikingly similar ways as their second child is born. The pressures they felt in combining full-time paid work and caring for a new, second baby are described in the following extracts:

But I felt quite close to [baby] I think, but also was abdicating responsibility for her. (Rebecca)

I just felt that I neglected [baby] quite a bit and also I ran out of milk very early and I breast fed her for five weeks. Then you know I was just so tired and just, so that was sad really. So I think again this whole sort of bonding issue, I don't know whether I had that with [baby] because I knew I had to go back to work again, it was quite a difficult time and I actually got really, really bad postnatal depression. (Kathryn)

The terms 'abdicate' and 'neglect' are not usually associated so readily with self-narrations of mothering practises but here powerfully convey a sense of not doing mothering – or caring – in ways both women assume they should (have). Even so, it is unlikely such language would have been risked in the earlier interviews. It is also hard to imagine a father sharing similar sentiments about full-time working (see Chapter 3). At the time these second babies were born (now aged 12 and 16 years, respectively) maternity leave in the United Kingdom was shorter,[5] and there were not the same opportunities as today to share paid parental leave with the father (see Chapter 2).

---

[5] Under legislation introduced in 1999 in the United Kingdom, maternity leave consisted of a 'right to 18 weeks ordinary (paid) maternity leave and 29 weeks additional (unpaid) maternity leave'.

The women talk of regrets too, but these are also (sometimes) reconciled ('*I did what I had to do*') within their narratives, which also invoke cultural ideals of how family lives and child-rearing should be practiced. For example, Sheila reflects on her divorce and her sense that boys need a father figure:

Well obviously I would have liked to have been able to stay in a marriage, I would have liked to have been with my ex-husband, I would have liked to have been able to be in a partnership, because that I think would have helped especially as they are boys. Anything else? No because I did what I had to do. (Sheila)

In the following extract, Rebecca continues to reflect back on how her mothering and (teaching) career have unfolded and in so doing acknowledges the fluid and embedded aspects of cultural expectations ('*accepted thing wasn't it in our day*') and her own sense of challenging these ('*I'm the full-time working mum, aren't I amazing*'):

Yeah we both, when first baby was born, we just decided that it would be me [who stayed home]. I think I just, because that was the kind of like accepted thing wasn't it in our day that the mother would stay at home, so we didn't really think about another way of doing it and it was easier for me to go part time … but when the other two were born, because then I had the full-time job and husband was already part time, that was why we decided I stay full time. But actually I think I probably would have preferred to have been the full-time carer, although at the time I probably had this thing of well I'm the full-time working mum, aren't I amazing, but actually I'm not sure I was, I just felt I did everything badly. (Rebecca)

The costs of trying to challenge societal conventions at a time when fewer mothers worked full time is evident in Rebecca's reflections and the personal costs to her of feeling she did 'everything badly'. In contrast, Kathryn feels she has worked through any conflicting feelings from being a full-time working woman and mother ('*I like who I am now*') but only after a course of therapy:

I like who I am now. I'm at peace with my body, I'm at peace with the fact that I'm good at my job. No I'm at peace with myself and that is such a good feeling. It's probably since that course … it just allowed me to get rid of all the baggage, to get rid of the fact that I was a mother and that I had failed my children because I hadn't been a stay-at-home mother. (Kathryn)

Kathryn, who in earlier interviews has described herself at different times as 'not very maternal' and 'very maternal' ('*I am very maternal, I just go completely gooey about babies*'), then goes on to reflect on the ways in which her full-time job has shaped how she could mother and the type of (working) mother she became:

Well I would have liked to have had another child and not gone to work or I'd have liked not to have had to work. Maternity leave is now a year I think and [I had] only 6 months for each of the children, I took the maximum amount, they were so precious. And I felt very jealous of friends, a lot of the children's friends mothers didn't work and they were all meeting up at the school gates and meeting up for lunch and I really, I don't think I resented that but I just felt I was missing out a lot. (Kathryn)

Kathryn depicts a happy scene of other mothers who didn't (have to) work meeting up and having lunch and implies she has missed out in some way, especially as she did not feel she had a choice ('*liked not to have had to work*'). In many ways the picture that Kathryn paints again appeals to ideals of motherhood that, if the surface were scratched, were probably much less idyllic for the full-time mothers involved than simply meeting at school gates and for lunch. A sense of 'damned if you do and damned if you don't' pervades these extracts, as the confounding aspects of trying to do mothering in circumstances that at the time may have been less typical (full-time employment) lead to a sense of personal guilt and regret (Romito, 1997).

The continued and ubiquitous conflation of the terms 'woman' and 'mother' is well recognised, as is the notion that a women's sense of an individual self can become subsumed within the 24/7 responsibility of doing mothering. It is interesting then to consider across these later interviews – coinciding with the mothers' firstborn child also anticipating a new, less dependent phase in their lives – how the women narrate aspects of their selves that are not about mothering: this turns out to be a difficult endeavour. There are only glimpses of the women doing things that are just for themselves ('me time'). The following extract implies a hierarchy of needs in women's lives:

But I always put the kids first and I always try and, my last ounce of energy is for them and my work comes second and I come right down the bottom, so there is never any me time. (Rebecca)

When her three sons were all at primary school, Sheila returned to study for a professional qualification at her local college, which she describes in the following extract as having been 'brilliant':

Brilliant, I felt great but I had pushed myself and I also felt that I hoped they would take something from it.... I think initially I was Mum, but I don't, by the end of it, no, I was me. So I think I grew as a person and I mean that was, really for me to be totally away from children and away from, I mean I know I was in a college with a lot of teenagers, but mine were little, mine weren't teenagers then. So yeah no I definitely, I did change as a person. (Sheila)

But even though being at college enabled Sheila to 'grow as a person' and achieve a qualification that now allows her to work from home and support her sons, she has worries about her actions ('*I wasn't there for them*') on her children and their schooling:

but I don't know it's just, I do beat myself up because I think doing that when they were at that age.... I don't know whether I've had an impact on their schooling because I was... because I wasn't there for them, I don't know. (Sheila)

Gillian, who has worked part time as her two daughters have grown up, feels that her sense of her self as a woman and mother are now 'moulded together', but for Gillian this is 'happily' so:

But I'm happy to be Gillian the mother, so Gillian the mother isn't a derogatory thing for me, it's not something that I want to get away from. I don't feel the urge to leave my mothering to go back to being Gillian the woman if you see what I mean. They are all moulded together quite happily. (Gillian)

For Felicity becoming a single parent to her four children[6] has focused how she sees her responsibilities to her children, but going to work she says enables her to also 'have my own life':

Being a mother of four is a huge part of me, but it is not the only thing about me and that is one of the nice things about returning to work is that because after number four was born, I became a single parent, I didn't feel that I could then change the way, or have my needs met at that point. Their needs being met, them feeling safe, them going through and having as normal a

[6] It is interesting that when Felicity, now a biological mother to four children, was interviewed after the birth of her first baby, she said with feeling (after a long and difficult birth) that 'I wouldn't mind adopting a child or fostering a child, but I will never give birth to another one'.

pattern, was the priority. It was only the fact, I don't know if that would have changed, whether I would have returned to work until they'd all left, I don't know. It was only the imperative of having to earn some money that focused it. But I'm glad it did, I think I'm a better person for it. I think I'm probably a better mother as a consequence of going back to work, because I do have a focus which is something other than them and I think it's less pressured for them in a weird way, that I do have my own life. (Felicity)

All the women in their different ways help to illuminate the confounding aspects of being a mother: the weighing up, balancing and also feeling weighed down by responsibilities to children, husbands/partners (lack of partners/new partners) and paid work. Even as the women describe things that are more singularly about themselves, they simultaneously reflect on these in relation to their children and being a mother. For example going to work also makes Felicity a 'better mother', Rebecca ensures that her needs are the last to be met (the 'selfless' mother), Sheila is able to work flexibly from home in her own small business but worries that her own studies had an impact on her sons 'schooling' because she 'wasn't there' (even though they were physically at school). At the time of the interview, Kathryn (who is divorced and recently engaged) is also contemplating 'my time' with a new partner and a house move, but in the following extract acknowledges that this is not straightforward:

So, [eldest child] is going off to university, his sister will be you know going soon behind. I feel it's now my time with [new partner] to enjoy my life. I'm looking forward to my time because I feel that I've worked hard. I really feel that I've been a good mother and that I've done my best as far as I think I could have done in the circumstances for my children, you see I'm qualifying it again aren't I? And I think, I mean my parents still say you know you've got to make sure that [younger child] has finished school before you carry on and look after your own life and don't you think you're being a bit selfish and I think sod it, no, this is my life now.... [later] but you know should I be taking a back seat now, or should I just be there for the next 2 years and would I forgive myself if I wasn't here for the next 2 years and something went wrong and blah, blah, blah. So I've got all that going on at the moment. (Kathryn)

Interestingly, Kathryn notes her own self-surveillance ('*I'm qualifying it again aren't I?*'), but also her parents response to her desire for 'me time': that she is being 'a bit selfish'. Even though she wants to reject such ideas, it is also clear that she feels that not being there (even though the child's father would be), for her younger (16-year-old) child could be risky (*'and something went wrong'*).

Is it possible then to escape these ways of storying and so narrating motherhood (by mothers themselves and others)? Are other story lines possible, for example the successful worker, when discourses in relation to 'good' mothering are so embedded, pervasive and narrowly defined?

Looking Back and Forward: Preparing for Hands-Off Mothering

As noted earlier the passage of time enables the women to reflect back and talk more candidly (*'and I mean to be completely honest'*)[7] and poignantly about their mothering experiences as they also anticipate a time when they will not mother so intensely. Lillian confides that she has not been a *'mumsie'* mum, but has *'done alright'*:

I'm not a mumsie, mumsie you know like making cakes and things like that. Maybe I'd quite like to have been a bit more like that, but I think we've done fun things as well. So no, I think I'm quite alright with you know.... But that's my point of view, 'I've done great'... but it's a minefield really I think ... but I've done alright. (Lillian)

It is interesting that Lillian uses the term 'minefield' to convey the terrain of motherhood. Other women talk of the boring aspects of mothering (*'I just couldn't be a full-time mother, I just wouldn't have had the patience'*) and look forward to days that are less occupied with the relentlessness of 'being there' and being responsible. There are conflicted reflections on paid work as the mothers try to imagine not having had to work, as in the following extract from Sheila and the poignant reflections from Rebecca:

I mean it would have been great if I'd had loads and loads of money and I didn't have to work, I would have been able to give them more, but that is really all... I wouldn't have worked.... I love my work and I don't know whether, I can't say if money was no object would I still have worked, I don't know, but I think...I would have liked the idea of not having to work so that I can just be here and give everything that they need. (Sheila)

---

[7] See Chapter 7 for discussion of how narratives are constructed and re-edited and thoughts on how selves are presented in areas so morally inflected.

You kind of think oh they need you when they are little, which they do, but I think they need me now, you know like [daughter] really needs me now because she's struggling with friendships. . . . I'm always playing catch up with her because I feel like I should have been there when she was little, so I'm damn well going to be here now for her. . . . My son, the same, the same, I should have been there a lot more with him. (Rebecca)

Rebecca's reflections are heartfelt and will be recognised by many working mothers, as they feel compromised and guilty about actions they have taken. But these actions and apparent 'choices' are always contextual and not made in isolation. In contrast, and again reflecting the contingent dimensions of caring, some of the fathers in the earlier chapter were more likely to feel that they were letting down colleagues in the workplace rather than their family at home (see Chapter 6; Miller, 2017b). But for Felicity, who has spent several of the past years parenting four children, there are no such recriminations:

I have always told them that when they get to 18 and they go to university or go wherever they will go, but they won't come back. . . . By then it will have been something like 24 years (of parenting) and that is enough. I've always helped them or expected them to stand on their two feet, they've never had, the fact that they've come from separated parents, as an excuse for anything. I expect them to get on and make a success of their life.

Felicity later conveys a sense of the relentless responsibility she has felt as she has parented largely alone:

I want some life then (after they leave). It's not that I haven't had a life, it's just that it's been emotionally, as I said earlier, emotionally and physically and financially and spiritually and every other 'lly' that you can imagine, hugely demanding and I just want it to stop. I just want to be able to stand still. (Felicity)

Even though young adulthood may be culturally signalled on reaching 18 years of age, research shows that young people in the United Kingdom are continuing to stay in the family home beyond this age (Office for National Statistics, 2016). However, there was a strong sense through the interviews that their children finishing school and turning 18 marked a shift in their mothering and immediate caring responsibilities, even if not in the decisive way envisaged by Felicity. Their 'hard work' would be put to the test as these young adults were 'launched' on the world or encouraged to make plans for their adult futures. But of course this does not mark the end of maternal and parental caring but rather begins to indicate generational shifts and slowly reconfigured, reciprocal caring responsibilities. As a 2-hour interview with Sheila (mother to three boys) drew to a close, I asked my final question:

TINA: Okay, so my final question, what does the word 'future' mean to you now?
SHEILA: [Laughs] Getting rid of them!

Conclusions

In the original Transition to Motherhood Study and in this later exploration of women's experiences of mothering and motherhood, the intention has been to enable maternal voices and accounts of caring to be heard on their own terms (Ruddick, 1989). But the unfolding and reflexive narratives of mothering that emerge show how keenly the moral imperative to be seen to be a good mother is felt so as to seem (almost) inescapable for women. The women have successfully raised families, managed paid work and taken on the mental work of orchestrating (and gatekeeping?) family caring, but there remains a sense of guilt and regret as they are caught among powerful maternal discourses, managing everyday demands and their own selves and needs. They have cared for their children as ideals of parenthood and 'cultivation' practices have become intensified, and they, like many parents, have responded to changed 'constructions of children's needs and mothers responsibilities' (Wall, 2013:163). This has involved them in helping their children achieve in school and outside school as an array of enrichment activities are undertaken and children's individual 'success' – and so parental behaviours by implication – is increasingly measured. They also perceive the world that their young adult children have to negotiate as more pressurised and riskier than in previous times – risks they have to some extent helped their children navigate to this point. But there is a sense too that they have done their best and that their children are ready for this next phase of their lives. Letting go after many years of agentic practices and thinking configured in relation to prioritising the needs of others is both dreaded and, for some, eagerly anticipated.

5 | *Parenting Separately?*

Post-Separation Experiences

There is never a good time, well from what I can see there is never a good time, to separate or get divorced.

(Gillian, separated, Motherhood study)

So we just, for lots of reasons really we stopped doing things together and making an effort together and yeah I started seeing somebody else.

(Joe, separated, Fatherhood study)

So it was just me with four young children and everywhere we went, everything we tried to do, there would always be happy or seemingly happy mummy and daddies everywhere, doing things together ... so that was a very, very hard time.

(Felicity, divorced, Motherhood study)

As noted in earlier chapters, the studies in this book originated in research undertaken as first births were (mostly) planned and happily anticipated. The advent of a baby was associated with making a family and a sense of familial permanence (*'I'm looking forward to you know a proper little family'*). But things don't always work out as expected, and in the intervening years some of the couples are no longer together. Statistics on rates of divorce in England and Wales show that in 2013 42% of marriages ended in divorce[1] and that almost half of these involve children aged 16 years and under (Office for National Statistics, 2015). Divorce or separation of course do not mean that mothering or fathering ends but rather that the daily and weekly logistics of parenting usually have to be negotiated and managed in different ways and across different domestic settings (Gatrell et al, 2015). Other aspects of parental relationships and the configuration of caring

---

[1] Separation in cohabiting couples is not captured in national statistics. All participants in this chapter had been married.

responsibilities are redefined as well (Philip, 2014; Ribbens McCarthy et al, 2003). Across the Motherhood and Fatherhood studies, more than a third (6 of 17) of the women in Motherhood study were known to be divorced or separated by the time their eldest child reached 16 years of age; in the Fatherhood study, 3 of the 17 fathers were known to have separated or divorced by the time their firstborn child reached 6 years of age.[2] Given these changes, this chapter explores understandings of parenthood, responsibilities and parenting practises and relationships across households, discernible in the experiences of mothers and fathers who no longer live together. Through the rich empirical data, questions about caring, residency, perceptions of responsibilities and the daily practices of negotiating parenting and relationships are explored as original family formations have changed. This focus includes examining the ways in which practises of parenting after separation or divorce coincide with prescriptive ideals of involvement and intensified parenthood, constructions of moral identities and 'being there'.

Looking at experiences of the mothers and fathers who are now living separately from the father/mother of their children is not to imply this is in any way less of a 'family', but rather offers an opportunity to explore from a different perspective how caring dynamics and mothering and fathering responsibilities are claimed/(re)constructed and practised. Nevertheless, representing experiences of separation and divorce risks being seen to be partial and uneven in their retelling, but my aim has been to be sensitive in using data to provide insights into this often conflictual area of familial care. The notion of 'being there' in both a physically present and emotionally attuned and hands-on way has been an enduring thread running across the data. It has been cited by the fathers as evidence of their involvement from the first antenatal interview and is mostly assumed and implicit in the narratives of the mothers (where else would they be?). Being there has crystallised as a motif in the longitudinal data denoting the 'mental work' and '24/7 thinking responsibility' taken on (mostly) by the mothers and physical presence and tasks and activities undertaken by the fathers, through which their paternal subjectivity and fathering involvement could be

---

[2] These figures could be higher because not all the original participants could be contacted. See Chapter 1.

made visible. But what happens to 'being there'[3] and its moral associations with 'good' and intensified parenting when separation changes the ways in which households are organised and parenting becomes practised? What does 'not being there' or 'being there differently' look like, and how is it narrated? As Sevenhuijsen has observed, 'women and men land up in all kinds of forms of mutual dependence when they have children together and want to care for these children in a relational context, whatever form that may take' (Sevenhuijsen, 2003:109). So how are caring relationships for children and 'mutual dependence' in changed relational contexts managed (including maternal and paternal claims, 'gatekeeping' and 'letting go') across households after separation and divorce?

Over many years, research has emphasised the importance of trying to maintain good, supportive relationships between parents, and parents and their children, in separated families. The 'material and emotional costs of this to children, fathers, mothers and governments' of not doing so is also evident (Philip and O'Brien, 2012; Smart and Neale, 1999). However, managing supportive relationships will be dependent on numerous factors, including length of separation/divorce and the circumstances in which it arose (*'ex is still very angry, he blames me for the divorce', 'he had an affair with somebody else and I threw him out', 'Well 18 months and £60,000 later it is finally all over', 'we weren't happy and I did a terrible thing and started seeing someone else', 'and it hasn't been a very nice divorce'*). This chapter draws on the experiences of six of the participants from the two original studies who now live in post-separation or divorced households: Sheila, Kathryn, Gillian and Felicity from the Motherhood study and Joe and James from the Fatherhood study. These six (unrelated) parents have a total of 14 children between them, aged from 3 to 18 years, at the time of these interviews. Both Sheila and Felicity have been separated (and divorced) for approximately 10 years, but the advent of separation is a much more recent occurrence in the lives of the others, including for

---

[3] The term 'being there' is ubiquitously present and described in all types of fatherhood and motherhood research. For example, when fatherhood is anticipated, it is a way for men to describe their intentions of closeness and ongoing connection to their child. But it is a term used much more by fathers because the normative assumptions that mothers (of course) will always be there does not need to be voiced.

Joe, whose emotionally raw interview is recorded only 3 months after he left his wife and two young daughters (*'every time I'm dropping them off or leaving, so every time it happens, my older daughter just holds onto my leg and doesn't want to let go . . . so yeah its really, really hard'*). But problems between some couples are retrospectively identified as having been ongoing for years before separation occurs (*'but we went through a really rocky time, ending up separating, then went to Relate'*, *'the cracks started showing in the relationship between me and my ex'*, *'I don't think he's been happy for a long time with himself and then I don't think he was happy with me either'*).[4] So for some, the navigation and management of separation and parenting has become an everyday practice, while for others, patterns of (new ways of) caring (or feeling excluded from caring) are only just being established, fought over or muddled through. Post-separation arrangements also shift as older children are able to express their own preferences (*'she's ever so careful about being fair'*), jobs and geographical locations change and new partners and (family) relationships are constituted (*'My Mum said, "how will you feel about someone else bringing up your children?"'*).

Paramount across the data is a clear sense that children should not be disadvantaged because their parents have separated (*'and the fact that we don't live together is not ideal, but they don't miss out'*, *'we've always put the children first'*, *'their needs being met was the priority'*, *'the girls are always going to be the priority'*). Given the moral context in which parenting is undertaken, it would be hard to imagine the parents positioning their intentions in any other way, even though acts described in terms of 'selfishness' rather than as 'selfless' may have provoked the separation (*'it's awful what I did'*). In the sections that follow, the practical aspects of navigating co-parenting relationships after separation are described. This is done from the perspectives of the mothers and fathers and their reflections on capacities of selves and ex-partners to undertake caring. Across different family formations from those originally established, changed parental trajectories,

---

[4] Talking about who left who in separation and divorce cases of course over-simplifies the action and its history (as will be clear in the data presented in this chapter), but for purposes of positioning the accounts of the participants, it is worth noting that three of the participants (Kathryn, Joe and Sheila) instigated the separation/divorce and three participants describe being the ones who were left (Gillian, James and Felicity).

practises, hopes and moral intentions – as well as assumptions – about maternal and paternal caring, are explored.

Putting the Children First: 'Being There' and 'Not Being There'

In their narrations of navigating co-parenting after relationship breakdown and separation, most parents spoke of wanting to protect their children from any unsettling and disruptive effects of changed homes and parenting contexts. Prioritising their children's needs over their own, which for some are put on hold (*'I vowed when our marriage fell apart that I would put their needs first until they left home'*) are held up as paramount. No one wants his or her children to suffer (*'having as normal a pattern, was the priority'*). Subsequent co-parenting arrangements are arrived at informally (*'it was just something we arranged. I didn't particularly want to go down the CSA route, get divorced, anything, I just thought, I just wanted to go'*) as well as through expensive legal process (*'so we went through quite a long legal process on every front'*). Parenting arrangements for the participants now involve sharing care equally across households (Kathryn and Gillian), or across weekends, some weekdays and school holidays (*'so I only see her 103 days a year, which is pathetic'*, James). In all but one case (where housing was tied to a husband's job), the mothers have remained in the family home, and the fathers have moved out. In part this reflects the 'moral criteria' that differently mark out societal expectations of mothers and fathers 'in relation to the level or nature of commitment to both children and the co-parental relationship' they may be expected to have (Philip, 2013). Across the narratives, these differently morally inflected assumptions are discernible, both in relation to expectations about fathers in the narratives of Joe and James (*'Well it's not fathering anymore is it?'*, James), as well as in the accounts given of their ex-husband's or partner's in the mothers' post-separation narratives.[5] New caring arrangements can make visible fathering practises that may have been regarded as optional or invisible previously (*'he's done*

---

[5] It is recognised that narratives can only be partial accounts of a shared 'reality' and that as Catherine Kohler-Riessman (1990) has shown in her work on divorce, competing accounts of the same event are almost inevitable. It is acknowledged then that the narratives included in this chapter provide firsthand and secondhand experiences and perspectives on relationship breakdown, separation and divorce.

an awful lot more parenting since we've been apart', Gillian) as well as reinforce gendered moral expectations, for example in relation to paid work and assumptions about primary residence and that mothers would be 'selfish' if they ever thought of putting their own happiness above that of their children (as discussed later in this chapter).

Continuing to 'be there' as a significant presence in his young daughters lives (now aged 6 and 3 years) is a priority for Joe, who only 3 months post-separation (and leaving the family home) is still in the very early stages of working out separation and caring arrangements. In an interview conducted in an earlier phase of the Fatherhood study when his firstborn daughter was a year old, Joe had described his close involvement with her and his desire to be the one to stay home to look after her full time (*'I would love to really have the roles reversed'*), but this was not vigorously pursued: *'I sort of said I'd like to and she was sort of like "no I'd like to", so it was never really a massive discussion'* (Miller, 2010:76). Whatever the accuracy of this sentiment, Joe, of the fathers in the original Fatherhood study, had been involved in his children's lives in ways more visible and measurable than some and more so than earlier generations of fathers (*'no as I say I can never remember my dad spending any sort of good parent/child time with me and my brother'*). Following the separation, Joe is determined to maintain his close relationship with his two daughters and has just managed to find accommodation where he can have them to stay:

and last weekend was the first time that they had stayed with me. So for the last 3 months, every weekend I've been taking them to my mum or dad's and staying there and last weekend was the first time they stayed in the flat where I am. So I'm just trying to keep everything routine based. But yes some things are a lot harder I guess. So even things like when the girls are asleep, even though they are asleep there, it's just nice them being asleep in the same house [as me] if that makes sense and I just fully never really.... Yeah, not thought. (Joe)

Being there for his daughters involves not only having a suitable physical space, but maintaining their routine as well.[6] Aspects of caring once taken for granted – his daughters being asleep – assumes new significance as their presence in his flat underscores his connectedness to his daughters and relationship as a dad. For Joe it also signals the potential

---

[6] All the fathers spoke about routines and the importance of having a routine in the earlier fatherhood book (Miller, 2010) and here in Chapter 3.

for there to be a new way of being in their lives, which is not determined by his everyday physical presence in the original family home. But it is still very early days in this unravelling parental relationship and Joe goes on to reinforce his intention to keep '*everything routine based*':

We have got everything routine based ... so I still do Monday and Wednesday before school, take them to school, collect one on Monday. I go back to the home on a Monday and Wednesday after work and [ex-wife] is not there and now on a Saturday I collect the girls at say four and drop them off at four on a Sunday afternoon. What is really hard is every time I'm dropping them off or leaving, so every time it happens, my elder daughter just holds onto my leg and doesn't want to let go and so yeah. . . . Really, really hard yeah. So it's really, really hard. I know, I've got a vision in my mind of where I want to get to, but yeah it's not going to be for a long time. So I'd like to get to a point where [ex-wife] is willing to share parenting, so the girls would stay with me for 3 days and with her for 4. If I could I'd want to have them the whole time but I would never do. . . . No it's not [an option]. Yeah, so. (Joe)

In contrast to Joe, James is further along a co-parenting trajectory after what he describes as a 'toxic' legal battle costing £60,000 following his wife's affair, his subsequent breakdown ('*I almost died*') and time off work. He is now '*living in a two-bedroomed flat in Slough*' with debts he says will take years to pay off ('*I'm probably exaggerating to say that I was married for 10 years and it will take 10 years to recover, but it was almost that scale*'). James is a father of one daughter whom he has custody of for 103 days a year. In the following extract, I've asked him to describe a typical weekend with his daughter:

Yeah, yeah I'd pick her up from school on Friday and so I always get off early and pick her up. So, it's changed slightly ... well it varies, it's difficult to say typical, because we always end up doing something different. But, so there isn't a typical day'.

TINA: Alright, well just a day, a Saturday.
JAMES: And some of them won't fall into the good parenting bucket I feel!
TINA: I want every type of experience.
JAMES: She is great. She is, so yeah we usually, so yeah we come over on a Friday and stop for a bite to eat on the way back or sometimes we'll go down to a club in Slough which is very good. It's one of these health and fitness clubs with a nice bar and food, tennis courts and swimming pools. So we get in a swim, a bite to eat, there are a few friends down there and some of the funniest days in the summer were down there.

> You know we were just, you know three or four other guys round this corner bar and then she's sat up and she's the centre of attention, they're all just.... It's just fun they are so good with her, it's fantastic. (James)

In earlier interviews before the separation, which has occurred 2 years earlier, James had also described his fathering involvement as mostly weekend based (due to long weekday working hours) when he would spend time out and about with his daughter, as this extract from an earlier interview when his daughter was 2 years old shows: '*I get up and take her to the coffee shop.... Yeah it's brilliant. I buy her a magazine a* Peppa Pig *magazine, she reads it through, chattering and looking at all the pictures and I'm reading the newspaper*'. So 'being there' described in this extract is, in practical terms, not so dissimilar to his earlier fathering experiences. But not being a presence in the home in which his daughter mostly lives, not knowing about aspects of her daily life that otherwise would possibly not even register – '*I don't know what her bedroom colour is*' – are now keenly felt by James. His partial (weekends and holidays amounting to 103 days a year) involvement have, for James, changed the dynamics of his relationship with his daughter and he no longer feels like a father:

> I mean I don't feel like a father now, I mean that's the reality of it... it's not fathering is it, it's you know, friend, I mean it's, she comes over and we have a good time and might do a bit of homework and you're engaged for that moment. You are not really there when she wakes up in the morning, you know, it's not the same it's just not, not, not parenting at all. It's not even called that is it, it's access isn't it, so it's not.... So the whole thing is rather, it leaves, yeah I'm really uncomfortable about the whole subject to be honest with you, I feel quite strongly about it now. (James)

In this powerful and candid extract, James redefines his now nonresident fathering relationship in terms of being a 'friend', where 'access' replaces being there and otherwise taken-for-granted aspects of parenting relationships (being there '*when she wakes up in the morning*'). James's narrative is both heartfelt and challenging because he has had to come to terms with a new relationship with his daughter that is defined for him by 'access' measures. He feels powerless and struggles to narrate a sense of a self as a father, finding his paternal identity difficult to hold on to in these circumstances, which are not of his choosing. For James, 'obstacles to maintaining fathering' are currently felt to be restrictive and overwhelming and he has (temporarily) ceded power

(Philip, 2014:230). But in the longer run he has (some) hopes of re-establishing his *fathering* relationship with his daughter on his own terms (Philip, 2014:230; see also Philip and O'Brien, 2012).

That's what everyone says you play the long game on these things. So eventually she's going to grow up and discover what's right and wrong in life and make decisions I think when she's.... So I'm, you know the way I'm looking at it, you know I've 40 years with her from the age of 18 onwards ... and this is just a small, little blip in the relationship. So you've got to be pragmatic, but it's difficult though. It's difficult to see that perspective though. (James)

As noted earlier, co-parenting arrangements after separation and divorce will be negotiated (or feel not to have been), managed and lived in contexts riven through with hurt, anger, disappointment, guilt, love, freedom and obligation and practically managed via texts, e-mails, messaging and solicitors (*'it is just over text or over e-mail'*, *'the only communication has been through solicitors'*). Even though Joe and James are now fathering (or feeling they are being prevented from doing so) in different circumstances, the importance of (the right) physical space is, in different ways, features of their perceived ability and inability to be present in their children's lives. So although it is important to note the ways in which 'the gendering of moral space' can significantly affect mothers and fathers in co-parental relationships, this extends to physical space too, including how court decisions and post-separation arrangements are determined, a finding reported in other research (Philip, 2014:231). A further aspect of how perceptions of moral and gendered caring orientations and claims can shape arrangements post-separation and divorce relates to gender equality. For example, Doucet and Lee (2014) have noted the contradictions that can arise in this complex and contested arena when feminists reframe their claims for gender equality in the light of potential post-divorce parenting arrangements, arguing not for equality but instead for these arrangements to recognise the 'gender differences in parenting' and are often reflected in post-divorce settlements (Doucet and Lee, 2014:358).

In the co-parenting arrangements that are more established and presented as working for the participants, parents geographical proximity (living within a few miles of each other) in physical spaces that can accommodate their children comfortably (*'yes he was so lucky to get that house just up the road, really lucky'*) enables continued parental (fathering) involvement. For Kathryn, Sheila and Gillian, their ex-husbands or partners all live in close proximity to either the original/new family home, and caring for the children across these households is shared, although not usually equally. Sheila left her husband, moving[7] with her then young sons (twins aged 6 years and a 3-year-old) to a house in the same town 12 years earlier. Gillian (*'the eldest was 17, yes but there is never the right time is there?'*) and Kathryn (*'At 13 and 15 years, the children have coped amazingly well'*) have separated more recently. Over many years, research has shown that maternal bodies have been conflated with 'being there' and having (essentialist) capacities to care in ways not so associated with paternal identities (Bobel, 2002; Chodorow, 1999; Hays, 1996; O'Reilly, 2008, 2016; Raith et al, 2015; Rothman, 1989; Ruddick, 1989). These assumptions have historically defined custody and care arrangements in favour of mothers (Collier and Sheldon, 2008). However, both Gillian (*'I mean the plan actually was that they would live with me and that they would visit him'*) and Kathryn and their ex-husbands have ended up in 'equally' shared co-parenting arrangements, which are detailed later in this chapter. Consideration of these illuminates how practices of 'gatekeeping', 'being there differently' and 'letting go' all challenge, and can reinforce, essentialist and gendered assumptions in relation to moral orientations and capacities to care.

Finding accommodation nearby has enabled Gillian's ex-husband to also share care for his two teenage daughters as Gillian describes:

So it's variable, she [16-year-old younger daughter] is ever so careful about being fair, they both are [older daughter is 18 years old]. You know they would have three or four nights a week here and then the next week it would be three or four nights a week with their dad, I mean the plan actually was that they would live with me and that they would visit him. But he managed to find this place just up the road, so that meant he, and he's got three bedrooms up there, so it meant that they had their own rooms up there and he could actually look after them. (Gillian)

But letting go and the loss of aspects of caring has been difficult for Gillian:

Awful to start with, yes, yes because I was just so used to it, it was just so weird not having them. . . . that is what to him, I said it's just what I do as a parent, it's, it is. So I found that really hard and I think because they're of an

---

[7] Sheila left the original family home as it was tied to her ex-husband's job.

age where they were quite happy to have gaps in the day where nobody quite knew where they were, then I didn't like that at all because that's not what we'd had in the past. I'd always, I'd always known exactly where they were, pretty well, as much as you can with a mobile phone.... But other than that I was always pretty aware as to which direction they were going after school and were they coming straight home or that sort of thing and which friends were they out with. So to lose that was quite a shock actually and not one that I had considered. So to have days and nights where actually you didn't know where they were, but you just knew that he knew where they were, that was tricky. But I'm much more used to that now because now we are 18 months down the line and they've survived. (Gillian)

Although Gillian has worked part time, she has still been caught up in the daily minutiae of her children's lives, in ways their father has not. Many would see knowing the whereabouts of your (young) children as a basic parental responsibility assumed of the primary carer, and so most often the mother. To have to let go of ('lose') that (singular) responsibility (even though her children are now older) and begin to share it has involved significant adjustment on Gillian's part and a gradual acceptance of her ex-husband's abilities (*'they've survived'*). But the shifting of their children between homes and navigating of old responsibilities in new ways, has created opportunities in which fathering is now seen to be practised in more expansive and involved ways. Gillian reflects on responsibilities shifting in the following extract:

So he has to do all that now, so he has to take them to school, make sure they've done homework, if they're doing sports, seeing friends.... I know all these things that are new to him, all those thing that he didn't have to do beforehand. It's not that he didn't do anything beforehand because he did, it's just **he didn't have to** do any of them, whereas now he does. He is definitely more involved. **He has to take responsibility now**, if they are staying with him overnight then he has that responsibility of where are they, should they be there, does somebody know where they are, what time are they coming back, are they coming here, are they being picked up, is he picking them up. (Gillian, emphasis added)

Interestingly, in this extract Gillian describes much of the largely invisible and taken-for-granted 'mental work' and 'being there' that mothers often undertake (and through practise become competent at) in heterosexual couple relationships, although not because men can't do them (*'it's just he didn't have to do any of them'*). As she sees her ex-husband doing '*an awful lot more parenting since we've been apart than he ever did when we were together*', Gillian is now reflective and questions, in retrospect, her 'gatekeeping' of particular responsibilities: '*I think maybe I've taken too much responsibility, maybe I could have shared the responsibility more*' (see Chapter 4). But there is a sense too of potential paternal gatekeeping here – '*you just knew he knew where they were*' – or at least different styles of caring and sharing of information. Again implicit assumptions about maternal and paternal responsibilities and expected types of engagement are illuminated in these extracts. In different (asserting, challenging and rejecting) ways these assumptions and responsibilities have run through the participant's narratives from the earliest antenatal interviews as the birth of their first children was anticipated.

After a divorce Kathryn feels torn between letting go and staying in the co-parenting arrangement she and her ex-husband have established. For the first year after their divorce, Kathryn and her ex moved in and out of the family home[8] on alternate weeks, so that any disruption to their children's lives (then aged 13 and 15) was minimised ('*we just felt that that would be the easiest and the kindest thing for them*'). Now the co-parenting arrangement involves alternate weeks in the father's new home (nearby) and the original family home, as Kathryn explains:

We now alternate week on, week off, he has them for one week and I have them for one week. . . . But it does mean that a lot of things get, fall down the middle and he, we had a big argument this week about something that he said he would do and that he didn't do . . . so I had to pick up the pieces . . . [Later] I think I'm much more laid back about things. **He's much more on their backs the whole time,** and I think it's probably because I'm on the pulse the whole time, so I know what's going on, so I can sort of gently steer them and he's not, he is just not. (Kathryn, emphasis added)

What is interesting here is how the practicalities of living between homes has the potential for things to '*fall down the middle*', with gaps or lapses that previously may not have occurred (or occurred but not have been seen as a problem) where someone had a primary (overarching), rather than shared-across-households, responsibility. But this resonates with Gillian's sense of 'letting go' of aspects of long and closely

---

[8] The family home was tied to Kathryn's full-time job.

held (mothering) responsibilities following separation. It can be hard to let go, especially if aspects of parenting are not accomplished by a father in the (exact) ways the mother thinks they should be (*'something that he said he would do and that he didn't do...so I had to pick up the pieces'*) (see Chapter 6). This also links with Sheila's assertion that her husband is too strict with their boys (see later). Giving up years of primary responsibility for the mental work of caring can be a difficult and painful process. But Kathryn's fear that her ex-husband is not as reliable (responsible?) a parent as she is (*'but this whole thing with me being on the pulse and him not being on the pulse'*) has made her think carefully about when she can marry her new partner (fiancé) and move away without the children (see Chapter 4). This raises questions again about what gets privileged in caring relationships and who is perceived as primarily responsible for their practise and continuity and when these intensive practices of being there can cease. For example, Kathryn's parents express recognisably normative ideas about the duration of intensive mothering responsibilities in the following extract:

I mean my parents still say you know you've got to make sure that [younger child, aged 16 years] has finished school before you carry on and look after your own life and don't you think you're being a bit selfish and I think sod it, no, this is my life now.... [Later] but you know should I be taking a back seat now, or should I just be there for the next 2 years and would I forgive myself if I wasn't here for the next 2 years and something went wrong and blah, blah, blah. So I've got all that going on at the moment. (Kathryn)

The question of when intensive parenting responsibilities are perceived to diminish ('able to take a back seat') is dependent on numerous factors, and it is hoped that family relationships more generally will endure. In many cultures and in the United Kingdom, adulthood is signalled by an 18th birthday, which coincides with other rites of passage, such as leaving school and being able to vote and marry without parental permission; it has been previously associated with leaving the parental home, although this is now much delayed in the United Kingdom (ONS, 2014). Kathryn's dilemma is that she feels pressure to put her younger child's needs above her own (regardless that there is a co-parenting father around to take on more responsibility) until school is finished and their youngest child reaches 18. It is interesting to pause and reflect here – and in other parts of this chapter– on how particular intentions or behaviours would be interpreted if they were undertaken by a father rather than a mother and vice versa – for example, if Kathryn and her ex were reversed in the preceding scenario. How (differently) do these actions look or feel then, and what responses would they garner?

Sheila is the mother of three boys and has been divorced for 12 years. Her ex-husband lives in the same town, and they now have an 'amicable' relationship (*'we are more friends now'*) as the following extract conveys:

He has always, always seen the boys every other weekend, never stopped. It was just something we arranged. I didn't particularly want to go down the CSA route, get divorced, anything, I just thought, I just wanted to go. I mean I was always very, I mean my neighbours are just going through a split and I mean as I said to them, just keep it simple, if they (the children) ask you questions, just answer it, but don't go into detail and that's what I did with my boys. . . . But I mean he's always round here anyway. Yeah, he's decorated most of this house, he's done all the bedrooms and things. (Sheila)

Interestingly, in the very first antenatal interviews in the Fatherhood study (2010), an intention of being there and a form of anticipated paternal caring was demonstrated (in gendered ways) through the men's DIY (do it yourself) activities. So it is noteworthy that Sheila's ex-husband has continued to undertake such practical activities of caring for his children. He is also the parental figure more associated with discipline (*'they do respect their father more than they respect me in the discipline side of things'*), but this is felt to go too far at times, which Sheila explains is due to his not being there 24/7 (*'because obviously he's not lived with them 24/7 and grown up with them'*). The co-parenting arrangements have shifted little through the 12 years, Sheila thinks in part because neither she nor her ex have re-partnered or married (*'I did see a couple of fellas'*). Since their divorce the boys have spent occasional periods staying with their dad, who is described as *'very domesticated'* and demonstrably capable of looking after his sons, as Sheila explains in the following exchange:

SHEILA: Their Dad, well I mean he is very domesticated, he is really good at all sorts of things like that. You know when he had the two of them [twin sons] on his own for those three months [GCSE exam period], he loved it, he absolutely loved it.

TINA: Was it your idea, or was it his [for two sons to move in with their dad during the exam period]?

SHEILA: I think it was more mine and he was more than happy to do it, but I couldn't wait to get them home and I wanted them home here before they went to their School Prom because I wanted them to go from here, because they're mine! [Laughs.] So they did literally move back in the day before they finished their last exam I think they came home.

TINA: So would, yeah would that arrangement ever have been extended, would either of them say well I want to live with Dad?

SHEILA: 'Oh no, no, no. No they wanted to come home. [Laughs.] No they didn't want to be with Dad . . . they love their dad, but they don't get on with their dad. It's a funny relationship they have.

The theme of residency and physical presence (as much more than having 'access', see James's story earlier in the chapter) and as a particular taken-for-granted way of 'being there' is further illuminated in these extracts. For Sheila it was important that her sons should leave for their school Prom (an event marking the end of secondary school) from her home – not for convenience but as Sheila says, *'because they're mine!'* It becomes clear that Sheila has organized aspects of the post-divorce parenting including residency and access in ways that don't appear to be available to her ex-husband. She acknowledges too that because 'he's not lived with them', he isn't (can't be) attuned to them in the ways she has become. Nevertheless he continues to (be allowed to?) have a traditional paternal presence in terms of discipline (*'and it's good that I have that deterrent'*) and house maintenance and Sheila affirms how he has *'loved his boys'*.

In much more acrimonious circumstances, Felicity now a mother of four children (aged between 12 and 18 years) is also sensitive to the contact her ex-husband has with the children, but she says to avoid their distress rather than determine the amount or form of that contact (*'I can't rely on anything'*). In similar ways to Sheila, and using almost identical language, in the following extract Felicity claims *her* children – *'they are my children'*:

So in terms of his intervention now, he sees the children alternate weekends, but it's got a lot less as they've become teenagers. . . . So they do see him regularly, they don't see him often and he doesn't have them, he has stopped now having them in any school holiday. So the pressure for me is 24/7 365 and sometimes he just doesn't turn up and he doesn't tell me when he's not going to turn up. So it's, I have to have this very fluid attitude to when they do or don't see him and I can't rely on anything, I can't plan anything. But that is okay, they are my children, I chose to have four children. (Felicity)

Interestingly Felicity uses the language of 'intervention' rather than access or visits or caring when describing her ex-husband's arrangements to see their children. The powerful term 'vowed' is also used to convey a sense of her absolute commitment to her children ('*I am the only person they can rely on*'), but this intensive commitment and associated (primary) responsibility is seen to have an end point too, when they reach 18 and leave home (see Chapter 4).

Felicity's sense of being the only reliable parent in her children's lives has made the work of parenting solitary and hard ('*It was the weekends that were the killer because then there was just me*'). But looking back over the years since the divorce ('*I never, ever thought I'd be a single parent. It never crossed my mind, never worried, never thought what I would do*'), Felicity feels '*positive in a weird way*' about the fact her children have had 'consistency' in their lives because only she has navigated their daily lives and so any 'boundaries' are hers alone ('*no good cop, bad cop, in terms of two different boundaries*'). Felicity is the only person to describe herself as a 'single parent', but also the only one whose ex-partner has remarried. Interestingly, in contrast to James who feels he has been forced out of fathering after his divorce and (reluctantly) now sees himself as a 'friend' rather than father to his daughter, Felicity is clear about her maternal identity and relationship with her children forged as the resident ('being there') and primary ('single') parent,

Yes and it's very, yes I am their mother, I am absolutely their mother, I am not their friend. There is that very distinct boundary, but we have a fantastic relationship with each of them and together that I don't think we would have had, had there been another adult there. (Felicity)

Having a sense of being the sole parent leaves Felicity feeling indispensable and so also fearful ('*even when they're with their father, I'm still on edge that something is going to go wrong*') both for the present, near future when her children have all reached 18 years of age and her own future when she can finally do '*all the things that I've put on hold*'. But her children each reaching their 18th birthday is set as a significant milestone (see Chapter 4) in how her mothering/parenting responsibilities are envisaged:

I have the fear that I have to be okay, I can't be ill, I can't break my leg, nothing can happen to me at the moment. So I try not to think of that bit of the future if you see what I mean because I have to cope, I have to be strong, I have to keep going until they all reach 18. (Felicity)

It is interesting that Kathryn, or more accurately her parents (see earlier), also assume that parental (especially mothering?) responsibilities should also be prioritised until a child reaches 18 years and early adulthood. James hopes that when his young daughter reaches early adulthood, she will be able to make her own decisions about him as her father (and by implication see that her mother was *'wrong'* to have had an affair). But the sense of wanting the pressure of parenting responsibilities to cease – have an end point – in such intensive ways (*'so the pressure for me is 24/7 365'*) is palpable in the homes where children have primary residency.

New Relationships and Sharing Children and Care

'Letting go' (unwillingly and/or willingly) of the daily minutiae of parenting relationships and patterns of caring, of partners, children and everyday proximity to loved ones and the 'family' home (*'I mean when the Child Maintenance Service tell you you're an absentee father, you kind of take exception to that and I got quite upset'*, James) can all be part of the fallout from separation and divorce. Navigating co-parenting also involves the possibility of introducing and sharing your children with a new partner, or an ex-partner doing this. Not surprisingly, the idea of 'sharing' your child with someone else, or a third party having 'influence' on your child, was regarded in different (sometimes apparently 'selfless') ways. As has become clear in earlier extracts from Felicity, her children will be her priority until they reach 18 years of age, and she is unequivocal in not wanting anyone else's input:

I would never, ever, ever, as a parent while the children live with me, I would never live with somebody else. I would never want, for lots of reasons, I would never want to share my children with anyone else. I would never want to have and this is, maybe this is the control freak, I would never want to have somebody's input into raising my children. They very much have been my life's work, they are the thing of which I'm most proud and fiercely protective over and I wouldn't want to have anything to interfere with that, so no. (Felicity)

Sheila also implies that the children have always been hers and her ex-husband's priority, taking precedent over possible new relationships:

I did see a couple of other fellas but there was never anything serious and it would only, I wasn't including the children, it would just be on the weekends when their dad would see the boys. . . . But then as years went by he did have a few partners, but nothing major because he didn't want to get any other children involved, he loved his boys and all he cared about was his boys and he wanted nobody else to start taking, which in a way is my feeling as well. (Sheila)

In contrast, James feels he has been forced to let go and become 'detached' from many aspects of his daughter's life following his ex-wife's affair. In the following extract, he recounts how he became aware of this, arriving home early from work and overhearing a phone conversation,

I could hear all the details of, which is why I mean the whole thing about me taking my daughter out on a Saturday, so it turns, yeah so she had been seeing this guy for years on Saturdays apparently. So it was all very painful . . . so yeah, so much so that they were going on holiday with [daughter] without me knowing about it. So they would meet up. My daughter said, 'Oh yeah we meet up with this guy called Peter' and I thought oh God! It was just horrific. (James)

James jokes that he wishes the new partner would move into the family home with his ex-wife (and daughter) to reduce his maintenance contributions and is hurt by knowing that his daughter was already acquainted with his ex-wife's new partner. But he also talks of his own subsequent relationships in which a new partner being a potential 'mother' to his daughter has been a consideration:

Yeah it's a weird thing, yeah, I mean I've sort of had two relationships since the, both very, very similar actually. Both started in the summer, both finished on or around Christmas and both I just think, I just couldn't see myself long term with them because of the whole, one of them had a child, the other one didn't have a child. The one without a child I couldn't really see her being a mother to [daughter] I think and yeah it just didn't, yeah maybe I don't know it's weird. Yeah I'd love to have another child, but age is against me massively on that front! [Laughs] (James)

It's interesting that James could be explicitly looking for a (another) 'mother' for his daughter as an aspect of any new relationship, while

Felicity, Gillian, Sheila and Kathryn are explicitly *not* looking for potential 'fathers' for their children. Kathryn's fiancé, for example, is described as part of *her* new life, but separate from her two teenage children (*'it's lovely because I have a week with them and then a week without them, concentrating on Simon* [fiancé]. *So I get the best of everything'*). While James could be regarded as quite functional in his approach to the criteria a new relationship must meet (*'I couldn't really see her being a mother'*), Joe holds on to the possibility of a new and additional emotional connection for his two young daughters, being provided by his new partner (who doesn't have children). In what follows, I ask him what his response was to a question his mother had asked him when he told her about the separation:

TINA: So what was your response to your mum's question? How would you feel about someone else bringing up your children?

JOE: 'Yeah, so um . . . I was thinking about it this morning actually, it's something that, yeah at the time my response was something like 'I know mum, I know'. But I guess now, that was like a day or two after it happened. . . . So it's not something I like the idea of at all, but obviously I accept that ex-wife is going to have the same, exactly the same I guess concerns from my partner I guess, exactly the same, so I recognise that. I've said in terms of the girls, it just means I think, like I say it's been really, really hard but hopefully one good thing is there's going to be somebody else there, another person in their lives that is going to love them and want to look after them. But yeah it's not something which I guess, there are lots of concerns and worries there about a stranger I guess obviously looking after them, but I have to put my faith in [ex-wife] and obviously I want her to be happy. So I just sort of accept and realise that she's going to have exactly the same concerns, worries, thoughts. (Joe)

In this extract, Joe is struggling as a newly separated father to convey a sense of being a responsible parent, but in the midst of changes to his family life that he instigated. Perhaps it is little surprise that he tries to see some positives for his daughters in his new relationship, *'but hopefully one good thing is there's going to be somebody else there, another person in their lives that is going to love them and want to look after them'*. So why do Joe and James positively position or seek out new partners who can also be 'mothers', while Sheila, Felicity, Kathryn and Gillian shield their children from their new relationships, or shun the idea of having a relationship with anyone while their children are still at home? Sheila and her ex have managed to establish a mostly amicable relationship after many years of living apart, but this would be different, according to Sheila, if they had re-partnered ('*Oh yeah I mean if there were partners involved I don't think we'd be like we are, no, no way*'). But what do these relationships and arrangements tell us about how moral identities and caring responsibilities in relation to children are constructed, enacted and narrated?

Managing Caring Relationships across Households

Having earlier phases of data collected in the longitudinal studies to refer back to and examine has made it possible to trace how caring responsibilities and parental relationships unfold (see Miller, 2005, 2007, 2010, 2012). Prophetically, as it turns out, James, in a much earlier interview (as his daughter approached her first birthday), described feeling pressured by the competing demands of a job, young daughter and having time with his wife as being a '*triangle that's difficult to square*'. This eventually led him to seek help for stress from his doctor (Miller, 2010, chapter 5). Both James and Joe now point to having not done things together as a couple or family ('*so it was being a dad or working and then the whole family thing didn't really mesh together*', James; '*we just got into a rut and like I say we stopped doing things as a couple . . . it was almost like two single-parent families and one home*', Joe) as they try to make sense of the breakdown of their relationships. For both James and Joe, like many fathers, their parenting/fathering involvement occurred in pockets of time – some mornings, evenings and (mostly) weekends around working commitments. Whereas for their (part-time) working ex-wives and for Sheila, Felicity, Kathryn and Gillian who also worked part time (except for Kathryn who worked full time) caring has been a primary and 24/7 thinking responsibility, visibly and invisibly occupying most of their time. The invisible 'mental work' of caring is taken on by the person with an overarching and so primary responsibility (obligation?) for the children, which is still mostly mothers. This positioning allows Felicity and Sheila to make the possessive and heartfelt claims they do about their children ('*they're mine!*'), while separated fathers James and Joe must make visible their relationship in other ways, through proximity and continuity (if possible), or seeking a new mother figure for their child or children. So even the fathers seem to assume the need for a mother (*maternal* care?) in their children's lives (Doucet, 2006). Interestingly, such deeply ingrained associations and practises related to mothers and children influence perceptions of behaviours seen as unmaternal, and ultimately 'selfish' (e.g. see Chapter 4).

Separation and divorce shake up family patterns of caring and demand that new configurations of parental relationships and practises be navigated and resolved, even if unwillingly. The 'significance of mundane family life' is thrown into relief as new ways of doing the minutiae of daily family living across households is contemplated and undertaken (Philip, 2013:233). The organisational and practical aspects are initially (and perhaps always) taken up in contexts of pain, love and sometimes continuing hurt, which makes decisions difficult, overwhelming and confusing. The passage of time can enable new ways of workably sharing care for their children to become established and normalised. Joe, who is at the very early stage of searching the Internet for information in the hope that he can get shared custody of his two daughters, feels this is some way off. He worries about how he can show he is the same dad, even though he no longer lives with his daughters:

It's hard for me to say or justify sometimes that I am the same dad to myself when I am not there on a Tuesday night at 7 o'clock when I'd be reading their story or taking them for a bath, it's hard for me to justify that I am the same I guess to what I was before. It's hard for me to say that, yeah. Myself I know I am, but it's hard I guess for the girls to understand that at the minute and other people to see that, but yeah it's hard to justify that, really hard to justify that. Yeah and if we can get to a point of shared parenting I'd see them every day so if they were to stay with me three nights a week, they would either be staying over that night or waking up and I'd be dropping them off so . . . (Joe)

Not being resident and having had to move away from the area where his daughter lives (for work and affordable housing), James now feels '*detached*' (and temporarily resigned?) from areas of his daughters life. As he explains,

I mean I'm very detached from it all now since, so I left home 2½ years ago now. So I try and stay engaged with school, but I live in Slough now, so it's an hour and twenty minute drive, so it's just tough really to stay in touch. So yeah I just contributed money wise to extra lessons and all this type of thing. (James)

When fathers (have to) leave the family home, fathering can be forced through circumstance (geographical proximity, a need for cheaper accommodation) to become practised in more intermittent and activity-based ways. But James notes his continued economic support for his daughters 'enrichment activities' (Ball and Vincent, 2007). Separation can also create new opportunities for father involvement when post-separation arrangements involve equally shared custody and geographical proximity. For example, Gillian talks about her ex doing more parenting now they are separated than he had ever done before, even though she has had to come to terms with this changing what she saw as her primary role as mother (*'to have days and nights where actually you didn't know where they were, but you just knew that he knew where they were, that was tricky'*). There are also new logistics to negotiate in how caring is organised between households. Kathryn describes their system as follows:

Logistically it's not too difficult because he's [father], only living 10 minutes away, so if they forget something, we can drop it off and I've got this chart, I don't know whether you can see it over there, one is yellow week and one is pink week, so it's incredibly organised. (Kathryn)

All the parents (except James) work hard to show their children have not suffered as a result of the separation or divorce (*'but they don't miss out on that, because they still get fathering and they still get mothering and they still get parenting'*, *'he is a very good cook and he teaches them to do cooking and he's a very good DIY so [daughter] can put together DIY furniture whereas I never could in my wildest dreams'*, *'it's given them more independence'*). But this can also involve working harder at caring to ensure the children are not (seen to be) disadvantaged (e.g. see Felicity in Chapter 4). But while the children must not suffer, the parent (mother?) might, as moral identities can be felt to be under heightened scrutiny.

Even though descriptions of relationship breakdown have been the focus of this chapter, positive caring attributes are still described in ex partners who have been left (*'she is a brilliant mum, she is fantastic'*, *'he was absolutely brilliant and he would often take them off for walks or do fantastic games with them or he would take them off for days to do things'*). In whatever ways parenting relationships and caring practises are managed across households, for most their seems to be a moral imperative to show that they are/have been 'good' parents (*'we never sort of fight or argue in front of the girls ever really', 'so I've been to all the school parents evenings', 'and like I say their lives are almost exactly the same', 'you know it was a very happy childhood they had').* This involves constructions of selves as parents in which moral identities ('*and actually I think I did pretty well*', '*I had done what I thought was the best at the time*') and ideas of 'being there' are reformulated and/or confirmed. There is a sense that separated fathers might be more insulated than mothers regarding expectations of (intensified) parenting, but they may also have to work harder to demonstrate and maintain their connection (claim and make visible) to their children ('*I want the girls to know that I will always be there for them, it doesn't matter how old they are, how old I am, and I'll always be there*') in contexts where maternal primacy, for a whole gamut of reasons, continues to be privileged.

Conclusions

This chapter has examined the ways in which practises of parenting post-separation/divorce are experienced and become managed. Cultural and gendered ideals of parenting and parenthood as well as types of parental involvement are revealed as practical arrangements of caring across households and spaces are navigated. Constructions of moral identities and being as good a parent as possible in compromised circumstances are conveyed in ways that affirm and challenge gendered assumptions and earlier parental divisions of care. Thus prescriptive cultural ideals of intensified parenthood and concerted cultivation of children become secondary to demonstrating that their children have not or will not be emotionally disadvantaged (as far as is possible) through parental relationship changes. But not all parents are in agreement about how to manage new family lives as their sense of being let down by an ex-partner (or letting a partner down) configure how they 'gatekeep', share or let go of aspects of care for their children. Imagined future trajectories for their children also feature, both as opportunities to demonstrate commitment (and hoped for reestablishment of a fathering relationship) and as liberation too, from the intensively felt demands of parenting/mothering alone. It becomes clear that in post-separation and divorce parenting, the mothers and fathers are 'subject to different moral criteria' (Philip, 2013:228). This is illuminated across the narratives in which continued, assumed, moral responsibilities of mothers can sit in contrasting ways to misplaced assumptions about fathers. However, parenting in post-separation or divorced circumstances also reveals how practices and responsibilities can be reconfigured in ways that refocus ideas around moral responsibilities and challenge assumptions around gendered capacities to care.

6 | *Unfolding Relationships*

Taking a Longer View of Moral Orientations, Mental Work and Gender in Family Care and Work

I think what I'm quite bad at is the predicting what's required as well. . . . So my wife is much better, I think it's her nature and it's also just that she lives with it all the time. . . . I don't have that gene I don't think, I'm not able to predict that in that sense, I just deal with the here and now.

(William)

This chapter is written as media coverage in the United Kingdom reports disappointingly low rates of take-up of the new shared parental leave (SPL) policy, 1 year after the legislation was first introduced.[1] Only a 'tiny proportion' of fathers have opted to take leave under this new scheme (Osborne, 2016). In many ways the explanations for this lack of take-up, which have included concerns over pay and a masculine 'duty' to provide, underscore the deeply rooted and contested aspects of caring and working illuminated in the earlier chapters. This chapter takes a longer view of unfolding relationships and care practices, made possible through the qualitative data, collected over time.[2] This extended perspective enables broader patterns as well as aspects of the minutiae of daily family caring and working to be traced: through narrations of antenatal intentions, the first year and starting school to young adulthood. Through these temporal accounts, practises of family care and paid work undertaken by mothers and fathers are examined in relation to the 'mental work' of caring responsibilities and care orientations. The question of *who* is doing the mental work and why

---

[1] Although take-up has been disappointingly low, there is debate about how the rates of take-up have been estimated. See https://select-statistics.co.uk/blog/1-fathers-taken-shared-parental-leave.

[2] The data draw on more than 200 hours of interviewing in 125 interviews (conducted over 18 years) and is informed by focus group and other related research materials. Taken together this archive provides a rich seam of unfolding relationships and fluid configurations of family lives and gendered selves, positions and narrations.

and how this thinking and moral orientation translates into responsibilities and becomes practised or shifts, is explored. How do patterns become established, and what constraints and occurrences can disrupt these (e.g. divorce as seen in the previous chapter)? Is it possible to share a primary caring responsibility for children *equally*?

Background

Significant scholarly work has for many years examined and theorised the interconnections among family life, paid work and gender equality. Recurrent themes have centred on moral orientations and cultural assumptions that permeate family care, paid work and gendered practises across these domains (Chase and Rogers, 2001; Doucet, 2006; Fox, 2009; Hays, 1996; Hill Collins, 1994; Hochschild, 1983; O'Reilly, 2008; Ruddick, 1989; Yarwood and Locke, 2016). Research has paid attention to multiple factors and potential causal mechanisms and relationships between aspects of these domains as broader structural changes have simultaneously occurred. For example, more than 20 years ago American academic Walzer addressed interactional and institutional (structural) processes in her research on the 'invisible, mental labor that is involved in taking care of a baby' (thinking, feeling and interpersonal work) and the physical tasks and activities associated with care (Walzer, 1996:291). Most readers will not be surprised by Walzer's conclusions: that differentiated gendered care practises are socially constructed, regarded as 'women's work' and 'reproduced by men and women through their interactions as parents with each other' (Walzer, 1996:230). Reeling forward over the intervening years, the structural features of many Western societies have shifted so that the majority of families are dependent on two incomes (when there are two parents), and this has become a normative model. But as noted in earlier chapters, mothers increased activity in the workplace has not been exactly mirrored by an increase in men's activities in the home, where gendered divisions continue and are more marked in some countries (Lyonette et al, 2011; Norman and Elliot, 2015; Pedulla and Thébaud, 2015). To theorise and thus understand aspects of these fluid *and* obdurate domains more clearly, it is necessary to consider 'how and under what circumstances women and men reproduce, break or transgress gender norms' in the context of family care and work arrangements (Björnberg and Kollind, 2005:126; Miller, 2012). A concern with trying to understand this area further has led researchers to focus in more precise ways on daily practices, which either reproduce/reinforce or reduce gender differences, as well as to question *where* (cultural ideologies and structural influences) and *how* (e.g. using a 'maternal lens') we look for evidence of change (Bass, 2015; Deutsch, 2007; Miller, 2012; Risman, 2009; Shirani et al, 2012).

The term 'parenting' is regularly invoked and applied in broad, brushstroke ways in political assertions about family lives 'and rarely depicted explicitly' (Lee et al, 2014:viii). Similarly, 'the main audience' for the policies and programmes increasingly being rolled out to address assumed deficits in parenting are regularly framed as 'gender-blind' (Daly, 2013:172) in a discursive context of parental responsibilities and obligations (Morgan, 2014). However, as noted in earlier sections of the book, there is a need to be vigilant in the use of the generic term 'parenting' because so much research has demonstrated its gendered dimensions and associated inequalities. Significantly, these histories lead to different 'habits', consequences and 'dividends' for women and men as they become mothers and fathers (Connell, 2005:205; Ruddick, 1997:213). They also lead to mothers and fathers being aligned and associated with assumed different moral orientations in relation to caring and working (see earlier chapters). Although the language of 'moral orientations' can invoke ideas of biological determinism as part of natural dispositions to care – for example as an aspect of what it is to be human – practices are socially and historically located, culturally overlaid and structurally influenced. Indeed the very meaning of care itself is gendered (Holloway, 2006). Moral orientations include notions of 'choice' and intentions being expressed and actions taken. But these are far from gender-neutral in relation to maternal and paternal caring and working opportunities, expectations and practises.

Earlier theorisations of individual orientations, 'preferences' and choices have been limited and limiting (Doucet, 2016; Hakim, 2000; Lewis et al, 2008; McRae, 2003). More recent research shows again the ways in which 'institutional constraints' rather than individual choices 'may affect work-family preferences' (Pedulla and Thébaud, 2015:119). Similarly and importantly, it has been noted that both men and women 'are constrained in their "choices" by structural factors' (Lyonette et al, 2011). Developing this further, Gerson found in her research in the United States that men and women both express a preference for long-term, egalitarian relationships in which paid work and care work are *equally* shared (Gerson, 2011, emphasis added). However, this shared ideal preference is also recognised as being 'unattainable' in the context of current demands made on workers and parents. This returns us to the earlier observation that just as family labour market participation has increased, so too have idealised expectations of intensified parenting (Chapter 1).

A significant and well-documented gendered difference in men and women's work lives involves the 'patriarchal dividend', in which men have benefitted economically (and in other ways) through less often interrupted/uninterrupted work careers and assumptions about 'ideal worker norms' and 'successful' hegemonic masculinities (Bass, 2015; Connell, 2005; Ranson, 2012). So even though theorisations of 'masculinity', 'masculinities' and 'men' are subject to ongoing critique and revision, the concept of 'patriarchal dividend' continues to usefully draw attention to the terrain on which care and paid work arrangements have been erected, are navigated and become practised (Brandth and Kvande, 2016; Connell, 2005; Elliott, 2015; England, 2005; Hearn, 2004; Ruddick, 1997). And this leads to the resulting conundrum: why should men prioritise caregiving, 'when it is clear that men, in general, still reap a 'patriarchal dividend' from *not* caring'? (Doucet, 2016:7, emphasis in the original), a position further underscored by the 'wage penalty' associated with women's lives and motherhood (Budig and England, 2001; Costa Dias et al, 2016; Johansson et al, 2005).

Even though decisions about 'being there' and developing caring relationships with our children should not be reducible to the economic principles of the market, this is exactly where many discussions on work–life balance begin. The pressing question is how family lives become fitted into work lives, rather than the other way around. Some men, once they had become first-time fathers in the Transition to Fatherhood Study (2010), spoke of their concerns about managing work and family life and so 'fitting fathering in' and 'not being able to cope' (see Miller, 2010, chapters 4 and 5). But many two-parent households in the United Kingdom cope by having mothers 'balance' *their* work–family life and working part time, as a consequence of unequal earning histories (Gatrell, 2005; Perrons, 2009; Radcliffe and Cassell, 2015). Recent research also suggests that such arrangements may be put in train many years before the advent of parenthood. Developing further the concept of 'mental work' outlined earlier in

Walzer's work, Bass recently found in research conducted in the United States that because men are 'unlikely to engage in the mental work of anticipating parenthood, they were also free from its emotional and behavioural consequences' and this included making career plans that assume uninterrupted career trajectories (Bass, 2015:362). In contrast, for women gendered, educational choices, career aspirations and expectations continued to be formed against the cultural backdrop of assumed reproduction,[3] followed by intensive mothering. Bass (2015), like Walzer many years before, posits that 'women worry and prepare for parenthood, *because* their partners do not' (p. 381, emphasis added; Walzer, 1996). In the sections that follow, the ways in which the often invisible mental work of caring unfolds beyond babyhood in families is explored. In doing so, the original concept of mental work is extended to include the '24/7 thinking responsibility' (Miller, 2012) and future-focused planning that has characterised the intensive caring expected of parents in neoliberal times.

Returning to Antenatal Anticipations

It is interesting to rewind to the original antenatal interview data in both the Motherhood study (2005) and Fatherhood study (2010) to examine the ways in which parenthood is anticipated. The all-encompassing 24/7 thinking responsibility experienced once a baby is born cannot yet be felt and only barely imagined. In fact, this leads to some similarities across the two data sets, as both men and women appeal to ideas of 'nature' and 'instincts' as they anticipate the birth and their caring. For the women this includes hoping that their instincts will get them through the birth and help them cope with their early mothering, while the men find comfort in assuming that 'nature' and 'maternal instincts' will get their wife/partner through this too. The women are also prompted to think about their future mothering through antenatal preparation classes (provided universally in the United Kingdom by the National Health Service) and the materials provided at these. As Angela, one of the study participants, explains,

---

[3] Childlessness and choosing to remain 'child-free' are patterns of fertility increasingly observed in the United Kingdom (www.ons.gov.uk/peoplepopulationandcommunity/birthsdeathsandmarriages/conceptionandfertilityrates/bulletins/cohortfertility/2013–12–05) and United States (www.census.gov/newsroom/press-releases/2015/cb15-tps33.html).

'*I think I read it through that Health Authority book and then . . . cos it gets your mind going and thinking is there anything else I should be asking about?*' Angela illuminates an experience encountered by most of the mothers, that they were expected by others (e.g. doctors and midwives) to already know, somehow intuitively, about motherhood even though they were anticipating *first-time* motherhood. Gillian, in the following extract conveys a sense of not knowing and talks of having a sense of 'trepidation',

Trepidation really because I don't know what it will be like, you know it's such a change in your life, I mean I haven't booked anything for at least 6 weeks after, I'm just thinking it's going to take us 6 weeks at least to get the hang of, you know, getting up in the middle of the night, feeding and just being parents. (Gillian, Motherhood study antenatal interview)

It is interesting here how 6 weeks – a relatively short period – is used to frame the anticipated time it will take to '*get the hang of it*'. The men also cannot know what being a father will be or feel like, but they are able to narrate their ideas and futures about being a parent from a position that does not assume instincts or *primary* caring capacities. In the following extracts, Dean and Ben anticipate their impending fatherhood:

I'm a . . . seize-the-day type, I think one day at a time, you can't know what hurdles life is going to throw at you. You plan for the future monetarily and fiscally and morally but I don't know what tomorrow will bring. God willing our baby will be perfectly healthy and everything else, but I have no way to know that and if not we will deal with that as it comes. (Dean, Fatherhood study antenatal interview)

I know it is a big responsibility you know doing the kind of, I don't have the most stable sort of career set up in all of this, so I am just kind of . . . I do know there is kind of more of a sense I hope . . . that all of that pans out well so that we can just provide a good home and everything for the child. (Ben, Fatherhood study antenatal interview)

Future orientations for the fathers include having money, career stability and an ability to provide a good home. But among the fathers-to-be there is also a generally expressed intention to be involved with their children in more emotionally engaged and hands-on ways. For example, in the following extract, Stephen talks about generational changes he sees and anticipates how he will be involved:

My Dad, he's definitely not a hands-on guy with small babies. And I know I'm going to be completely in there and doing all the stuff with the baby and playing about and bathing it you know everything again involved as much as possible so that would be the main difference.... I think some of the stereotypes have broken down over the years, definitely, and a lot of things have changed.... I work 5 minutes down the road and wife's job is half an hour away, so I'll be more around the kids probably when it comes to work and I'm 5 minutes down the road and I can just nip home and look after them and things like that. (Stephen, Fatherhood study antenatal interview)

Although all the fathers anticipated greater involvement with their children, compared with their memories of their own fathers' involvement, only 2 of the 17 fathers anticipated changing their work patterns to facilitate this.[4] Graham is one of them:

the idea of flexible working is accepted [at work], and I think that if things crop up then the manager's supportive about staff having to deal with domestic issues, they're quite good at that. But I suppose I'm thinking about I suppose more what I find acceptable in myself you know and I sort of feel that I sort of feel at the moment that I'm further behind with things and making less of an effort than I feel that I should in some ways. (Graham, antenatal interview)

It has been suggested that men (before they become fathers) view 'their future careers through an unmuddled career focused lens' (Bass, 2015:370). But this orientation may also be supported or reinforced by a wife or partner, which Philippa in the Motherhood study (a graduate working full time in advertising) demonstrates as she thinks ahead to how parenting will unfold following the birth of their first child:

I just think, I think his work is a lot more important to him than mine is to me, so I suspect that he'll.... I don't really mind that, I mean ... say I'll do more or less equal ... I'll probably do a bit more than he will. (Philippa, Motherhood study, antenatal interview)

Dylan in the Fatherhood study is clear who may end up doing most of the 'parenting' but anticipates involvement:

but right from the start I would like to negotiate work so that I have you know sort of a day off work a week to be a father and to do childcare and to

---

[4] The fatherhood data was collected after the introduction of 2 weeks' paternity leave in the United Kingdom (2003) but before the introduction of Shared Parental Leave (2015).

be involved and I would really like to be able to maintain that throughout my working life if possible. It could be that Lisa is doing most of the parenting. My job isn't very flexible. (Dylan, Fatherhood study, antenatal interview)

In this extract Dylan's unremitting responsibility is to his job, not a new baby, although he is hopeful of carving out time across his 'working life' to be an involved father. But the gendered assumptions implicit in how we are able to position and narrate ourselves as women/mothers and men/fathers is powerfully demonstrated if we substitute Lisa (the mother) for Dylan (the father) in the extract, describing her anticipated involvement in mothering. The data collected during the antenatal phase in both studies suggest that at this time (1996–2006), the women's short-term horizons extend to getting through the birth and the very early weeks (in which mothering will be mastered). For the men it is career and future focused in terms of the need for job stability, economic provision (a good home) and having quality time to engage in activities with the baby and 'share' care in generationally different ways. But nothing can fully prepare parents for the birth of their first child.

Early Experiences of First-Time Motherhood and Fatherhood

After births, which often do not go as hoped for or according to the 'birth plan',[5] the parents leave hospital.[6] For several of these parents there is a sense of mystification and confusion that they are able to leave the hospital with their new baby, alone, and without supervision or more instructions (Miller, 2014). They are now parents, and after all the months of 'expert' instruction, preparations and imagining, they begin their mothering and fathering journeys with a baby who makes demands on them from the moment of birth. The initial days and weeks after the birth see the new mothers and fathers (who have taken 2 weeks' paternity leave and sometimes saved additional days of annual leave) muddling through together (*'we did the classes, we read and stuff and I don't think it prepared us in the slightest'*, *'but nothing*

---

[5] 'A birth plan is a record of what you would like to happen during your labour and after the birth' according to the National Health Service in the United Kingdom. See www.nhs.uk/conditions/pregnancy-and-baby/pages/birth-plan .aspx.

[6] Except for one homebirth in the Fatherhood study.

can prepare you for this'). The data in this section span the first year in the Motherhood study and the first two years in the Fatherhood study.[7]

During the early days and weeks, both parents together work out the practicalities of caring for a new baby – feeding, cleaning and all trying to get some sleep; but then the fathers return to work. Some return reluctantly and some more happily, but all wondering how their wife or partner will manage alone with a new baby who has required both their attention (*'I wonder whether she can cope when she has to do it all day on her own'*). What happens next is that patterns of caring, which quite quickly become embedded, taken-for-granted and invisible, fall into place. In particular the mothers become proficient at meeting their baby's needs and the fathers are constrained from becoming as proficient because they are physically at work. Whether the proficiency of the mother is interpreted by the fathers as being a result of successful *'bonding'* and *'natural, maternal instinct'* or as a consequence purely of time (*'She had obviously built up perhaps a stronger bond with baby because I wasn't there all the time'*), the impact is the same: the mother is placed as the primary carer and so takes on the mental work of caring. This early mental work involves rapidly coming to feel a sense of 24/7 responsibility, but not at this early stage, longer term planning (too tired, overwhelmed and uncertain for that).

Fathers too, are committed and involved in caring through this period, especially when breastfeeding ceases, but in pockets of time around their jobs, so mostly evenings and weekends (*'I'm much more involved in that I can feed him because he's eating solid food. I look after him on a Thursday morning now wife's back to work, so we have time just together'*, Ben). Their intermittent caring requires that they are debriefed about the routine and the ever-changing needs of their developing baby as they provide a supportive, rather than primary carer role (*'but oh the first few times I had care of her, was just shattering. I'm sure everyone says that! But you know just handing her back, the relief, and then I'd go and lie down for a while'*, father). For both parents, the early weeks and months are absorbed with coming to terms with the demands of being a parent and managing this with paid work, especially once maternity leave ends and the mothers also return to work.

---

[7] A decision to extend the original Fatherhood study beyond the first year was taken in part because of the lack of data on men's experiences of fatherhood beyond the first year.

No one was able to fully appreciate before becoming a parent that a physically small baby would be able to occupy so much thinking and physical space. Even once the mothers return to work[8] and child-care may be outsourced to grandparents, childminders and workplace nurseries, these patterns of primary thinking and planning and 'helper', 'supporter' roles are continued (Miller, 2012).

But this is not to suggest that the fathers aren't competent at caring for their baby or young child, although they are much less subject to assumptions that they should be caring ('*your mums not here, what do you do?!*' See below), but rather that their full-time work and greater ability to choose their practises of involvement (the physical activities and tasks), and smaller timeframes in which to undertake them, constrain and shape their perceptions of expertise. At the same time practices are contingent and so wives and partners will also have developed their ways of doing caring, which may differ to their husband's approach, as Gillian explains:

So yes I've had two mornings away with husband in charge, and when you come home . . . he was trying to watch the Grand Prix on TV at the same time in the lounge, but he was feeding baby in the high chair in the kitchen, so this was blaring, all the doors and windows were open and the place looked as though a bomb had hit it and the baby was screaming because she didn't want whatever it was that she had [laughter] and he looked a bit stressed. But I mean they'd had a lovely morning together so it didn't really matter, it's just different . . . different to what I do. (Gillian, Motherhood study, postnatal interview at 9 months)

It's interesting that Gillian talks of leaving her '*husband in charge*', implying a temporary exchange of responsibilities. She describes a scene that will be recognisable to many parents and ends by noting that her husband's style of caring is '*just different . . . different to what I do*'. But this observation is key to understanding how responsibilities become demarcated and potentially claimed and protected through for example, 'maternal gatekeeping' (Allen and Hawkins, 1999; McBride et al, 2005; Puhlman and Pasley, 2013; Schoppe-Sullivan et al, 2008, 2015). Not all mothers would so cheerfully accept that their partner just cares for the baby or child in different ways, but would see it

---

[8] Of the 17 mothers in the original Motherhood study, 15 returned to work after maternity leave. The majority returned to part-time work, but (at least) 3 of the 15 worked full time.

as the wrong way (*'in general terms I consider myself very confident with my daughter, qualified by my inability to pick the right clothes for her to wear still and maybe not provide her with the right food'*, William). Women's caregiving has also been noted to occupy more time as they also orchestrate the care work (Gerstel and Gallagher, 2001). But caring acts are of course also embodied practises, and Gillian Ranson has recently drawn attention to the physical differences in masculine practices of caring for young children and noted the neglect of research on men's experiences of embodied caregiving (Ranson, 2015).

Nevertheless, as soon as fathers return to work, mothers have sole care for the baby on a daily basis, whereas for the fathers this occurs less frequently, as Ian and Mike describe:

If wife leaves me with baby [9 months old] for a morning or afternoon at the weekend, whatever, you know I do feel a little that I'm getting things wrong and not doing them at the right time and that kind of thing... she gives me a list of what to do and when or tells me what to do and when but of course baby may decide to do something different that morning so the list may not entirely apply. So we haven't quite worked out our strategy for that kind of handover. (Ian, Fatherhood study, postnatal interview at 9 months)

On Monday afternoon I took baby [9 months old] out for the first time in the car on my own and went over to, into Peterborough to see a couple of friends and their family and they were like is this the first time you've been out without [wife] and I was like yeah it is actually. I just kind of did it, I didn't actually think about it and it wasn't until they said that I was like 'oh yeah flipping heck, your mums not here what do you do?!' But again you know it was just really cool and natural instinct seemed to take over. It was nice that I now kind of know that I can, you know I feel more confident, you know go out on my own and maybe, I'm not too sure about going into town on my own just yet, I'll maybe build up to that. But yeah it's good. (Mike, Fatherhood study, postnatal interview at 9 months)

It is interesting to note the assumptions implicit and explicit within these extracts. For example, Mike invokes his *'natural instincts'*, and Ian's caring is orchestrated by his wife via a written list or verbal instructions. But these fathers relate caring scenarios that confirm men's capacities to care, even if this involves *'getting things wrong'*. They also again highlight aspects of caring that are explicitly regarded as maternal or paternal responsibilities.

The doing of mental work in the form of thinking about and planning for and around a baby and growing child's needs is not complicated, but it is a form of responsibility and engagement that is omnipresent even when not consciously or conspicuously so. However, using data collected in the first 2 years after the birth of a baby, it is noteworthy how aspects of this mental work are ascribed to, or rejected by, mothers and fathers. In the Fatherhood study, there was a mismatch between earlier antenatal *intentions* and how fathering became practised on a daily basis, partly as a consequence of full-time work, but it became clear too that other factors such as having differently gendered choices, were at play as well. In the following extracts, particular dimensions of caring involvement, mental work and maternal–paternal differences are described:

I'm doing plenty of childcare [but] Ros is taking responsibility for her [the baby's] future orientation of where we will be going next.... It's not that I couldn't do that but I'm not doing that ... men can't do it because men can't do practical things, actually it is easy to feed the baby but knowing what to feed her tomorrow is difficult. (Richard, Fatherhood study, interview at 2 years after the birth)

I definitely see myself as a breadwinner and you know kind of because she's obviously what she does for a living [teacher], I think she's basically better qualified to bring up children than I am, having studied and worked with children like she has. (Gareth, Fatherhood study, interview at 1 year after the birth)

In these extracts a 'maternal' expertise is privileged by the fathers in relation to mothers 'knowing' and planning what to feed a baby or child and being *'better qualified'* to care through education and practice. Even though the men are more involved, they are also able to express culturally and morally acceptable preferences as fathers, including invoking maternal expertise, in ways not so readily available to women as mothers (Bass, 2015; Gerstel and Gallagher, 2001; Miller, 2005, 2011; Pedulla and Thébaud, 2015; Thébaud, 2010). The fathers are also able to make claims of (masculine) incompetence (*'getting things wrong and not doing them at the right time and that kind of thing'*) that would not be made, or would be unacceptable, in other domains of their lives (e.g. the workplace). However, this is not to suggest that a father's love for his children is any less than a mother's, as Joe explains in the following extract as he talks about his daughter:

It's just really strange, you can't really explain it, but there was just a bond when she was first born, I don't know why that is, it's just strange. It's an immediate protectiveness really and that's sort of grown over the time. The love has got a lot stronger and the protectiveness has got a lot stronger as well. (Joe, fatherhood study, interview at 1 year following the birth)

Joe here conveys a sense of caring and protection as a recognisable, shared universal orientation (see Chapter 2). But the data from the earlier phases of the studies show how claims and rejections and particular moral orientations (to provide and protect) can be taken up by fathers in ways that would be (normatively) unacceptable if it were a mother describing aspects of such pick-and-mix caring. Through this early period of first-time parenthood, orientations in relation to the mental work of care become clearer and are associated with physical presence and perceived competence and incompetence. Someone has to take on the primary responsibility and associated mental work for a baby over the first weeks, months and year, and this turns out to be a *singular* endeavour, still mostly taken on by mothers.

Growing Children and Caregiving: Practises of Maternal and Paternal Gatekeeping?

In this section I return to the most recently collected data from the interviews undertaken with the fathers as their firstborn child started school (see Chapter 3), followed by the mothers talking about their teenage children (see Chapter 4). This is to see how caring relationships and practices are experienced and explained *over time* and how and whether the mental work of caring shifts as children and families grow. Most of the fathers and mothers have had additional children born since their last interview, and so new birth and preparation stories still feature in the interviews as well as the logistics and demands of fathering and mothering older children alongside younger ones. The theme of how far the thinking mental work of caring continues to be enacted in singular and primary (maternal) ways as children grow is examined in this section.

In an earlier chapter (see Chapter 3) the term 'interchangeable' was used by two of the fathers to signify how they felt their parenting was sufficiently shared that their caring roles could be swapped in straightforward ways. But does caregiving become increasingly interchangeable between parents as their children grow, or do earlier patterns continue to define areas of expertise? The concept of 'maternal gate-keeping' emerged in research literature in the 1990s to theorise 'mother–father boundaries' and attitudes and behaviours associated with father involvement with their children and how this is restricted or enabled by mothers (Allen and Hawkins, 1999; McBride et al, 2005). Since then, and corresponding to broader changes in family lives, divorce, parenting and work, the concept has been further developed – and critiqued, revised and reconceptualised (Fagan and Barnett, 2003; Puhlman and Pasley, 2013; Stevenson et al, 2014). This has involved the use of 'family systems theory', 'feminist theory' and analysis of data leading to models and types of maternal gatekeeping (for example the identification of '8 types of maternal gatekeeping'; Puhlman and Pasley, 2013:182). Even though maternal gatekeeping has more recently been recognised as 'both restrictive and facilitative', the language of 'gatekeeping' still implies restriction on the part of the mother. But less attention has been given to how micro-processes of family arrangements unfold and the detail of low-level, everyday parental interactions or their practise over time. Similarly, there has been a lack of scholarly attention given to the possibilities of 'paternal gatekeeping'; rather the focus has continued instead on practices of maternal 'control', 'encouragement' and 'discouragement' and how mothers 'block' or facilitate father involvement. From the data collected across the motherhood and fatherhood studies, it is clear that practices of caregiving, parenting and working are supremely contingent: mothers in the studies can affect fathering, and the fathers in the studies can affect mothering.

The subject of gatekeeping of areas of parental caring involvement also requires consideration of theorisations of 'preferences' and choices in relation to how caring in families becomes organised and the potential for types of gatekeeping to occur. The ways in which preferences and choices have been assumed as relatively neutral practices of agency and/or essentialist responses has led to critique and calls for more precise explorations of how choices are/can be made (Doughney and Leahy, 2006; Miller, 2012). Matters of gendered histories and differential power that is operationalised, assumed and etched through maternal and work spheres provide a complicated backdrop to modern family lives. What becomes shared or defined and held on to as maternal or paternal areas of expertise, and how practises can be rejected, ignored or not seen, are all aspects of caring evident in the

data collected in the longitudinal motherhood and fatherhood studies. This is a more complex area than some theorisations of 'maternal gatekeeping' have conveyed. In this section practices of caring
that influence patterns of maternal and paternal involvement – over
time – are explored. These illuminate the ways in which overlapping
aspects of control, competency/incompetency, visibility/invisibility and
physical presence shape family caring arrangements and can inform
theorisations of maternal *and* paternal 'gatekeeping' in more precise
ways.

Practises of taking 'control' are evident in various ways in the data
from both studies and emerge quite quickly, because mothers in the
United Kingdom are the ones most likely to stay at home to care for a
new baby.[9] Their expertise develops more quickly during this time, and
so they come to share and orchestrate baby care information with the
father. This can involve lists and verbal 'briefings', and fathers practises
are likely to be overseen, as they more slowly (because of time and practise) become accomplished at aspects of caring. Different practises of
embodied care may also be a feature here as well (Ranson, 2015). There
are many opportunities for fathers to be seen to get things 'wrong' as
caring may be undertaken in different ways. For example, Sheila, now
a mother of teenage sons, talks of having 'standards' (*'and also on the
controlling side ... really I shouldn't do it to myself, but I do. I still
do have my standards and I like to keep to my standards'*). Rebecca
also talks of individually orchestrating her children's activities and having *'to hold it all in my head'* and being *'in charge of the transport
and I'm always in charge of the arrangements'* and that *'her husband
wouldn't have a clue, not a clue'* (see Chapter 4). But does the control
here emanate from Rebecca being a 'control freak' (a term used earlier
by Felicity to describe herself), or does she feel she has to act in this way
because her husband has not demonstrated his competence in taking
on the overarching mental work necessary in families (even though he
works part time and Rebecca works full time)? Has he tried and got
it 'wrong' and not met Rebecca's 'standards', and has she had to *'pick
up the pieces'*, as Kathryn described earlier? Could his style of organisation just be different rather than wrong? Or by being seen to be
incompetent, has he avoided activities he doesn't want to do? Clearly,

---

[9] This could change in the future as it becomes more acceptable and financially
practicable for couples to share Shared Parental Leave (introduced in 2015).

aspects of apparently controlling or 'gatekeeping' behaviours are multifaceted and differently construed depending on whose vantage point is taken.

With hindsight and after separation, Gillian, who happily sees herself as having been the primary carer (*'that was my job'*) for their two daughters, now wonders why she held on to the responsibilities in such a singular way. In their shared custody arrangements (see Chapter 5) she now sees her ex-husband competently caring for their teenage children. But in the following extract, Gillian reflects on the optional involvement he had earlier been able to choose:

No, no I always felt that I, as a primary carer, I would always do all the things for the children, that was my job, particularly because I didn't really go to work very much, even, I was only sort of working 2 or 3 days a week when he left so I had to increase that. So, yes I was always on standby for them if you see what I mean.... But other than that, no he did things when he wanted to ... and I think he always had the capacity, but he didn't have to.... [Later] So he was involved when he wanted to be involved. I think he had the choice thing because he didn't have to have that responsibility time and he did the physical things like that with them. (Gillian)

It becomes clear that control and practises of 'maternal gatekeeping' are also contingent on the willingness and perceived competency of the father, who can also be seen to have 'choices' (*'he had the choice thing'*). Because of time and leave policies in the United Kingdom that have until recently provided considerably more maternity leave than the statutory 10 days paternity leave, caring competencies are (often) developed more rapidly by the parent at home, the mother. Across the data the fathers can make claims of incompetency as well as be chastised for getting things *'wrong'* and *'not having a clue'* by their wives or partners. In the following extract, Lillian conveys the fraught aspects of early caring, taking control, feeling pressure as a mother to get things right, and her sense that her husband can be too involved (as far as she is concerned) and sometimes *'needs to back off'*:

But I think it was more me that done the survival of them, you know the ... I mean he loved him, but I did more of the ... you take control don't you and being in control that is what gives you the pressure I think to do everything right ... [Later] I wouldn't be able to stop it [but] I think some fathers stand back and let it just happen don't they? But I think sometimes he's in too much, he just needs to back off, yeah. (Lillian)

Notes

how is parental care imagined,
pren ded for
shared
narrated
justified

— & & what consequences
a situation changes this?
intentions vs behaviour.

welfare regimes; social care policies
eg state provision of pre-school
care for children

vs care resps on the individual
p34 a pr work unit the 'greek matter
able to manage these competing
demands with little state
support.
gendered
Conffirmations of care + paid work

Interestingly, Lillian shares her perception that '*some fathers stand back and let it just happen*' and so hints at the optional ways in which father engagement can be taken on – or not. In the fatherhood study, William has a theory about how couples come to manage family life:

One of my theories is that as a couple, you become quite polar, polar opposites in terms of how you manage things.... So if I'm thinking and I'm not being flippant, but I mean we will always have big discussions about Alice's stuff, but if I know [wife] is on the case with clothing for instance and what she needs to buy the next size up of course I'm not going to be doing that, because it's silly us both doing it. (William)

Left to our own devices I think each of us would just get on with Alice in slightly different ways and I think we'd just make it happen. There's a, probably a good tension otherwise, because there is always a little bit of pushing and pulling and whereas I would have allowed Alice to eat a sweet or something, [wife] may say well she doesn't need that she just had a you know something and I say well I didn't know she just had that. (William)

The observations and exchanges relayed in William's descriptions illuminate further how aspects of managing (or 'gatekeeping'?) care can be seen as optional ('*I'm not going to be doing that*') as well as based on incomplete knowledge on which to make a (primary) decision ('*well I didn't know she just had that*'). Knowledge or lack of knowledge about the minutiae of their children's needs (especially in relation to clothes and feeding: '*it is easy to feed the baby but knowing what to feed her tomorrow is difficult*') and acceptable claims of care acts being optional (because someone else has the overview, rather than necessarily the control?) are expressed in the following extract from an early interview with Gus (who works in a catering business) at 1 year after his child's birth:

Because one of the roles that Anna, one of the things that she does regularly is she gets his food ready for the next day. So (she) goes into the freezer, gets out a cube of whatever, puts it all into pots... it's something she does every night. I should probably do it but I never do... I think you know it's always said to me that blokes can switch off a little bit more. (Gus)

Narrating aspects of incompetence seems to be more acceptable for the fathers to do: the mothers are much more alert to the possibilities of how they will be perceived and what may be felt to be at risk ('*the pressure I think to do everything right*', '*If I'm away, I have to write it all down'*). But being responsive and knowledgeable – and so competent – is also linked to time and physical presence in the home (*'I'm quite bad at is the predicting what's required as well. . . . So my wife is much better, I think it's her nature and it's also just that she lives with it all the time'*). In the United Kingdom, although most families are working families, it is still more likely that fathers will work full time and mothers work part time and more flexibly to accommodate caregiving demands. Ian, now a father of two children, has recently moved from a home-based job to going out to a workplace, as he explains in the following extract:

> I was still at home most of the time until July when second baby (a daughter) was 8 months or whatever, then during that time I think I was as involved as much as I was with our son. Yeah I think there are different rewards because very much when I come home there is a little girl who says 'daddy' and you know that's a daily meeting that you don't get if you are there all the time. . . . So it's nice to come home. [On] Saturday yes we both, I think we are equally involved on Saturdays. I perhaps have slightly more things that I do out of the house than Polly does, so the balance might not be quite as I think it is, because when I'm not there, I don't take that into account. (Ian)

While Ian notes physically being there (and the joys of being welcomed home by his young daughter), it is the possibility that when he is not physically at home he does not 'see' or at least can be unaware of aspects of caring work (*'I don't take that into account'*). So visibility and the possibility of invisibility by not being physically there are also facets of how caregiving involvement and responsibilities can become taken on or can be resisted.

It becomes clear then that definitions of 'maternal gatekeeping' as 'mothers' preferences and attempts to restrict and exclude fathers from childcare and involvement with children' (Fagan and Barnett, 2003:1021) are overly simplistic. By teasing apart and juxtaposing parental narratives of caregiving and giving consideration to the contexts in which lives are historically embedded, gendered and lived, it becomes clear that practices of caregiving are complex, contingent and dynamic. Both parents are able to exert forms of control or behaviours that 'block' and/or facilitate care. For example, 'paternal gatekeeping' might be defined through behaviours and attitudes that involve not taking on or avoiding longer term planning and thinking (*'I just deal with the here and now, maybe a week ahead planning, but nothing years ahead*') and prioritising outside activities and the 'fun stuff' while optionally declaring incompetence in relation to some activities and not 'seeing' others. These forms of 'gatekeeping' of course have implications for how mothering and fathering become taken on and how caregiving becomes choreographed in households by *both* parents.

But, regardless of how caring becomes taken on, conveying the emotional and relational elements of becoming a parent before a baby is born is retrospectively seen as an (almost) impossible task. In the following extract, Nick (now father of two children) responds to a question I have asked about his thoughts on the need for preparation for becoming a parent:

I'm not sure that there is [a need]. I think we spoke to people, we did the classes, we read and stuff and I don't think it prepared us in the slightest and I think when friends of ours have had children, we have shared our experiences, they have watched our experiences but I don't think it prepared them. I think it is just one of those things that you cannot prepare people for and I guess that's largely about you can't describe a relationship. You can't. Superficially you can, but you can't describe the depth of that relationship and you can't describe the emotional impact of that relationship, you have to experience it . . . you are caught in that dependent relationship and I don't think you can prepare for that. (Nick)

The emotional impact and relationship parents come to have with their children is (one hopes) deeply felt, enduring and almost impossible to convey. But there can be experiences of almost unimaginable sadness as a parent too.

Caregiving in Its Purest Form: The Loss of a Baby

So far this and earlier chapters have reflected upon the ways in which orientations and practices of caring for our children become enacted in everyday contexts of family life. But what can be seen when elements of these structural demands are suspended and familial caring relationships are revealed at their most intense and poignant? In the course of any research, unexpected things can occur, and this is especially true in longitudinal research; this was the case when I returned to interview Sean as his first child (born in an earlier phase of the Fatherhood study) reached school age. Like most of the other fathers in the study,

Sean[10] had news of a subsequent birth in the family to relate. But unlike the other fathers, Sean's second baby, Jack, had died at 4½ months of age. An intense account of birth, love and loss crystalized into a short life was conveyed simply and eloquently in Sean's interview. As the interview unfolded, Sean reflects upon his and his wife's relationship with their son and any possible differences. Their fathering and mothering relationships unfold over 4½ months in an environment (a special care baby unit in an NHS hospital) where the otherwise normal demands of everyday life are largely suspended and the major focus is on the baby. The lengthy extracts that follow encompass themes drawn across the preceding chapters about caring orientations, practices and how these become enacted in gendered or other ways. In the following extract, Sean talks about how he had been involved with his new baby son:

I can't think of anything that I haven't done, again apart from the breastfeeding. There is a difference and Jack taught me the kind of difference between a mum and dad, just in terms of when your baby is that small, a lot of the time you don't really realise whether they know who you are, or whether you are significant, but you get the feeling that they must do. But with Jack because everything was so medical, Ella initially was really worried about never being able to bond. Because he wouldn't breastfeed, and in the early days he was fed through tubes, in fact he was fed through tubes up until the end, but later on she tried to breastfeed him and then to try and feed him solids and things. But Ella was really worried about that and when you look back it became very, very clear that Jack knew who she was, as in he didn't know 'mum' or 'mummy' but he knew that she was obviously something significant. There was obviously a bond, a very strong bond, and that came about because, out of everyone he would settle better on her than anyone else. He'd be playing up and he might play up in her arms, but he'd be a lot more comfortable with her than anybody else, that was true compared to me as well. However, I did get the feeling that he felt pretty secure and comfortable with me and there were lots of times where it wasn't necessarily just about settling, it was that I would come along and pick him up and cuddle him or we'd dance to music around the room or something – I'd probably treat him in a way that either a lot of other people wouldn't because they were scared of all of his tubes and wires, or the nurses didn't really, because they had a million other things to do. So I think he seemed to know me, but

[10] Sean has kindly given permission (separate and subsequent to the informed consent form he initially signed) for the lengthy extracts about his son Jack to be used in this way in this chapter.

it wasn't the same.... You could tell that there was a difference with Ella, but it didn't really matter is the other thing and it didn't mean that Ella got more of something than I did. We tended to be there as much as each other we just had to stagger it, to cover home.

Yeah, I mean he's been so influential to everything. I mean he's not here, but he's still a very key part of the family. And what's wonderful is that [first child] still talks about him a lot, she still can remember a lot, and she wasn't even 2 when he first was born. But she did, it wasn't until I guess she was just about 2 when she spent more time and she was allowed to see him in the hospital and she does remember, she will recognise things from pictures and she will point out things as well. So he is still very much there. But as a result of that, we now do a lot of fundraising for the hospital in the neonatal unit . . . the neonatal unit is being expanded, we are supporting that and the reason why it's them as opposed to anywhere else is because when Jack was born he was just so sick. We had the 'don't expect him to last' conversations, we had those kind of conversations many, many times and he did and they stuck him back together well enough to go for heart surgery. So you kind of, although he didn't win overall, he survived that period when nobody expected him to survive, so he's a small miracle and you have to be grateful. They gave us four and a half months which we wouldn't have had, had they not done as well and just reacted as well as they did. So we are very grateful for that. It was, it's odd to say it was a wonderful time and it's the after effect that's been the hard bit, but at the time it was very stressful and it was very sad for most of it, but then you realise actually it was also such a special time.

Sean then returns to contemplate possible differences between his and his wife's embodied, visceral and tactile interactions with the baby:

But it was very, it's very strange and maybe it's just that [wife] was more comfortable with it, she's kind of got more lumps and bumps and more comfy bits for him to lay in, whereas I was a bit more gnarly and old. I don't know, maybe it was something as simple as that, so he could actually physically just get more comfortable. Who knows? It was clear and if he had just been born, then it would have been easier to explain because it would have just been normal, but because there was a break in that time, and I mean we weren't able to hold him – I think it was round about 6 days until we were able to actually get him out and give him a cuddle. So it's quite difficult to understand why but it seemed to be there anyway. But then, as I say, I think over the course of time it did come, an obvious bond or an obvious kind of closeness did develop because it was clear that he knew that I was important in his life somehow. I was a nice person to him and I would react to him when he cried, help him, make him feel better and try to comfort him, dance with him and whatever it might be. So obviously it did, there was something that did develop and he did become more comfortable. Initially I think there was an element of him wanting just to be cuddled quite a lot. But yeah, as I say, he was still far more comfortable on Ella, always.

These extracts convey the intensity of reciprocated, tactile and embodied feelings associated with forming a relationship with a baby who is living with a very unclear trajectory. 'Normal' life is suspended, and caring for and about the baby becomes the major orientation for both parents. Even so, Sean reflects on this intense period as having been a 'wonderful time', in which time, relationships and futures exist in heightened ways. In the course of his retelling, Sean explains and ponders the differences he could see between Jack and his mother and he with Jack. He reflects on opportunities to 'bond' being initially compromised, as they could not hold their son for 6 days, but that his son could then be readily comforted by his wife. Sean reflects on various explanations for this, including physical differences between their bodies. The caring practices Sean describes in the baby unit involve him reacting to Jack when he cried, comforting him and dancing with him to 'make him feel better' and are narrated in a language of intimacy in which 'closeness' and reciprocal connection is conveyed. And over time *'an obvious bond or an obvious kind of closeness did develop'*. Even though Sean sees small differences in their interactions with Jack and abilities to comfort in differently embodied (and gendered) ways, significantly he notes that *'it didn't really matter is the other thing'*. Even though some other aspects of daily living had to be managed (care for their older child), for the most part Sean and his wife were absorbed in comforting their baby son in different ways, but with the same unconditional love and hope.

The experiences that Sean describes sharing with his baby son are embodied and palpable and convey a lyrical rhythm of gentle caregiving, even though the family are cocooned in a high-dependency neonatal hospital unit. Most importantly, outside pressures are suspended as comforting and getting to know their baby son is the shared primary focus. It's a brief period in which the demands and constraints that shape the organisation of caregiving, parenting and working in the outside world are deferred. But it also shows caregiving and love as raw, basic human emotion conveyed through bodies that are lumpy and bumpy in different ways, that are hard to escape, but that here don't matter.

Conclusions

This chapter has explored the question of *who* is doing the mental work in caring and why and how this relates to notions of gendered, moral orientations and practices in households. It has shown how relationships and caring practises unfold and become practised in (usually) less equitable ways than originally intended. The reasons for this can be multiple and are interrelated, operating at the interpersonal and broader structural, political, policy and cultural levels. A baby or dependent child has needs to be met, but not necessarily by the mother. Even so parenting is undertaken and choreographed in highly gendered and politicised contexts, and only gradually are socially constructed care arrangements being challenged and reconfigured. It is also apparent that men's understandings and practices of parenting do not mirror exactly those of women, but this makes them different and differently embodied, rather than wrong (Rehel, 2014:111; see also Doucet, 2006; Ranson, 2016). The need for a more critical engagement with dimensions of the powerful and fluid concept of maternal gatekeeping, in conjunction with possible paternal gatekeeping behaviours and attitudes has also become clear. The question remains, then, of whether and how sharing a primary caring responsibility for children – the mental work of caring – can be achieved *equally*. How might more egalitarian family relationships, be achieved and work and family life be made more compatible? These questions are now considered in the concluding chapter.

7 | Conclusions and Reflections

And I kind of think, I've probably done a good enough job, not brilliant, but good enough that she will be successful and she's had a good enough start in life and that's what I want for all of them and that they will remain close to me and my little refrain to all of them at bedtime is, I'm always here for you, you know ... oh, it's making me tearful thinking about it.

(Rebecca)

This chapter draws together the arguments developed through the preceding chapters and returns to consider orientations to care, gender and practices of agency and narration. Through these related conceptual frames and perspectives, the question of whether a primary caring responsibility can be shared equally between parents is further examined and findings theorised. The qualitative longitudinal data explored across the earlier chapters show that even though caring practises are increasingly shared between parents, the undertaking of the mental work – the 24/7 thinking responsibility of caring for children – is not and continues to be taken on by mothers in heterosexual, dual-earner households. By closely following the unfolding practices of family caregiving as babies have grown into school-age children and then older teenagers, more precise versions of caring practises, thinking and responsibilities in the families have been revealed. This has involved focusing on different ages of children and stages of parenting in couple households as well as where forms of co-parenting now occur across households following separation and divorce. What becomes clear is that in working families, the fathers in the study have become competent caregivers sharing in a range of aspects of childcare. Their practical involvement has continued after its initiation in the very early hours and days of first becoming a father and captured in the first interviews in this longitudinal research. This resonates with recent quantitative research findings which reported 'that fathers in the United Kingdom who share childcare when the child is nine months old are significantly

146

more likely to share childcare when the child is three years old' (Fagan and Norman, 2016). However, intentions of sharing equally in caring for their children have not been realised as family and workplace demands collide. Data collected across both studies and at different stages of unfolding parenting relationships help to affirm, explain and challenge why having a primary responsibility in relation to caring for our children continues to be a maternal act.

Increasingly intensified ideals of what practices constitute 'good parenting' were considered in the opening chapter of the book. The paradox that these ideals have become further heightened at a time when more families than ever before in the United Kingdom are also working, meeting labour-force demands and covering household budgets was also noted. This is a phenomenon increasingly witnessed across many developed countries (Craig et al, 2014; Jacobs and Gerson, 2016; Lee et al, 2014). The balance between meeting work and family demands has most often been achieved by mothers' working flexibly, although there is recent evidence to show this could be changing to a model in which both parents work full time (Connolly et al, 2016). Not surprisingly, parents describe feelings of being time-squeezed and under pressure but are also caught up in arranging and transporting their children to extra 'enrichment activities' as these are perceived to be (among these participants) normative aspects of responsible parenting (Craig et al, 2014; Henderson, 2012; Vincent and Ball, 2007; Wall, 2013). Family time – all being together socially – is also difficult to achieve in packed weekdays and weekends (*'we try and go on a family walk, I'm really big on that, they all moan like anything'*). Parents narrate typical days, in which boundaries between school and home are felt to be more porous than in their own childhoods. Homework (for those beginning school) and homework and exam pressures (for those preparing to finish school) are activities into which parents have increasingly felt drawn. Trying to help your child succeed in education falls beyond the school gates, and homework occupies weekend (family) time. There are concerns about the risk of failure, both in terms of being able to help older teenage children with schoolwork and in relation to younger children being seen as 'successful'; for example being seen as lacking a 'competitive' spirit is expressed as a concern (*'he claims to love football more but he's given up football because he couldn't really hack it'; 'I'm not saying she needs to be competitive, but she needs to try and she just gives up so easily'*).

An overview of existing literature in the United Kingdom concludes that 'warm, authoritative and responsive parenting is usually crucial in building resilience' (in children) and that 'parents who develop open, participative communication, problem-centred coping, confidence and flexibility tend to manage stress well and help their families to do the same' (Utting, 2007:2). Building warm and supportive relationships with their children was exactly what all the parents in the studies were occupied in trying (in different ways) to do, but alongside and around other demands in their lives, which configured and constrained how family lives became managed over time. The contradictions felt between the values of parenthood and the values of the marketplace were evident in how participants constructed gendered accounts of their selves as carers and workers and what was privileged (Hays, 1996; Miller, 2017b). Choices and preferences were narrated in ways that underscored paternal capacities to care for children and significant (sometimes main breadwinner) maternal activity in the workplace. But these generationally different behaviours were narrated in ways that still drew upon more traditionally gendered binaries. Paid work was privileged in the fathers accounts (but) alongside caring activities too, while the women prioritised aspects of their maternal selves even when working full time, seemingly unable to escape the moral dimensions of being seen to be a 'good mother'.

Gender Matters: Moral Orientations and Embodied Practices of Caregiving

A concern across the chapters has been to trace how practices of family caregiving and responsibilities unfold once babies have reached school age and the teenage years. Earlier considerations of care orientations and work (Chapter 2) noted that care work is often invisible, under-valued and has been a largely feminised responsibility, in households as well as when commodified and/or outsourced. The debates around moral and ethical dispositions and orientations to care were also considered as a 'relocation' of care from women to men and from private to public domains had become evident, if partial (Sevenhuijsen, 2003:15; Williams, 2010). This movement indicates possibilities of change in how care becomes practised, more visible, valued and theorised as a human and so universal value and capacity. This, according to Tronto (2010), requires change to 'the educational and familial institutions that are responsible for making the differences between justice and care gender specific' (pp. 662–3). Others too have drawn attention to the possibilities of the 'moral transformation caregiving could produce' if men are more central actors in its thinking and practise (Ranson, 2015:6; Rehel, 2014). Examining practices of caregiving across the chapters and how these occur in concrete daily experiences has shown how men can and do care for their children, but not in ways that exactly mirror or replicate mothering practises: different, but not wrong. Practices of caring for children in families continue to be orchestrated by mothers who take on the mental work of 24/7 thinking in ways that (most) fathers do not (have to).

However, men's orientations to care were evident across the data and most visceral as Sean described the early days and weeks spent with his baby son Jack in a neonatal hospital unit (Chapter 6). He reflected on how he and his wife (Ella) comforted their seriously ill baby son and acknowledges that *'you could tell that there was a difference with Ella, but it didn't really matter is the other thing and it didn't mean that Ella got more of something than I did'*. There has been a general lack of research attention to the ways in which parental practices of caring are also embodied practises, noting the different physicality of how maternal and paternal bodies impart care. An exception to this is the expansive research on breastfeeding and research in which men's perceived 'risky' bodies have been a concern. But there are notable and more recent important contributions to theorising fatherhood and caring as embodied, emotional and relational practises. For example, in Lupton's work on 'interembodiment' and 'skincraft', which fathers can develop and experience through touch and skin proximity with their baby or child (Lupton, 2013:41) and 'intra-actions' in Doucet's (2006, 2009) work that draws attention to the intertwined entanglements of caregiving bodies. Most recently, the 'body techniques' and 'particular physical capital' that fathers bring to their embodied, masculine practices of caring and potential mental work have been explored by Ranson (2015:177). There is need, then, to rethink where, and from which perspective, fathering involvement and forms of caring have been considered. For example, the potential problems of using a 'maternal lens' to explore practises of paternal agency and subjectivity has also been noted (Shirani et al, 2012). On the other hand, the structuring and intersectional features of gender and policies and workplace expectations have received considerable attention in attempts to theorise individual and household patterns of work and caring. The need to wrest parental caring from its historical and unequal 'gender load' and examine ways that enable possibilities of caring differently, where choices are more equitable, has been a focus of scholars and (some) policy makers, but this ambition returns us to fraught and contested territory.

The question of whether men's equal involvement (and choices) in parental caregiving is desirable sits at the core of feminisms and feminist debates, which also pursue competing agendas and seek different outcomes. On the one hand, gender equality achieved through a reconfiguration of unequal caring and household arrangements is a (primary) goal, set beside those who privilege the maternal–child bond and maternal 'preferences' to care or regard the promotion of men's rights (especially in this domain) as contrary to feminist goals (Doucet and Lee, 2014; Firestone, 1971; Gilligan, 1982; O'Reilly, 2016; Rich, 1976; Ruddick, 1989). Indeed the position taken in this book has been to prise apart the concept and everyday practises of caring for children to see where and how fathers become involved – not only in the activities and tasks of caring but the mental work too. Although there is general agreement in fatherhood research findings in Western countries that fathers are significantly more involved in practices of caring, it is the overarching responsibility and orientation of carrying the mental work (*'and I have to hold it all in my head'*) that continues to be an aspect (and burden) of caring most resistant to change. This orientation is least likely to be shared or given up in couple households. And for some women the idea of relinquishing the mental work of caring to fathers may be felt to be a step too far, a position that may be underscored following separation and divorce (see Chapter 5).

Different approaches to shifting the 'gender load' so that work and family life become more compatible or egalitarian have been achieved through policy mechanisms such as shared parental leave, most significantly in Scandinavian countries (Feldman and Gran, 2016; O'Brien, 2013; O'Brien et al, 2014; Wissö and Plantin, 2015). Although the United Kingdom lags behind these northern European countries in relation to such policies, it is ahead of other industrialized countries (e.g. Ireland and the United States), where breadwinning and caring continue to be more differentiated, in theory if no longer so much in practise. For example, in the United States it has been lamented that despite broader economic and cultural shifts and so patterns of intensified work and parenting, a 'viable framework' that can support new arrangements of caring and work has not emerged (Jacobs and Gerson, 2016). Where political commitment exists and policies (that can work) have been introduced, they have supported opportunities for more equitable patterns of working and caring.

It has been argued that the 'most direct and far reaching policy to encourage father involvement' and so promote shared parenting and gender equity more broadly, is through paternity leave policies (Feldman and Gran, 2016:96; Klinth, 2008). Over the years since their introduction and refinement (for example in Sweden; see Chapter 2), parental leave policies have had positive and measurable associations in terms of father–child engagement in couple households. This has been shown to continue into later years and also includes more sharing of household labour (Fagan and Norman, 2016; Feldman and Gran, 2016). The mantra of 'work–life balance' has become part of political rhetoric even though policies can confound the possibility of achiev- ing a workable balance that does not leave people feeling stressed through pressure and lack of time. Even though much more evidence is now available on what types of policies (and welfare states) facili- tate gender equity and work–life balance, the introduction of new poli- cies is mediated by a range of broader political and economic factors. This was the case when Shared Parental Leave was introduced in the United Kingdom in 2015 (Moss et al, 2012; O'Brien and Koslowski, 2016). But if work–life balance is a serious political objective, then a broader range of 'family-friendly' initiatives is required, with policies that join up (and do not leave gaps, for example, in childcare provision as is the case in the United Kingdom). As scholars have noted, 'poli- cies must provide for paid leaves, care services and "family-friendly" working hours if reconciling work and care is to be family centred and promote gender equality' (Lewis et al, 2008:22). In father-focused policies, high levels of income replacement during periods of leave are also key in achieving higher levels of uptake (Featherstone, 2009; O'Brien, 2009).

Shifts in men's practices and involvement in caregiving as fathers have been theorised in relation to acknowledging alternative ways of doing masculinities, in which more emotionally responsive and practical aspects of being a man are emphasised and increasingly culturally acceptable. Theoretical developments have been particularly influenced by the work of Connell, who among much else observed that normative definitions of masculinity do not reflect many men's actual practises (Anderson, 2011; Connell 1995, 2005; Connell and Messerschmidt, 2005; Hearn and Pringle, 2006; Peterson, 1998, 2003; West and Zimmerman, 1987). Connell's earlier unpacking of the concept, identity and practice of gender and its structuring capacities has been significant in how gender is understood and used theoretically. Drawing on more expansive, plural understandings of multiple and fluid masculine ways of being has provided frames through which to examine empirical data collected in different settings and further develop theory (see Chapter 2). This has included visions 'of a new care-oriented masculinity' and the 'nurturing man' developed in theorisations of father involvement in caring (Johansson and Klinth, 2007:2; Vuori, 2007). More recently, in their research on Norwegian fathers who stay home on parental leave, Brandth and Kvande (2016) report that through practise, they develop 'competence' and 'self-worth'. Their findings support theorisations of 'caring masculinities', which are increasingly recognisable and permissible masculine positions reported especially in the Scandinavian context and gradually more apparent in the United Kingdom as well (Dermott and Miller, 2015; Wissö and Plantin, 2015). However, men's practices as (usually new) fathers are most often developed in time-limited periods (10 days' paternity leave in the United Kingdom, daddy quota months in Sweden), and so their fathering is also developed in a context where a return to paid work, looms (Miller, 2012). Looking at fathers who (have to) take on full-time caring for their children (as a consequence of circumstances) provides a more comprehensive view of fathering competencies and so contributes to theorisations of gender, masculinities and femininities (Doucet, 2006, 2016; Ranson, 2015). From this vantage point, it is interesting to note that in Doucet's (2006) major study on Canadian primary-caregiving fathers, one thing the fathers were certain they were not doing, was 'mothering' (p. 217). On this point it is useful to recall how two of the separated fathers, James and Joe (in Chapter 5) both envisaged future relationships with women who could also be a 'mother' to their respective children.

It is clear that father involvement in caregiving has increased in many countries and masculinities, both as theory and practice, are being gradually redefined and traditional, binary and oppositional patterns of gender disrupted. It is also apparent that fathers' caring is not the same as mothering, or mothering the same as fathering. But both parents are capable of giving loving care, delivered in ways which are best described and differentiated as 'parenting like a man' and 'parenting like a woman' (Ranson, 2015:178). But it is important that these different ways of caring and thinking are not glossed over in relation to how parenting responsibilities are perceived and taken up or avoided. Björnberg and Kollind (2005) have noted that 'creating equality in everyday life' becomes a possibility only as and when 'gender' is done differently (p. 131). It remains important to be alert to how gender and power (now) play out in this domain and how these are done and undone in relation to caring responsibilities associated with parenthood (Miller, 2012, 2017a). Thus it continues to be necessary to examine the contours and detail of maternal and paternal caring rather than slip into politically convenient and generic assumptions about parenting and parenthood.

Across the chapters of the book, the mothers' and fathers' descriptions and reflections on caring for their children have been woven into everyday stories of caring, work and relationships. It is apparent from the longitudinal data that tendencies to link caring 'with the symbols and norms of femininity' (Sevenhuijsen, 2003:21) are not so assumed when compared with the first transition interviews as babies were anticipated and the participants were first interviewed but are also not completely absent either. Thus, gendered histories and practices continue to shape in households both what is practised and how, as well as what can and cannot be narrated. For example, in an interview with Joe as his eldest daughter reaches school age, and only 3 months after he has separated from his wife, he describes his emotional state:

Yeah exactly right, but it's hard, yeah, hard. I haven't been emotional for years and years and years and I guess over the last three months I have been about twenty times. But it's all, it's just, it's hard. (Joe)

In this extract Joe is talking about crying ('*about twenty times*'), but seems unable to bring himself to use the word, even though it has been a frank and emotional interview. He goes on in a later part of the interview to talk about how his fathering features in talk with his friends:

But there is not that much we speak about the children, like I say it's still very much a case of 'everything okay?', 'yeah, yeah, good'. You know literally a 2- or 3-minute chat, everything okay, whereas yeah for the next sort of three hours we talk about football or sports or something. (Joe)

Joe, like all the fathers in the study, is involved in significant ways with caregiving for his two young daughters but narrates practises of a masculine self (emotional, but not crying) with reference to 'football or sport' being dominant topics with his friends over discussion of his children (see Miller, 2010, chapter 5). Many women too might want to talk about football or anything else other than their children when out socially, but it's a topic that more easily creeps back into conversations (linked to the all-encompassing sense of responsibility associated with the mental work of primary carer). In the following extract, Joe again confirms the opportunity to reflect that the interview facilitates and prompts (five interviews over a six-year period):

And like I say in terms of when I've spoken to you before I've sort of found it really enlightening because I don't really speak about fears or hopes and those sorts of things, it's still a case of you sort of say, everything is okay, good yeah. (Joe)

It is interesting then that aspects of men's lives and theorisations of masculinities have changed in significant ways to encompass caring masculinity as practice and identity (Anderson, 2011; Brandth and Kvande, 2016; Elliott, 2015; Westerling, 2015; Wissö and Plantin, 2015). But individual narrations are also culturally framed and may be slower to reflect shifts and so (in the context of Joe's life) these are narrated through perceived normative and culturally acceptable discourses and masculine practices of agency – here through sport and not crying. But this is in contrast to recent research findings in Sweden, which note that work colleagues 'provide daily opportunities [for fathers] to talk about both the joys and concerns of parenthood' (Wissö and Plantin, 2015). It may be that this reflects the much longer history of efforts to promote gender equality found in Sweden. It is interesting to think about how individual selves become subsumed into identities and assumptions, as they become mothers and fathers and how even if emotional responses may be the same, cultural ideal and normative practices can continue to shape and be shaped in relation to wider structural influences.

Maternal and Paternal Gatekeeping: Claims of Competency and Incompetency

Even the language of primary carer used to convey caring arrangements and responsibilities in families and households infers a hierarchy of carer. 'Primary' suggests that something or someone is secondary in couple relationships, and this is of course how parental caring arrangements had been managed, up until the more recent period of increased involvement by fathers. The secondary and 'supporting' father still continues to be recognisable in the United Kingdom and was how many of the fathers in the earlier chapters described themselves. Being secondary, or perceiving yourself in a supporting role, often due to employment outside the home and pressures of time, can lead to practices of parenting (as a man) being evaluated as *'wrong'*, *'not the right way'*, *'too harsh'* or *'too indulgent'* by the mother, who has the (primary) overview. Even where caring was described as shared (in some cases equally), the mental work of holding the overarching 24/7 responsibility together was still taken on (or claimed) by the mothers. In Chapter 6, the ways in which this continued maternal caring responsibility is thought about, planned and practised was critically examined through the concept and language of 'gatekeeping', a term singularly applied to mothers. Using the qualitative longitudinal data a more nuanced and broader view of any gatekeeping practices, both maternal *and* potentially paternal was urged in an attempt to point out the contested and contingent terrain on which caring and apparent 'gatekeeping' is undertaken. For example, when does taking on caring responsibilities tip over into 'maternal gatekeeping'? Indeed across the data there was evidence of gatekeeping or 'blocking' behaviours being described in the narratives of the mothers *and* fathers, especially in relation to claims of competency and incompetency (Fagan and Barnett, 2003; Miller, 2017b; Puhlman and Pasley, 2013). Claims of incompetency could free up a father from an activity (see Ian, Chapter 2), but equally with time and practise an incompetency could become a competency, just as would be expected in the workplace or other setting when learning a new skill set. But mothers would also have to let the fathers in (even though it may be felt to be quicker to do the task themselves) and so accept practises that may be achieved in a different (and differently embodied) way to how they have otherwise been done. But is this power that mothers want to relinquish, and does it have to be given up or shared in ambitions for greater gender equity or 'gender symmetry' in family lives? These are key questions for sociologists to consider further.

The moral dimensions and associated scrutiny of parenting still weighs more heavily on mothers, as maternal subjects, than on fathers. But this is not necessarily how fathers want things to be (Doucet, 2006; Ranson, 2015). However, even given the shifts towards realigned gendered relations in caring arrangements over the past 30 years, the mothers position caring in more dominant ways over their careers in their narratives (see Chapter 4), while the fathers do not, and paid work remains a dominant thread running across their narratives (Bass, 2015; Miller, 2017b). Despite significant changes in women's increased participation in the workplace, the normative worker identity continues to be more strongly associated with men and ideals of particular, dominant types of hegemonic masculinity also associated with more highly valued occupations and perceived practices (Perrons, 2009). It continues to be the case that in the United Kingdom women who are mothers are more likely to work flexibly around family commitments (Gatrell, 2005; Thébaud, 2010). The language of the 'working mother' is culturally recognisable, but the concept of the 'working father' much less so because masculine workers are already normatively assumed (Ranson, 2012). This operates in the same way for women who are (and are not) mothers: maternity, motherhood and associated natural orientations are assumed in ways that parallel the working man/father. I was reminded of this when writing Chapter 4 of this book in which the women's experiences of being mothers of teenage children was considered. This followed directly on from writing the chapter on men's experiences of being a father to a primary school–age child in Chapter 3. I was struck when writing about the women that it was not necessary to use the word 'caring' when writing about mothering because it is *so* implicit in our culture, whereas when writing about the fathers, their practices of care had to be made visible and distinct from their paid work and working selves. This reminds me too of the much earlier data collected when the men first became fathers and their fathering was immediately described in optional (not less loving) ways when compared with the mothers (*'you know sort of a day off work a week to be a father'*). They could talk of 'fitting fathering in' or wondering how they would be able to be an involved father and ambitious, successful worker as well.

It continues to be the case then that mothering and fathering are contingent and gendered practices but have been shown to be responsive to political and policy interventions as evidenced in northern European countries. Cultural and economic change has also led to an increased number of mothers in the workplace and men's greater involvement as fathers in caring. But the gender equality 'revolution' awaits completion as institutional constraints persist (Pedulla and Thébaud, 2015:116). Economic logics of work still privilege masculine workers and, importantly, ideas of uninterrupted career trajectories. So it continues to be the case that 'patriarchal habits' are still evident and entrenched in some areas of social life (Bass, 2015; Ruddick, 1997:213).

Narratives and the Longer View: Researching Unfolding and Unravelling Relationships and Practices

There is something particularly illuminating in following unfolding, individual experiences of everyday caring and working in longitudinal research when trajectories cannot be known. It can be the glimpses that emerge in the 'normal' to-and-fro of everyday lives, which across the years can illuminate behaviours and practices in new ways – ways that cannot be captured in single, snapshot interviews. Taking a longer view provides descriptions and narratives of change and continuities that, through their accumulation and layering, come to tell stories which are different perhaps from those originally intended or sought. Everyone grows, including the researcher, and his or her analytic and reflexive skills. The longer view provides an opportunity to look back across the twists and turns of lives and to document what might have changed and what remains embedded – and why. But taking a longer view and inviting participants to (once again) reflect back across episodes in their lives, which were captured in earlier phases of a the study, raises a number of issues for the researcher. One is a practical concern about re-establishing contact with participants and the ethical concerns associated with this undertaking.[1] Next, the accumulation of new data may provide alternative or contradictory versions of aspects of the earlier

---

[1] See Miller (2015) 'Going back: "Stalking", talking and researcher responsibilities in qualitative longitudinal research' for further details and reflections on going back in the original Motherhood study.

research (e.g. experiences of transition to first-time motherhood and fatherhood) and so prompt questions about what constitutes 'the data', and and how subsequent events are interpreted (Miller, 2015). Additionally, the (re)ordering of past events, collected in earlier interviews, can offer the researcher novel opportunities to ask new questions of previous data, providing fresh analytical insights through the analysis of cumulative (over a longer time period) and so more richly layered and textured episodes of experience and narration. Indeed, this has been the case here, as caring orientations have been examined specifically as a consequence of the 24/7 mental work of caring that has emerged but that, in a single interview, would not have been so apparent. Going back into lives and experiences that have unfolded in unexpected ways and reminding the participants of earlier versions of their selves, can enrich theorising of temporal subjectivity – for example in relation to understandings of the storied human self – but also may be (unintentionally) uncomfortable or painful for the narrator – and listener.

The process of undertaking narrative research has become a well-recognised research approach and is popular in different social science and other disciplines. The term 'narrative' has been widely applied in research approaches but not always so carefully aligned to particular philosophical or theoretical frames (Miller, 2017b). The original motherhood and fatherhood studies were designed to explore selves, identities and practices of agency through the (potentially disruptive) life event of becoming a first-time parent and how this is made sense of over time (see Miller, 2005, chapter 1, for further details). The particular social, cultural and, importantly, moral contexts that underpin contemporary experiences was also a focus. So too, what can and cannot be voiced in relation to experiences of being a mother and being a father and associated gendered responsibilities. Returning to collect later accounts of experiences (especially 17 years later in the Motherhood study) underscores the work that we individually engage in to make sense of events and produce what we think are coherent and culturally acceptable narratives. Going back offers opportunities to edit earlier versions of selves presented as a new father, a good worker, a divorced mother, a caring parent, as experiences over time have accumulated, changed ideas or been forgotten. The (re)ordering of events, together with current orientations and future trajectories are usually perceptible in strands of narrative, as selves are made sense of and an account of a moral and acceptable self is narrated. As human beings we are storytelling animals, and through the active production of narrative accounts, we present ourselves to others in what we anticipate are culturally appropriate ways (e.g. the 'involved' father and 'good' mother).

In analysing the data, it is interesting to see what the passage of time facilitates in how experiences of motherhood, fatherhood and parenthood are narrated (Oakley, 2016). Even though the studies involve small numbers of participants, especially compared with quantitative approaches, it is the intensity of the data, added to as phases of transition and parenting journeys have unfolded, that provides unusual depth and facilitates analysis and theorisations to be made. But the lapse of time also shows how memories and recall can work to provide alternative or contradictory accounts of an earlier event or experience and how these can be revised and re-narrated in the light of other changes. For example, a key finding in the Fatherhood study was that intentions to share caregiving in ways that were implied to be 'equal' with their wife or partner were revised once the reality of having a new baby was felt (Miller, 2012). Narrations of new fatherhood shifted to emphasise ideals of masculinity, in which the importance of economic provision and worker identities were dominant as well as, simultaneously, caring masculinities and being there in supporting ways. Earlier findings also revealed gendered differences in the freedoms the mothers and fathers felt in narrating their experiences, which for the mothers involved treading a metaphorical tightrope of feeling it was only acceptable to present and narrate a self as a good mother, while feeling like a not very good (new) mother (Miller, 2007). This time around and 17 years later, the women now preparing for their teenage children to leave home, have *lived* mothering in all its dimensions and they are 'successful' mothers. They and the children and family have got to this point, even if not in the ways originally envisaged as family formations change. There are candid revelations (without the same fear of sanction as in the earlier motherhood interviews) and as before 'disclosures' in both studies (*'and not that my boss next door knows yet, but I won't be staying, I will be leaving and I've already got a new job'*). There are contradictions too, looking back at how 'maternal' journeys are narrated and what the women retrospectively have begrudged, felt guilty about, poor at providing and what they look forward to as child–parent relationships shift (see Chapter 4). The descriptions of unfolding family lives are filled with other people, subsequent children and significant and mundane events (*'and I remember when I was going through really bad postnatal depression following the birth of [second baby] and ringing the Samaritans'*) and all these cast light on developments, change and continuities in aspects of family and work lives and intimate relationships. There is gratitude for the opportunity to talk, as Sheila (mother of three sons) notes, *'I've talked for god knows how long, almost 2 hours! ... I think we've talked about everything. Is there anything else – I don't think so. ... It's nice just being able to talk about me'*. The ways in which this type of research can be experienced as 'therapeutic' are again evident as one father says *'we're just blokes, we don't really speak about it, like well I do when I speak to you'* (Birch and Miller, 2000). The (unusual) opportunity to 'take stock' in time-squeezed lives is also evident and appreciated.

It is always interesting to consider how those who are most vital to our research – the participants – view the enterprise in which they have agreed to participate. As the interview wound down with Nick in the Fatherhood study (a fifth interview as his eldest child reached school age), the following exchange unfolded;

NICK: So how old was [son] when you first came, 2?
TINA: So he was just over 2 at the last interview.
NICK: Two and a half last time?
TINA: Yeah I mean so obviously he wasn't born when I first came, but...
NICK: I had forgotten that.
TINA: That was the transition part of the project.
NICK: Oh that's probably a good transcript, 'oh it will be fine, it will be great, it will be really easy'.

This is interesting in part because Nick had completely forgotten about the first interview, a key interview from my perspective for the study overall, as it was where first-time fatherhood and intentions were imagined and explored as transition was anticipated. But also the fact that he has forgotten underscores the enormity of the shifts that occur in lives when individuals become parents and it's hard to recall a pre-baby life and self. And Nick's final jesting comment about the possible content of the forgotten interview – *'oh it will be fine, it will be great, it will be really easy'* – confirms a shared but misplaced view that caring for a baby is straightforward, but now in the knowledge of just how difficult the first year with his new baby had turned out to be (see Miller, 2010, chapter 4). This links to a further point about participants and researchers in studies that focus on family lives and relationships, which is that 'researchers are already involved with their subject matter' (Morgan, 2014:29). Experiences of family lives is, at some level, inescapable regardless of how varied and different our (versions of our) experiences may seem to be and there are ethical and other considerations as a result. These include how families are assumed and framed in the research, beginning with very initial research ideas and including how and where recruitment is conducted, up to questions in longitudinal research about when a study ends (Miller, 2013a).

The woven together accounts of everyday experiences, narrated from different vantage points through parenthood journeys and explored across the earlier chapters, have illuminated subjectivity as moving and reflexive. Across these accumulated interviews, unfolding, individual stories have revealed tenuous selves in which 'core' and recognisable aspects of subjectivity are edited and re-narrated over time (Thomson, 2009). For example, it was interesting to see how the mothers anticipate life 'after children' and contemplate their selves at this juncture in their lives. Importantly, time 'is central to the task of creating a moving picture of the lifecourse' (Neale, 2015), and the longer and moving view taken here helps to illuminate the twists, turns and messiness as individuals 'negotiate' what at the outset are envisaged as unproblematic life-course (becoming a parent) trajectories – and now look back.

Concluding Thoughts

It is clear that expectations of more intensive and child-centred parenting have become politically and professionally normative, against a backdrop of neoliberal notions of choice, individualism and competitiveness. This sits in stark contrast to what the families in this book say they need, which is time, time together and a level of work and family compatibility and support, which leaves them feeling less stressed by work, care and other demands. Even so, the mothers and fathers are engaged in what they perceive as good parenting (and especially mothering), which is interpreted as investing in the future success of their children, not only at school, but also through a range of enrichment and cultivation activities. Does anyone just spend time at home doing nothing anymore? It is not a surprise that this more privileged group of parents (in terms of their social class) should be so caught up in such activities (Fox, 2009; Klett-Davies, 2010; Lareau, 2003). But this confirmation of perceived intensified parenting responsibilities is only one small thread that runs through the rich stories of mothering and fathering, narrated and shared as their parenting journeys have unfolded.

Taking a longitudinal approach to the study of unfolding family lives is endlessly fascinating. In research terms the fluidity and constancy around practices of agency, perceived responsibilities, changing identities and how selves are narrated at different junctures through a life provide valuable insights into how family lives are made sense of – again and again, as circumstances and relationships change and children grow. The durability of families – being there and being together – within accounts is evident in the data, even when original families are no longer physically together. Children's needs remain a priority, even at a distance. The participants in the studies have made sense of their parenting experiences in the knowledge that some behaviours are seen to constitute 'good parenting' and others not. But there are differently gendered experiences of these, and mothers continue to have less lassitude in relation to how their actions may be interpreted. For example, ideas that a ('selfish') mother might leave her children (especially for a new relationship) is regarded negatively, but the same behaviour by a man would not reflect so entirely on his paternal self and fathering. Gendered differences persist, although to a lesser extent than in previous generations, but can be sharply apparent in some caring and working circumstances if the nouns 'mother' and 'father' are swapped. Being alert to where change is slower and where resistance to change by men or women through various actions, inactions and claims requires vigilant monitoring and further research.

There is now growing international evidence that well-funded government policies can overturn structural constraints and significantly facilitate work–family compatibility and address the 'parental gap' in employment (Connolly et al, 2016). This means that choices in relation to managing caregiving and working should not assume essentialist 'preferences', which in turn raises questions about the acceptability of how we proceed in relation to a more universal-caregiver model. In terms of calls for gender equality, equity, egalitarianism and symmetry, this is the way forward, but how will mothers and fathers feel about particular losses and gains and are 'egalitarian family relationships' possible (Doucet, 2016)? Indeed is it possible to fully envisage these from maternally and paternally inflected positions and embedded perspectives? What is clear is that men, like women, in neoliberal welfare states 'are constrained in their "choices" by structural factors, such as lack of statutory support for working families' (Lyonette et al, 2011:46). It has also been identified that the amount of time that a new father can spend with a baby after its birth has implications for how caregiving becomes shared and practised longer term (Fagan and Norman, 2015; Feldman and Gran, 2016).

This book began with an overview of contemporary parenthood, associated practices of parenting and (continued) scepticism and concern about the political rush to professionalise and scrutinize people's lives as they are occupied bringing up their children. It is clear that the gaze of political and policy interventions falls much more trenchantly on some individuals and much less so on the kinds of mothers and fathers who have shared their experiences in this and the earlier books. But it is essential to note both the variety in how caring and managing family lives is practised and what good-enough parenting might actually look like. The following extract helpfully conveys elements of what children might need: 'at least one loving and attentive parent. Having two parents helps to share this difficult and time-consuming task, but there is no clear evidence that the gender of either of these matters to children's outcomes' (Morton and Viry, 2015). In the mix of heterosexual, couple and (now) co-parenting households explored in this book, the mothers and fathers are both caught up in the minutiae of caring and some are envisioning futures as their young adult children leave home.

The qualitative longitudinal data shared in the earlier chapters in this book and the earlier books on the motherhood and fatherhood studies leads to a concluding observation. This is that practises of parental caring that indicate fathers' increased emotional engagement and possibilities of change as well as maternal and paternal 'gatekeeping' of particular practises have emerged. Patriarchal habits and dividends and motherhood wage penalties continue to underscore the terrain. But it is the daily, micro-processes of caring, documented over many years, that shows the ways in which gendered practises become accepted, reinforced and quite quickly 'invisible' and where inequalities *and* gatekeeping co-exist. Even though it must be possible (mustn't it?) for a 24/7 thinking and caring responsibility to be shared *equally*, why is this equation so hard to balance in relation to parental caring? Rather than focus on the division of tasks, their type and hours spent on them, in trying to promote more gender-equitable choices in home and work spheres, at the heart of these matters sits the assumed *singularity* of a primary responsibility. For all the sharing, it is this singularity – so obdurately attached to constructions of motherhood and 'good mothering', that demands our continued critical attention if meaningful change is to be finally achieved. Men can care too.

References

Acocella, J. (2003) 'Little people'. *The New Yorker*. August 18:138–42.

Adkins, L. (2002) *Revisions: Gender and Sexuality in Late Modernity*. Buckingham, UK: Open University Press.

Allen, G. (2011) *Early Intervention: The Next Steps*. London: Cabinet Office.

Allen, S. M. and Hawkins, A. J. (1999) Maternal gatekeeping: mothers' beliefs and behaviors that inhibit greater father involvement in family work. *Journal of Marriage and the Family*, 61:199–212.

Anderson, E. (2011) *Inclusive Masculinities: The Changing Nature of Masculinities*. London: Routledge

Andrews, M., Squire, C. and Tamboukou, M. (Eds) (2013) *Doing Narrative Research*. 2nd ed. London: Sage Publications.

Arendell, T. (2000) Conceiving and investigating motherhood: the decade's scholarship. *Journal of Marriage and Family*, 62:1192–207.

Aries, P. (1962) *Centuries of Childhood. A Social History of Family Life*. New York: Vintage.

Asher, R. (2012) *Shattered: Modern Motherhood and the Illusion of Equality*. London: Vintage Books.

Awsiukiewicz-Tomczak, A. (2009) *Motherhood Experiences through Transformations: Narratives of Intergenerational Continuities and Changes in Post-Communist Poland*. Unpublished PhD Dissertation, Oxford Brookes University.

Bailey, J. (2012) *Parenting in England c. 1760–1830: Emotions, self-identities and generations*. Oxford: Oxford University Press.

Bailey, L. (2001) Gender shows: First-time mothers and embodied selves. *Gender & Society*, 15:110–29.

Bass, B. C. (2015) Preparing for parenthood? Gender, aspirations, and the reproduction of labor market inequality. *Gender & Society*, 29:362–85.

Ben-Galim, D., Pearce, N. and Thompson, S. (2014) *No More Baby Steps: A Strategy for Revolutionising Childcare*. London: Institute for Public Policy Research (IPPR).

165

Ben-Galim, D. and Thompson, S. (2013) *Who's Breadwinning? Working Mothers and the New Face of Family Support.* London: Institute for Public Policy Research.

  (2014) *Childminding the Gap: Reforming Childcare to Support Mothers into Work.* London: Institute for Public Policy Research. www.ippr .org/publications/childmind-the-gap-reforming-childcare-to-support-mothers-into-work.

Biblarz, T. and Stacey, J. (2010) How does the gender of parents matter? *Journal of Marriage and the Family,* 72:3–22.

Birch, M. and Miller, T. (2000) Inviting intimacy: The interview as therapeutic opportunity. *International Journal of Social Research Methodology,* 3:189–202.

Björk, S. (2013) Doing morally intelligible fatherhood: Swedish fathers' accounts of their parental part-time work choices. *Fathering,* 11:221–37.

Björnberg, U. and Kollind, A. (2005) *Individualism in Families: Equality, Autonomy and Togetherness.* London: Routledge.

Bobel, C. 2002. *The Paradox of Natural Mothering.* Philadelphia: Temple University Press.

Bornat, J. and Bytheway B. (2014) Grandparenting across the lifecourse. In J. Holland and R. Edwards (Eds), *Understanding Families over Time* (Palgrave Macmillan Studies in Family and Intimate Life). London: Palgrave Macmillan, pp. 176–93.

Bowlby, J. (1971) *Attachment and Loss. Volume 1: Attachment.* London: Penguin Books.

Brandth, B. and Kvande, E. (2016) Masculinity and fathering alone during parental leave. *Men and Masculinities,* doi: 10.1177/ 1097184X16652659.

Brannen, J., Moss, P. and Mooney, A. (2004) *Working and Caring over the Twentieth Century.* London: Palgrave Macmillan.

Bruer, J. T. (1999) *The Myth of the First Three Years: A New Understanding of Early Brain Development and Lifelong Learning.* New York: Simon & Schuster.

Bryson, C., Brewer, M., Sibieta, L. and Butt, S. (2012) *The Role of Informal Childcare: A Synthesis and Critical Review of the Evidence. Full report.* Nuffield Foundation. www.nuffieldfoundation.org/sites/default/ files/files/The_role_of_informal_childcare_FULL_REPORT.pdf

Budig, M. and England, P. (2001) The wage penalty for motherhood. *American Sociological Review,* 66:204–25.

Burgess, A., Goldman, R. and Davies, J. (2017) *State of the UK's Fathers: Full Report.* London: Fatherhood Institute.

Charles, N., Davies, C. and Harris, C. (2008) The family and social change revisited. In R. Edwards (Ed), *Researching Families and Communities: Social and Generational Change*. London: Routledge.

Chase, S. E. and Rogers, M. F. (2001) *Mothers and Children: Feminist Analyses and Personal Narratives*. New Brunswick, NJ: Rutgers University Press.

Chodorow, N. (1999) *The Reproduction of Mothering Psychoanalysis and the Sociology of Gender*. Berkeley: University of California Press.

Christopher, K. (2012) Extensive mothering. *Gender & Society*, 26:73–96.

Clegg, N. (2014) Nick Clegg at the launch of Cityfathers on Shared Parental Leave [speech delivered 23 April 2014]. www.gov.uk/government/speeches/nick-clegg-at-the-launch-of-cityfathers-on-shared-parental-leave.

Collier, R. and Sheldon, S. (2008) *Fragmenting Fatherhood: A Socio-Legal Study*. Oxford: Hart.

Coltart, C. and Henwood, K. (2012) On paternal subjectivity: a qualitative and psychosocial case analysis of men's classed positions and transitions to first time fatherhood. *Qualitative Research*, 12:435–52.

Connell, R. W. (1995) *Masculinities*. Cambridge: Polity.

Connell, R. W. and Messerschmidt, J. W. (2005) Hegemonic masculinity: Rethinking the concept. *Gender & Society*, 19:829–59.

Connolly, S., Aldrich, M., O'Brien, M., Speight, S. and Poole, E. (2016) Britain's slow movement to a gender egalitarian equilibrium: Parents and employment in the UK 2001–13. *Work, Employment and Society*, 30:838–57.

Correll, S. J. and Benard, S. (2007) Getting a job: Is there a motherhood penalty? *American Journal of Sociology*, 112:1297–339.

Costa Dias, M., Elming, W. and Joyce, R. (2016) *The Gender Wage Gap*. London: The Institute for Fiscal Studies.

Craig, L., Powell, A. and Smyth, C. (2014) Towards intensive parenting? Changes in the composition and determinants of mothers' and fathers' time with children 1992–2006. *The British Journal of Sociology*, 65:555–79.

Crespi, I. and Miller, T. (Eds) (2013) *Family, Care and Work in Europe: An Issue of Gender?* Macerata, Italy: University of Macerata Press.

Crespi, I. and Ruspini, E. (2016) *Balancing Work and Family in a Changing Society: The Fathers' Perspective*. New York: Palgrave Macmillan.

Crompton, R., Lewis, S. and Lyonette, C. (2007) Introduction: The unravelling of the 'male breadwinner' model and some of its consequences. In R. Crompton, S. Lewis and C. Lyonette (Eds), *Women, men, work and family in Europe*. Basingstoke: Palgrave Macmillan.

Crompton, R. and Lyonette, C. (2007) Reply to Hakim. *The British Journal of Sociology*. doi: 10.1111/j.1468–4446.2007.00143.x

(2008) Who does the housework? The division of labour within the home. In A. Park and J. Curtice, K. Thomson, M. Philips, M. Johnson and E. Clery (Eds), *British Social Attitudes: The 24th Report*. London: Sage.

Crossley, S. (2015) 'Realising the (troubled) family', 'crafting the neoliberal state'. *Families, Relationships and Societies*, 5:263–79. doi: 10.1332/204674315X14326465757666.

Curtice, J. Phillips, M. and Clery, E. (2016) *Britain Divided? Public Attitudes after Seven Years of Austerity*. London: British Social Attitudes. www.bsa.natcen.ac.uk/?_ga=1.43472613.1332573774.1467244789.

Daly, M. (2013) Parenting support policies in Europe. *Families, Relationships and Societies*, 2:159–74.

Davidoff, L., Doolittle, M., Fin, J. and Holden, K. (1999) *The Family Story: Blood, Contract and Intimacy*, 1830–1960. Harlow, England: Addison Wesley Longman.

Davies, B. and Bansel, P. (2007) Neoliberalism and education. *International Journal of Qualitative Studies in Education*, 20:247–59.

Department of Health (2016) *Early Years High Impact Area 1 – Transition to Parenthood and the Early Years*. www.gov.uk/government/uploads/system/uploads/attachment_data/file/413128/2903110_Early_Years_Impact_1_V0_2W.pdf.

Dermott, E. (2008) *Intimate Fatherhood: A Sociological Analysis*. London: Routledge.

Dermott, E. and Miller, T. (2015) More than the sum of its parts? Contemporary fatherhood policy, practice and discourse. *Families, Relationships and Societies*, 4:183–95.

Dermott, E. and Pomati, M. (2016) 'Good' parenting practices: How important are poverty, education and time pressure? *Sociology*, 50:125–42.

Deutsch, F. M. (2007) Undoing gender. *Gender & Society*, 21:106–26.

Deven, F. (2014) *Leave Arrangements in Europe: Major Trends, Challenges and Policy Issues 2014*. www.family2014.org/egmb/PD4-Deven.pdf.

Dorling, D. (2015) *Injustice. Why Social Inequality Still Persists*. Bristol, England: Policy Press.

Doucet, A. (2006) *Do Men Mother?: Fathering, Care, and Domestic Responsibility*. Toronto: University of Toronto Press.

(2009) Dad and baby in the first year: Gendered responsibilities and embodiment. *The Annals of the American Academy of Political and Social Science*, 624:78–98.

(2016) Is the stay-at-home dad (SAHD) a feminist concept? A genealogical, relational, and feminist critique. *Sex Roles*, 75:4–14. doi10.1007/s11199–016–0582–5.

Doucet, A. and Lee, R. (2010) Fathering, feminism(s), gender and sexualities: connections, tensions and new pathways. *Journal of Family Theory and Review*, 6:355–73.

(2014) Fathering, feminism(s), gender, and sexualities: Connections, tensions, and new pathways. *Journal of Family Theory & Review*, 6:355–73.

Doughney, J. and Leahy, M. (2006) Women, work and preference formation: A critique of Catherine Hakim's preference theory. *Journal of Business Systems, Governance and Ethics*, 1:37–48.

Dribe, M. and Stanfors, M. (2009) Does parenthood strengthen a traditional household division of labor? Evidence from Sweden. *Journal of Marriage and Family*, 71:33–45.

Duncan, S. (2007) What's the problem with teenage parents? And what's the problem with policy? *Critical Social Policy*, 27:307–34.

Duncan, S. and Edwards, R. (1999) *Lone Mothers, Paid Work and Gendered Moral Rationalities*. Basingstoke, England: Macmillan.

Duncan, S. Edwards, R. and Alexander, C. (2010) *Teenage Parenthood: What's the Problem?* London: The Tufnell Press.

Dunne, G. A. (2000) Opting into motherhood: Lesbians blurring the boundaries and transforming the meaning of parenthood and kinship. *Gender & Society*, 14:11–35.

Edwards, R. (Ed) (2008) *Researching Families and Communities: Social and Generational Change*. London: Routledge.

Edwards, R. and Gillies, V. (2011) Clients or consumers, commonplace or pioneers? Navigating the contemporary class politics of family, parenting skills and education. *Ethics and Education*, 6:141–54.

(2012) Farewell to family? Notes on an argument for retaining the concept. *Families, Relationships and Societies*, 1:63–9.

Edwards, R., Gillies, V. and Horsley, N. (2015) Early intervention and evidence-based policy and practice: framing and taming. *Social Policy and Society*, 15:1–14. doi: 10.1017/S1474746415000081.

Edwards, R., Gillies, V. and Ribbens McCarthy, J. (2012) The politics of concepts: Family and its (putative) replacements. *British Journal of Sociology*, 63:730–46.

Ehrenreich, B. and Hochschild, A. R. (Eds) (2002) *Global Woman: Nannies, Maids, and Sex Workers in the New Economy*. New York: Henry Holt.

Ekberg, J., Eriksson, R. and Friebel, G. (2013) Parental leave – a policy evaluation of the Swedish "Daddy-Month" reform. *Journal of Public Economics*, 97:131–43.

Elliott, K. (2015) Caring masculinities. Theorizing an emerging concept. *Men and Masculinities*, 19:240–59.

Elliott, S., Powell, R. and Brenton, J. (2015) Being a good mom: Low-income, black single mothers negotiate intensive mothering. *Journal of Family Issues*, 36:351–70.

Elvin-Nowak, Y. and Thomsson, H. (2001) Motherhood as idea and practice: A discursive understanding of employed mothers in Sweden. *Gender & Society*, 15:407–28.

England, K. (2010) Home, work and the shifting geographies of care. *Ethics, Place and Environment*, 13:131–50.

England, P. (2005) Emerging theories of care work. *Annual Review of Sociology*, 31:381–99.

England, P. (2010) The gender revolution. Uneven and stalled. *Gender & Society*, 24:149–66.

Eurostat. (2016) *Europe 2020 Indicators – Employment*. http://ec.europa.eu/eurostat/statistics-explained/index.php/Europe_2020_indicators_-_employment

Eydal, G. B. and Rostgaard, T. (2016) *Fatherhood in the Nordic Welfare States: Comparing Care Policies and Practice*. Bristol, England: Policy Press.

Fagan, J. and Barnett, M. (2003) The relationship between maternal gatekeeping, paternal competence, mothers' attitudes about the father role, and father involvement. *Journal of Family Issues*, 24:1020–43.

Fagan, C. and Norman, H. (2016) Which fathers are involved in caring for pre-school age children in the United Kingdom? A longitudinal analysis of the influence of work hours in employment on shared childcare arrangements in couple households. In I. Crespi and E. Ruspini (Eds), *Balancing Work and Family in a Changing Society: The Fathers' Perspective*. New York: Palgrave Macmillan.

Fagnani, J. (2007) Fertility rates and mothers employment behaviour in comparative perspective: similarities and differences in six European countries. In R. Crompton, S. Lewis and C. Lyonette (Eds), *Women, men, work and family in Europe*. Basingstoke, England: Palgrave Macmillan, Basingstoke.

Faircloth, C., Hoffman, D. M. and Layne, L. L. (Eds) (2013) *Parenting in Global Perspective: Negotiating Ideologies of Kinship, Self and Politics*. London: Routledge.

Featherstone, B. (2003) Taking fathers seriously. *British Journal of Social Work*, 33:239–54.

Featherstone, B. (2009) *Contemporary Fathering*. Bristol: Policy Press.

Featherstone, B., Gupta, A., Morris, K. and Warner, J. (2016) Let's stop feeding the risk monster: Towards a social model of 'child protection'. *Families, Societies and Relationships*. doi: https://doi.org/10.1332/204674316X14552878034622.

Feldman, K. and Gran, B. (2016) Is what's best for dads best for families? Paternity leave policies and equity across forty-four nations. *Journal of Sociology & Social Welfare*, XLIII(1).

Firestone, S. (1971) *The Dialectic of Sex*. London: Jonathan Cape.

Fisher, B. and Tronto, J. (1990) *Circles of care: Work and Identity in Women's Lives*. Albany: State University of New York Press, pp. 35–62.

Flood, M. (2002) Between men and masculinity: An assessment of the term "masculinity" in recent scholarship on men. In S. Pearce and V. Muller (Eds), *Manning the Next Millennium: Studies in Masculinities*. Perth, Australia: Black Swan Press.

Fox, B. (2009) *When Couples Become Parents: The Creation of Gender in the Transition to Parenthood*. Toronto: University of Toronto.

Frank, A. (1995) *The Wounded Storyteller*. Chicago: University of Chicago Press.

Furedi, F. (2001) *Paranoid Parenting: Abandon Your Anxieties and Be a Good Parent*. London: Penguin.

(2008) *Paranoid Parenting: Why ignoring the experts may be best for your child*. London: Continuum.

Gatrell, C. (2005) *Hard Labour: The Sociology of Parenthood*. Maidenhead, England: Open University Press.

Gatrell, C. J., Burnett, S., Cooper, C. L. C. and Sparrow, P. (2015) The price of love: The prioritisation of child care and income earning among UK fathers. *Families, Relationships and Society*, 4:225–38.

Gerson, K. (2011) *The Unfinished Revolution. Coming of Age in a New Era of Gender, Work, and Family*. Oxford: Oxford University Press.

Gerstel, S. K. and Gallagher, N. (2001) Connections and constraints: The effects of children on caregiving. *Journal of Marriage and Family*, 63:265–75.

Gillies, V. (2007) *Marginalised Mothers: Exploring Working Class Experiences of Parenting*. Abingdon, England: Routledge.

(2008) Childrearing, class and the new politics of parenting. *Sociology Compass*, 2/3:1079–95.

Gilligan, C. (1982) *In a Different Voice. Psychological Theory and Women's Development*. Cambridge, MA: Harvard University Press.

Golombok, S. (2000) *Parenting: What Really Counts?* London: Routledge.

Golombok, S. (2015) *Modern Families: Parents and Children in New Family Forms*. Cambridge: Cambridge University Press.

Grundy, E. and Henretta, J. C. (2006) Between elderly parents and adult children: A new look at the intergenerational care provided by the 'sandwich generation'. *Ageing and Society*, 26:707–22. doi: 10.1017/S0144686X06004934.

Grunow, D. and Evertsson, M. (Eds) (2016) *Couples' Transitions to Parenthood: Analysing Gender and Work in Europe*. Cheltenham, England: Edward Elgar

Haas, L. and Hwang, P. (2008) The impact of taking parental leave on fathers' participation in childcare and relationships with children: Lessons from Sweden. *Community, Work & Family*, 11:85–104.

(2016) "It's about time!": Company support for fathers' entitlement to reduced work hours in Sweden. *Social Policy*, 23:142–67.

Habib, B. (2012) The transition to fatherhood: A literature review exploring paternal involvement with identity theory. *Journal of Family Studies*, 18:4–21.

Hakim, C. (2000) *Work-Lifestyle Choices in the 21st Century: Preference Theory*. Oxford: Oxford University Press.

Harden, J., MacLean, A., Backett-Milburn, K., Cunningham-Burley, S. and Jamieson, L. (2014) Responsibility, Work and Family Life: Children's and Parents' Experiences of Working Parenthood. In J. Holland and R. Edwards (Eds), *Understanding Families over Time. Research and Policy*. Basingstoke, England: Palgrave Macmillan.

Hays, S. (1996) *The Cultural Contradictions of Motherhood*. New Haven, CT: Yale University Press.

Hearn, J. (2004) From Hegemonic masculinity to the hegemony of men. *Feminist Theory*, 5:49–72.

Hearn, J. and Pringle, K. (2006) *European Perspectives on Men and Masculinities: National and Transnational Approaches*. Basingstoke, England: Palgrave Macmillan.

Held, V. (2006) *The Ethics of Care: Personal, Political, and Global*. Oxford: Oxford University Press.

Henderson, M. (2012) A test of parenting strategies. *Sociology*, 47:542–59.

Hendrick, H. (2016) *Narcissistic Parenting in an Insecure World*. Bristol: Policy Press.

Henwood, K. and Shirani, F. (2012) *Extending temporal horizons*. Timescapes Methods Guides Series 2012. No. 4. www.timescapes.leeds .ac.uk/assets/files/methods-guides/timescapes-henwood-extending-temporal-horizons.pdf.

Henwood, K., Shirani, F. and Coltart, C. (2014) Investing in involvement: Men moving through fatherhood. In J. Holland and R. Edwards (Eds),

Understanding Families over Time: Research and Policy. Basingstoke, UK: Palgrave Macmillan.

Herrera, F. (2013) "Men always adopt": Infertility and reproduction from a male perspective. *Journal of Family Issues*, 34:1059–80.

Hicks, S. (2011) *Lesbian, Gay and Queer Parenting*. London: Palgrave Macmillan.

Hill Collins, P. (1994) Shifting the centre: Race, class and feminist theorising about motherhood. In E. N. Glenn, E. Chang and L. R. Forcey (Eds), *Mothering, ideology, experience and agency*. London: Routledge.

Hochschild, A. (1983) *The Managed Heart Commercialization of Human Feeling*. Berkeley: University of California Press.

(1989) *The Second Shift*. New York: Avon Books.

— (2003) *The Commercialization of Intimate Life: Notes from Home and Work*. Berkeley: University of California Press.

Hoff, A. (2009) *Families, Care and Work: Changes and Challenges*. Oxford: The Oxford Institute of Ageing, University of Oxford.

(2015) *Current and Future Challenges of Family Care in the UK. Future of an Ageing Population: Evidence Review* (Foresight Future of an Ageing Population Project). London: Government Office for Science.

Holland, J. and Edwards, R. (Eds) (2014) *Understanding Families Over Time: Research and Policy*. Basingstoke, UK: Palgrave Macmillan.

Holloway, S. L. and Pimlott-Wilson, H. (2011) The politics of aspiration: Neo-liberal education policy, 'low' parental aspirations, and primary school Extended Services in disadvantaged communities. *Children's Geographies* (Special Issue: 'Education and Aspiration'), 9:79–94.

Holloway, S. L. and Pimlott-Wilson, H. (2014) Any advice is welcome isn't it?: Neoliberal parenting education, local mothering cultures and social class. *Environment and Planning A*, 46:94–111.

Hollway, W. (2006) *The Capacity to Care: Gender and Ethical Subjectivity*. London: Routledge.

Inhorn, M., Chavkin, W. and Navarro, J. (Eds) (2016) *Globalized fatherhood*. New York: Berghahn.

Irwin, S. and Elley, S. (2011) Concerted cultivation? Parenting values, education and class diversity. *Sociology*, 45:480–95.

(2012) Parents' hopes and expectations for their children's future occupations. *The Sociological Review*, 61:111–30.

Irwin, S. and Winterton, M. (2014) Gender and work-family conflict: A secondary analysis of Timescapes data. In J. Holland and R. Edwards (Eds), *Understanding Families over Time: Research and Policy*. London: Palgrave, pp. 142–58.

Ives, J. (2014) Men, maternity and moral residue: Negotiating the moral demands of the transition to first time fatherhood. *Sociology of Health and Illness*, 36:1003–19.

Jacobs, J. A. and Gerson, K. (2015) Unpacking Americans' views of the employment of mothers and fathers using national vignette survey data. *Gender & Society*, 30:413–41.

James, A. and James, A. L. (2004) *Constructing Childhood: Theory, Policy and Social Practice*. Basingstoke, England: Palgrave Macmillan.

Jamieson, L., Simpson, R. and Lewis, R. (2014) *Researching families and relationships: Reflections on process*. Basingstoke, England: Palgrave Macmillan.

Jensen, T. (2010) Warmth and wealth: Re-imagining social class in taxonomies of good parenting. *Studies in the Maternal*, 2:1–13.

Johansson, M., Katz, K. and Nyman, H. (2005) Wage differentials and gender discrimination – changes in Sweden 1981–98. *Acta Sociologica*, 48:341–64.

Johansson, T. and Klinth, R. (2007) Caring fathers. The ideology of gender and equality and masculine positions. *Men and Masculinities*, 11:42–62.

Jones, C. and Hackett, S. (2011) The role of 'family practices' and 'displays of family' in the creation of adoptive kinship. *British Journal Social Work*, 41:40–56. doi: 10.1093/bjsw/bcq017.

Jones, J. (2014) Recomposing maternal identities: Mothering young adult children. In A. O'Reilly (Ed), *Mothers, Mothering and Motherhood Across Cultural Differences: A Reader*. Ontario, Canada: Demeter Press.

Kehily, M. (Ed) (2013) *Understanding Childhood: A Cross Disciplinary Approach*. 2nd ed. London: Open University Press and The Policy Press.

Kehily, M. and Thomson, R. (2011) Displaying motherhood: Representations, visual methods and the materiality of maternal practice. In E. Dermott and J. Seymour (Eds), *Displaying Families*. London: Palgrave Macmillan, pp. 61–80.

Kimmel, M. S., Hearn, J. and Connell, R. W. (2004) *Handbook of Studies on Men and Masculinities*. London: Sage.

King, M. L. (2007) Concepts of childhood: What we know and where we might go. *Renaissance Quarterly*, 60:371–407.

Kittay, E. (1999) *Love's Labor: Essays in Women, Equality and Dependency*. New York: Routledge.

Klett-Davies, M. (Ed) (2010) *Is Parenting a Class Issue?* London: Family and Parenting Institute.

Klinth, R. (2008) The best of both worlds? Fatherhood and gender equality in Swedish paternity leave campaigns, 1976–2006. *Fathering*, 6:20–38.

Lareau, A. (2003) *Unequal Childhoods: Race, Class and Family Life*. Berkeley: University of California Press.

Lash, S. (1994) Reflexivity and its doubles: structure, aesthetics, community. In U. Beck, A. Giddens and S. Lash (Eds), *Reflexive Modernization:*

Politics, Tradition and Aesthetics in the Modern Social Order. Cambridge: Polity Press.

Lawler, S. (2000) *Mothering the Self: Mothers, Daughters, Subjects.* London: Routledge.

Lee, E., Faircloth, C., MacVarish, J. and Bristow, J. (2014) *Parenting Culture Studies.* London: Palgrave.

Lewis, J., Campbell, M. and Huerta, C. (2008) Patterns of paid and unpaid work in Western Europe: gender, commodification, preferences and the implications for policy. *Journal of European Social Policy,* 18:21–37.

Lewis, J., West, A., Roberts, J. and Noden, P. (2015) Parents' involvement and university students' independence. *Families, Relationships and Societies,* 4:417–32.

Lowe, P., Lee, E. and Macvarish, J. (2015) Growing better brains? Pregnancy and neuroscience discourses in English social and welfare policies. *Health, Risk & Society,* 17:15–29.

Lupton, D. (2013) Infant embodiment and interembodiment: A review of sociological perspectives. *Childhood,* 20:37–50.

Lyonette, C., Kaufman, G. and Crompton, R. (2011) 'We both need to work': Maternal employment, childcare and health care in Britain and the USA. *Work, Employment & Society,* 25:34–50.

Mac an Ghaill, M. and Haywood, C. (2007) *Gender, Culture and Society: Contemporary Femininities and Masculinities.* Basingstoke, England: Palgrave Macmillan.

MacIntyre, A. (1981) *After Virtue.* London: Duckworth.

Macvarish, J. (2016) *Neuroparenting: The Expert Invasion of Family Life.* Basingstoke, England: Palgrave Macmillan.

Marsiglio, W., Roy, K. and Fox, G. L. (2005) *Situated Fathering: A Focus on Physical and Social Spaces.* Boulder, CO: Rowman & Littlefield.

McBride, A., Brown, G., Bost, K., Shin, N., Vaughn, B. and Korth, B. (2005) Paternal identity, maternal gatekeeping, and father involvement. *Family Relations,* 54:335–473.

McGregor, S. (2001) Neoliberalism and health care. *International Journal of Consumer Studies,* 25:82–9.

McRae, S. (2003) Choice and constraints in mothers' employment careers: McRae replies to Hakim. *The British Journal of Sociology,* 54:585–92.

Messerschmidt, J. W. (2009) "Doing gender": The impact and Future of a Salient Sociological Concept. *Gender and Society,* 23:85–88.

Miller, T. (2005) *Making Sense of Motherhood: A Narrative Approach.* Cambridge: Cambridge University Press.

(2007) '*Is this what motherhood is all about?*' Weaving experiences and discourse through transition to first-time motherhood. *Gender & Society,* 21:337–58.

(2009) Thoughts around the maternal: A sociological viewpoint. *Studies in the Maternal*, 1. www.researchgate.net/publication/241144728_ Thoughts_around_the_Maternal_A_Sociological_Viewpoint.

(2010) *Making Sense of Fatherhood: Gender, Caring and Work*. Cambridge: Cambridge University Press.

(2011) Falling back into gender? Men's narratives and practices around first-time fatherhood. *Sociology*, 45:1094–9.

(2012) Reconfiguring research relationships. In T. Miller, M. Birch, M. Mauthner and J. Jessop (Eds), *Ethics in Qualitative Research* (2nd ed). London: Sage.

(2013a) Messy ethics: Negotiating the terrain between ethics approval and ethical practice. In J. MacClancy and A. Fuentes (Eds), *Ethics in the field: Contemporary Challenges*. Oxford: Berghahn Books.

(2013b) Shifting out of neutral on parental leave: Making fathers' involvement explicit. *Juncture*, 19:258–62.

(2014) Anticipating and 'experiencing' birth: Men, essentialisms, and reproductive realms. In M. Nash (Ed), *Reframing Reproduction Conceiving Gendered Experiences*. London: Palgrave Macmillan.

(2015) Going back: 'Stalking', talking and researcher responsibilities in qualitative longitudinal research. *International Journal of Social Research Methodology*, 18:293–305.

(2017a) Doing narrative research? In J. Woodiwiss, K. Smith and K. Lockwood (Eds), *Feminist Narrative Research: Opportunities and Challenges*. Basingstoke, England: Palgrave Macmillan (in press).

(2017b) Making sense of motherhood and fatherhood: Competing moral discourses and logics of caring and work 'choices' in the UK. In B. Brandth, S. Halrynjo and E. Kvande (Eds), *Work-Family Dynamics: Competing Logics of Regulation, Economy and Morals*. London: Routledge.

Morgan, D. (2014) Framing Relationships and Families. In L. Jamieson, R. Simpson and R. Lewis (Eds), *Researching Families and Relationships*. Basingstoke, England: Palgrave Macmillan.

Morton, S. and Viry, G. (2015) Supporting dads in the context of gender inequality. Center for Research on Families and Relationships. http://crfrblog.blogspot.co.uk/2015/01/supporting-dads-in-context-of-gender_27.html.

Mose, T. R. (2016) *The Playdate, Parents, Children, and the New Expectations of Play*. New York: NYU Press.

Moss, P., O'Brien, M., Lamb, M., Miller, T., Burgess, A., Abse, S., Asher, R., Fisher, D. and Lammy, D. (2012) Think again on plans for parental leave. *The Guardian*, November 14. www.theguardian.com/lifeandstyle/2012/nov/14/think-again-plans-parental-leave.

Moss, P. and Wall, K. (2007) *International Review of Leave Policies and Related Research 2007* (Employment Relations Research Series No. 80). London: Department for Business Enterprise and Regulatory Reform.

Murphy, D. (2016) *Gay Men Pursuing Parenthood through Surrogacy: Reconfiguring Kinship*. Kensington, Australia: New South Publishing.

Neale, B. (2012) *Timescapes Methods Guides Series 2012 Guide No. 1. Qualitative Longitudinal Research: An Introduction to the Timescapes Methods Guides Series.* www.timescapes.leeds.ac.uk/assets/files/methods-guides/timescapes-methods-guides-introduction.pdf.

(2015) Time and the lifecourse: Perspectives from qualitative longitudinal research. In N. Worth & I. Hardill (Eds), *Researching the Lifecourse: Critical Reflections from the Social Sciences*. Bristol, England: Policy Press.

Nelson, M. (2010) *Parenting Out of Control: Anxious Parents in Uncertain Times*. New York: New York University Press.

Nilsen, A., Brannen, J. and Lewis, S. (Eds) (2013) *Transitions to Parenthood in Europe: A comparative life course perspective*. Bristol, England: Policy Press.

Noddings, N. (2003) *Caring: A Feminine Approach to Ethics and Moral Education*. Berkeley, CA: University of California Press.

Norman, H. and Elliot, M. (2015) Measuring paternal involvement in childcare and housework. *Sociological Research Online*, 20:7.

Oakley, A. (1979) *Becoming a Mother*. Oxford: Martin Robertson.

(2016) A small sociology of maternal memory. *The Sociological Review*, 64:533–49.

O'Brien, M. (2009) Fathers, Parental Leave Policies and Infant Quality of Life: International Perspectives and Policy Impact. *The ANNALS of the American Academy of Political and Social Science*, 624:190–213.

(2013) Fitting fathers into work-family policies: International challenges in turbulent times. *International Journal of Sociology and Social Policy*, 33. www.emeraldinsight.com/doi/abs/10.1108/IJSSP-05-2013-0060.

O'Brien, M., Brandth, B. and Kvande, E. (2007) Fathers, work and family life. Global perspectives and new insights. *Community, Work and Family*, 10:375–86.

O'Brien, M. and Koslowski, A. (2016) United Kingdom (country note). In A. Koslowski, S. Blum and P. Moss (Eds), *International Review of Leave Policies and Research 2016*. International Network on Leave Policies & Research. www.leavenetwork.org/fileadmin/Leavenetwork/Country_notes/2016/United_Kingdom.pdf.

O'Brien, M., Koslowski, A. and Daly, M. (2015) United Kingdom (country notes). In *International Review of Leave Policies and Research 2015*. International Network on Leave Policies & Research.

www.leavenetwork.org/fileadmin/Leavenetwork/Country_notes/2015/
UK.pm.pdf.

O'Brien, M., Moss, P., Koslowski, A. and Daly, M. (2014). United Kingdom Country Note. In P. Moss (Ed), *International Review of Leave
Policies and Research 2013*. London: Institute of Education, University of London. http://www.leavenetwork.org/fileadmin/Leavenetwork/
Annual_reviews/2013_annual_review.pdf.

Office for National Statistics. (2013) *Women in the Labour Market:
2013*. www.ons.gov.uk/employmentandlabourmarket/peopleinwork/
employmentandemployeetypes/articles/womeninthelabourmarket/
2013-09-25.

   (2015) Divorces in England and Wales: 2013. www.ons.gov.uk/
   peoplepopulationandcommunity/birthsdeathsandmarriages/divorce/
   bulletins/divorcesinenglandandwales/2013#divorce-rates.

   (2016) Families and households in the UK: 2016. www.ons.gov.uk/
   peoplepopulationandcommunity/birthsdeathsandmarriages/families/
   bulletins/familiesandhouseholds/2016.

O'Reilly, A. (Ed) (2008) *Feminist Mothering*. Albany, NY: SUNY Press.

O'Reilly, A. (2016) *Matricentric Feminism: Theory, Activism, Practice*. Perth,
Australia: Demeter Press.

Osborne, H. (2016) Tiny proportion of men are opting for shared
parental leave. *The Guardian*. www.theguardian.com/money/2016/apr/
05/shared-parental-leave-slow-take-up-fathers-paternity.

Park, A., Bryson, C., Clery, E., Curtice, J. and Phillips, M. (Eds) (2013) *British
Social Attitudes: the 30th Report*. London: NatCen Social Research.
www.bsa-30.natcen.ac.uk.

Pedulla, D. and Thébaud, S. (2015) Can we finish the revolution? Gender,
work-family ideals, and institutional constraint. *American Sociological
Review*, 80:116–139.

Perrons, D. (2009) *Women and Gender Equity in Employment: Patterns,
Progress and Challenges*. (Working Paper WP23). Brighton, England:
Institute for Employment Studies.

Perrons, D. (2010) Gender, work and 'market' values. *Renewel*, 18(1/2).
www.direct.gov.uk/en/Parents/Moneyandworkentitlements/WorkAnd
Families/Parentalleaveandflexibleworking/DG_10029416.

Peterson, A. (1998) *Unmasking the Masculine: Men and Identity in a Scep-
tical Age*. London: Sage.

Peterson, A. (2003) Research on men and masculinities. Some implications
of recent theory for future work. *Men and Masculinities*, 6:54–69.

Philip, G. (2013) Relationality and moral reasoning in accounts of fathering after separation or divorce; care, gender and working at 'fairness'.
Families, Relationships and Societies, 3:409–24.

(2014) Fathering after separation or divorce: navigating domestic, public and moral spaces. *Families, Relationships and Societies*, 3:219–33.

Philip, G. and O'Brien, M. (2012) *Supporting Fathers after or Divorce: Evidence and Insights*. Norwich, England: Centre for Research on the Child and Family, University of East Anglia.

Plantin, L., Mänsson, S.-A. and Kearney, J. (2003) Talking and doing fatherhood: On fatherhood and masculinity in Sweden and England. *Fathering: A Journal of Theory, Research, and Practice about Men as Fathers*. www.mensstudies.info/OJS/index.php/FATHERING/article/view/184.

Pruett, M. L., Arthur, L. A. and Ebling, E. (2007) The Hand That Rocks the Cradle: Maternal Gatekeeping after Divorce. Summer 2007 Symposium on the Miller Commission on Matrimonial Law. *Pace Law Review Volume*, 27:Article 8.

Puhlman, D. J. and Pasley, K. (2013) Rethinking maternal gatekeeping. *Journal of Family Theory & Review*, 5:176–93.

Radcliffe, L. and Cassell, C. (2015) Flexible working, work–family conflict, and maternal gatekeeping: The daily experiences of dual-earner couples. *Journal of Occupational and Organisational*, 88:835–55.

Raith, L., Jones, J. and Porter, M. (Eds) (2015) *Mothers at the Margins: Stories of Challenge, Resistance and Love*. Newcastle-upon-Tyne, England: Cambridge Scholars Publishing.

Ramaekers, S. and Suissa, J. (2012) *The Claims of Parenting*. London: Springer.

Ranson, G. (2012) Men, Paid Employment and Family Responsibilities: Conceptualizing the 'Working Father'. *Gender, Work & Organization*, 19:741–61.

(2015) *Fathering, Masculinity and the Embodiment of Care*. Basingstoke, England: Palgrave Macmillan.

Reece, H. (2013) The pitfalls of positive parenting. *Ethics and Education*, 8:42–54.

Rehel, E. M. (2014) When dad stays home too. Paternity leave, gender, and parenting. *Gender & Society*, 28:110–32.

Reynolds, T. (2005) *Caribbean Mothering: Identity and Childrearing in the UK*. London: Tufnell Press.

Ribbens, J. (1998) Hearing my feeling voice? An autobiographical discussion of motherhood. In R. Edwards and J. Ribbens (Eds), *Feminist dilemmas in qualitative research*. London: Sage.

Ribbens McCarthy, J. (2006) *Young People's Experiences of Loss and Bereavement: Towards an Inter-disciplinary Approach*. Buckingham, England: Open University Press.

(2012) The powerful relational language of 'family': Togetherness, belonging and personhood. *Sociological Review*, 60:68–90.

Ribbens McCarthy, J., Edwards, R. and Gillies, V. (2003) *Making Families: Moral Tales of Parenting and Step-parenting*. Durham, NC: Sociology Press.

Ribbens McCarthy, J., Hooper, C. A. and Gillies, V. (Eds) (2013) *Family Troubles? Exploring Changes and Challenges in the Family Lives*. Bristol, England: Policy Press.

Rich, A. (1976) *Of Woman Born*. London: Virago.

Ricoeur, P. (1984) *Time and Narrative*, Volume 1. Chicago: University of Chicago Press.

Riessman, C. K. (1990) *Divorce Talk: Women and Men Make Sense of Personal Relationships*. New Brunswick, NJ: Rutgers University Press.

(2008) *Narrative Methods for the Human Sciences*. Thousand Oaks, California: Sage Publications.

Risman, B. (2009) From doing to undoing: Gender as we know it. *Gender & Society*, 23:81–4.

Romito, P. (1997) Damned if you do and damned if you don't: psychological and social constraints on motherhood in contemporary Europe. In A. Oakley and J. Mitchell (Eds.) *Who's afraid of Feminism?* London: Hamish Hamilton.

Rothman, B. K. (1989) *Recreating Motherhood*. New York: Norton Press.

Ruddick, S. (1989) *Maternal thinking: Toward a politics of peace*. Boston: Beacon Press.

(1997) The idea of fatherhood. In H. L. Nelson (Ed), *Feminism and Families*. London: Routledge.

(1998) Care as labor and relationship. In Joram G. Haber and M. Haflon (Eds.), *Norms and Values: Essays on the Work of Virginia Held*. Lanham, MD: Rowman & Littlefield.

Rutter, J. (2015) *Childcare Survey 2015*. Family and Childcare Trust. www.familyandchildcaretrust.org/childcare-survey-2015.

Sanchez, L. and Thomson, E. (1997) Becoming mothers and fathers: Parenthood, gender and the division of labor. *Gender & Society*, 11:747–72.

Saxonberg, S. (2014) *Gendering Family Policies in Post-Communist Europe: A Historical Instituitional Analysis*. Basingstoke, England: Palgrave Macmillan.

Schoppe-Sullivan, S. J., Altenburger, L., Lee, M. A., Bower, D. J. and Kamp Dush, C. M. (2015) Who are the gatekeepers? Predictors of maternal gatekeeping. *Parenting: Science and Practice*, 15:166–86.

Schoppe-Sullivan, S. J., Brown, G. L., Cannon, E. A., Mangelsdorf, S. C. and Szewczyk Sokolowski, M. (2008) Maternal gatekeeping, co-parenting quality, and fathering behavior in families with infants. *Journal of Family Psychology*, 22:389–98. http://dx.doi.org/10.1037/0893–3200.22.3.389.

upho dale?

Scott, S. and Clery, E. (2013) *British Social Attitudes: The 30th Report.* London: National Center for Social Research. www.bsa.natcen.ac.uk/media/38457/bsa30_gender_roles_final.pdf.

Sevenhuijsen, S. (1991) The morality of feminism. *Hypatia,* 6:173–91.

(1998) *Citizenship and the Ethics of Care: Feminist Considerations on Justice, Morality and Politics.* New York: Routledge.

(2003). The place of care. The relevance of the feminist ethic of care for social policy. *Feminist Theory,* 4:179–97.

Sherwin, S. (1992) *No Longer Patient: Feminist Ethics and Health Care.* Philadelphia: Temple University Press.

Shirani, F., Henwood, K. and Coltart, C. (2012) Meeting the challenges of intensive parenting culture: Gender, risk management and the moral parent. *Sociology,* 46:25–40.

Sikorska, M. (2014) Changes in the area of family life in Poland. In Z. Rajkai (Ed), *Family and Social Change in Socialist and Post-Socialist Societies: Change and Continuity in Eastern Europe and East Asia.* Boston: Brill.

Skeggs, B. (1997) *Formations of Class and Gender: Becoming Respectable,* London: Sage.

Skills for Care. (2015) *The State of the Adult Social Care Sector and Workforce Report in England.* Leeds, England: Skills for Care. www.skillsforcare.org.uk/stateof2014.

Smart, C. and Neale, B. (1999) *Family Fragments.* Cambridge: Polity Press.

Sparrman, A., Westerling, A., Lind, J. and Dannesboe, K. (2016) *Doing Good Parenthood: Ideals and Practices of Parental Involvement.* London: Palgrave Macmillan.

Stephenson (1999)

Stevenson, M. M., Fabricius, W. V., Cookston, J. T., Parke, R. D., Coltrane, S., Braver, S. L. and Saenz, D. S. (2014) Marital problems, maternal gate-keeping attitudes, and father–child relationships in adolescence. *Developmental Psychology,* 50:1208–18.

Sweet, S. (2011) Anticipated and unanticipated consequences of work-family policy: insights from international comparative analyses. *Community, Work and Family,* 14:117–18.

Thébaud, S. (2010) Masculinity, bargaining, and breadwinning: Understanding men's housework in the cultural context of paid work. *Gender & Society,* 24:330–54.

Thelen, T. and Haukanes, H. (2010) *Parenting after the Century of the Child.* London: Ashgate.

Thomson, R. (2009) *Unfolding Lives: Youth, Gender, Change.* Bristol, England: Policy Press.

Thomson, R., Kehily, M. J., Hadfield, L. and Sharpe, S. (2011) *Making Modern Mothers.* Bristol, England: Policy Press.

Tronto, J. (1989) Women and caring: What can feminists learn about morality from caring? In A. M. Jaggar and S. Bordo (Eds), *Gender/Body/ Knowledge: Feminist Reconstructions of Being and Knowing.* New Brunswick, NJ: Rutgers University Press, 172–187.

(1993) *Moral Boundaries: A Political Argument for an Ethic of Care.* New York: Routledge.

(2005) Care as the work of citizens: A modest proposal. In M. Friedman (Ed), *Women and Citizenship.* New York: Oxford University Press, 130–145.

Tyler, I. (2008) Chav Mum, Chav Scum: Class Disgust in Contemporary Britain. *Feminist Media Studies*, 8:17–34.

Unpaid Parental Leave. Gov.UK. www.direct.gov.uk/en/Parents/Moneyand workentitlements/WorkAndFamilies/Parentalleaveandflexibleworking/ DG_10029416.

Utting, D. (2007) *Parenting and the Different Ways It Can Affect Children's Lives: Research Evidence.* York, England: Joseph Rowntree Foundation.

Vincent, C. and Ball, S. J. (2007) 'Making up' the middle-class child: Families, activities and class dispositions. *Sociology*, 41:1061–77.

Vuori, J. (2007) Men's choices and masculine duties. Fathers in expert discussions. *Men and Masculinities*, 12:45–72.

Wall, G. (2010) Mothers' experiences with intensive parenting and brain development discourse. *Women's Studies International Forum*, 33:253–63.

(2013) 'Putting family first': Shifting discourses of motherhood and childhood in representations of mothers' employment and child care. *Women's Studies International Forum*, 40:162–71.

Wall, K. (2007) *Leave Policy Models and the Articulation of Work and Family in Europe: A Comparative Perspective.* Paper presented at the 8th ESA Conference, Glasgow, Scotland, September 2007.

Walzer, S. (1996) Thinking about the baby: Gender and divisions of infant care. *Social Problems*, 43:219–34.

Wastell, D. and White, S. (2012) Blinded by neuroscience: Social policy, the family and the infant brain. *Families, Relationships and Societies*, 1:397–414.

West, C. and Zimmerman, D. (1987) Doing gender. *Gender & Society*, 1:125–51.

Westerling, A. (2015) Reflexive fatherhood in everyday life: the case of Denmark. *Families, Relationships and Societies*, 4:209–23.

White, C. and Office for National Statistics. (2013) *2011 Census Analysis: Unpaid Care in England and Wales, 2011 and Comparison with 2001.* http://webarchive.nationalarchives.gov.uk/20160105160709/http:// www.ons.gov.uk/ons/dcp171766_300039.pdf.

Williams, J. F. (2010) *Claiming and Framing in the Making of Care Policies: The Recognition and Redistribution.* Geneva: United Nations Research Institute for Social Development.

Willoughby, B. J., Hersh, J. N., Padilla-Walker, L. M. and Nelson, L. J. (2015) 'Back Off!' Helicopter parenting and a retreat from marriage among emerging adults. *Journal of Family Issues*, 36:669–92.

Wissö, T. and Plantin, L. (2015) Fathers and parental support in everyday family life: Informal support in Sweden beyond the auspices of the welfare state. *Families, Relationships and Societies*, 4:267–80.

Working Families. (2014) Shared Parental Leave. Briefing for Employers. www.workingfamilies.org.uk/wp-content/uploads/2015/03/Working-Families-SPL-briefing-paper.pdf.

Yarwood, G. and Locke, A. (2016) Work, parenting and gender: The care–work negotiations of three couple relationships in the UK. *Community, Work & Family*, 19:362–77.

Index